The Emotionally Intelligent Financial Advisor

The Emotionally Intelligent Financial Advisor

Hendrie Weisinger, Ph.D.

Dearborn™
Trade Publishing
A **Kaplan Professional** Company

This publication is designed to provide accurate and authoritative information in regard to the subject matter covered. It is sold with the understanding that the publisher is not engaged in rendering legal, accounting, or other professional service. If legal advice or other expert assistance is required, the services of a competent professional should be sought.

Vice President and Publisher: Cynthia A. Zigmund
Acquisitions Editor: Mary B. Good
Senior Project Editor: Trey Thoelcke
Interior Design: Lucy Jenkins
Cover Design: DePinto Design
Typesetting: Elizabeth Pitts

Published by Dearborn Trade Publishing
A Kaplan Professional Company

Printed in the United States of America

04 05 06 10 9 8 7 6 5 4 3 2 1

Library of Congress Cataloging-in-Publication Data

Weisinger, Hendrie.
    The emotionally intelligent financial advisor / Hendrie Weisinger.
      p. cm.
    Includes bibliographical references and index.
    ISBN 0-7931-9187-4
    1. Financial planners—Psychology. 2. Investment advisors—Psychology. I. Title.
    HG179. 5.W45   2004
    332.024—dc22

                        2004009567

Dearborn Trade books are available at special quantity discounts to use for sales promotions, employee premiums, or educational purposes. Please call our Special Sales Department to order or for more information at 800-245-2665, e-mail trade@dearborn.com, or write to Dearborn Trade Publishing, 30 South Wacker Drive, Suite 2500, Chicago, IL 60606-7481.

To all the Bulls and Bears—may you feast on all the Pigs!

Contents

I am in the top one half of one percent of the brokers in the country and it's because I have worked hard to develop my emotional intelligence. Doing so has helped me think about investors' needs, how they select advisors to help them, how to address their needs, and the dynamics of successful relationships. It paid off as the people around boardroom tables, one by one, became my clients and helped me build my business. It has also allowed me to stay motivated in rocky times, turn setbacks into comebacks, and continue to be happy, healthy, and productive at work.

In this book, Hendrie Weisinger, Ph.D., explains emotional intelligence and how to put it to work to achieve success in our business. You will learn how to assure yourself a positive attitude, communicate your ideas effectively, remain confident and calm in the heat of the moment, stay focused, and respond effectively. You will understand how to avoid being nervous and unsure. You will be able to avoid losses of self-confidence. You will be in a position to energize yourself, inspire others, work out conflict, and win trust.

As we face new situations, or changing circumstances in old situations, we do not always have the skills, knowledge, or understanding needed. Emotional intelligence helps us get through, often capitalizing on the opportunity presented by change. If there is one form of intelligence that enables all others, creating personal value in the marketplace, it is emotional intelligence. It will serve you well in your office's conference room and an investor's living room, and get you into the corporate boardroom.

William Nicklin, Chairman, Horsesmouth, LLC

The Emotionally Intelligent Financial Advisor

When you become an emotionally intelligent financial advisor (EIFA), you come to work each day with positive attitudes, ready to increase your bottom line. You find it easier to manage your emotions, enabling you to stay motivated in difficult times, bounce back faster from setbacks, and increase your results-oriented behavior. While others struggle to keep clients, you can enhance and develop your client relationships by communicating your ideas more effectively, responding productively to your clients' criticisms, and being adept at retaining and handling emotionally aroused clients, especially in times of volatile markets. You leave work feeling energized and productive, with lots of positive anticipation for the next day, irrespective of whether the market tanked or rallied.

This book helps you become an emotionally intelligent financial advisor by teaching you how to develop and apply your emotional intelligence (EI) in the daily scenarios that determine your success. What might be some of these scenarios? Here are a few in which applying your emotional intelligence spells success, and a lack of it spells disaster.

- It is your first meeting with the client—the Moby Dick to your Ahab, the big fish you really want to land. You feel nervous and unsure of yourself, but you're determined not to show it. You tell yourself to just ignore the butterflies and everything will be fine. During the meeting, though, your anxiety starts to rise. You feel the telltale signs: your heart pounds, your breathing speeds up, and your palms start to sweat. In this keyed-up state, you begin fidgeting nervously with your pen. Whatever your words say, your behavior has just sent a loud and clear message about your lack of self-confidence.

- You're giving a seminar on a new topic to a large group of prospects tomorrow. Your manager will be there, so it's a great chance to showcase your skills and knowledge. As you try to prepare your talk, though, you just can't seem to get rolling. The very thought of PowerPoint sends you running for the water cooler, and you wind up wasting the whole morning chatting with coworkers, tidying up your desk, and calling an old friend you haven't talked to in six months. The next day, you stumble through an ill-prepared presentation. Half of the prospects leave before you've even finished your talk, and your manager looks decidedly unimpressed.

- The latest nosedive by the market has set off a fresh wave of panic among your clients. By the time you get your fifth frantic phone call of the day, you're feeling an anxiety attack of your own coming on. Before you know it, you feel the same doom and gloom as your clients. When the sixth call comes, you don't even want to take it.

The common denominator in these situations—and hundreds of others that I have collected from financial advisors (FAs)—is that you can avoid the disastrous outcomes if you apply your emotional intelligence.

In the first, applying *self-awareness* and *managing your emotions* would help you remain confident and calm, thus increasing your chances to hook Mr. Big. In the second, if you know how to *self-motivate* and *time lock* your task, you will end up having a *Wow!* presentation. In the third, if you can *emotionally immunize* yourself to your clients' distress, you might not make any more sales, but at least you are going home in a better mood, fostering a positive attitude for tomorrow.

Note that in all of these situations, it's not your technical skills—product knowledge, familiarity with financial formulas, understanding of global economics, analysis of specific market sectors—that makes the difference. These are important, but are of little help when clients are yelling at you or your audience is bored with your presentation. Rather, to achieve success in these situations—and hundreds of others that you will experience—being a top producer requires you to apply your emotional intelligence.

WHY IT PAYS TO BECOME AN EMOTIONAL INTELLIGENT FINANCIAL ADVISOR

Emotional intelligence, specifically, refers to *your ability to use your emotions, moods, and feelings—and those of others—to enhance your results.*

For you, emotional intelligence means being able to turn setbacks into comebacks, to respond effectively to emotionally aroused clients—especially those that are angry and anxious—and to stay motivated and focused during turbulent times. It means enhancing your productivity by giving positive criticism to your assistants and team members, taking criticism in a manner that helps you develop, and managing your anger when a client is late or blames you for a bear market. It also means being able to jazz up those you work with, to remain calm when your clients panic, and to work out conflict, whether it is with a client, a fellow advisor, or your branch manager. In short, to you emotional intelligence means success.

LEVERAGING YOUR ASSETS

The idea driving the emotionally intelligent financial advisor is that *emotional intelligence is a valuable asset.* Like any asset, it is always a sound, solid, and effective strategy to leverage it for the purpose of maximizing its value.

Emotional intelligence has five key components and leveraging each helps you become more productive. Here is a prospectus on each component.

1. *High self-awareness.* High self-awareness is the foundation on which all other emotional intelligence competencies and skills are built. High self-awareness is about tuning in to information

about yourself. With high self-awareness, you can monitor yourself, observe yourself in action, and influence your actions to make sure that they are working to your benefit. High self-awareness increases your results-oriented behavior.

2. *Managing emotions (mood management).* Managing your emotions means making your *emotional operating system*—your thoughts, physical arousal of emotion, and behavior—work for you. Unlike suppressing your emotions, which deprives you of valuable information that those emotions provide, managing your emotions means understanding them and using that understanding to deal with situations productively. Managing anger, anxiety, disappointment, and fear do not have to derail you from the track of success or create havoc in your life. Quite the contrary; they can all positively impact your bottom line—if you apply your emotional intelligence.

3. *Self-motivation.* This is the ability to get yourself started, to energize yourself. To be a top producing financial advisor, you have to be highly focused. You do research, talk with people on the phone, go out to see clients, give presentations, and much more. Where does all the energy come from? How do you energize yourself when the market is bad and a client says, "Liquidate everything! I am making a change!" Self-motivation is what gives you the tenacity to stay focused and keep to the task at hand. It allows you to stick to the issues, get your mission accomplished, and turn setbacks into comebacks. Setbacks are a daily occurrence for most financial advisors, and much of your success depends on how well and how quickly you can bounce back and prevent an emotional downswing from killing your productivity. When you are bombarded with stressful situations and interactions that can leave you in a bad mood, those moods are toxic to productivity. Thus, part of self-motivation is the ability to quickly transform your toxic moods into positive energy.

4. *Interpersonal expertise.* At work, you do not live in a world of "me." You relate to your manager, your support staff, your

coworkers, and, of course, to your clients. Conflicts arise, and you'd better be able to work them out, lest you see your business decline. You have to know how to take criticism from your manager, and give it positively to your support staff, if you want their support. Most importantly, you have to win the trust of other people—this is the basis of building your book and maintaining your business. To build trust these days, you must respond effectively to the emotional state of the client. Your interpersonal expertise allows you to handle these daily job tasks.

5. *Emotional mentoring.* This is helping other people deal with their emotions, communicate effectively, solve their problems, resolve their conflicts, and become motivated. Emotional mentoring requires that you use your emotional intelligence skills to help your managers and coworkers. In particular, the skills can help you on down market days when you are dealing with upset clients who demand answers.

WHAT'S THE ROI?

Investing in your emotional intelligence will take time and energy, so the return on investment (ROI) should be substantial—and it is. Here are a few of the results you can expect from leveraging your emotional intelligence assets.

- Quickly gain the trust of prospects and clients.
- Stay focused and manage anxiety in turbulent times.
- Deal effectively with emotionally aroused clients.
- Respond positively to clients' criticism in order to increase client trust.
- Turn setbacks into comebacks.
- Enhanced office relationships.
- Stay motivated for the long haul.
- Significantly increase your bottom line.
- Be healthier and happier at work and at home.

The goal of *The Emotionally Intelligent Financial Advisor* is to help you realize these results, and more, by giving you the nuts and bolts for developing and applying your emotional intelligence in the context of your daily activities.

You begin by growing your EI portfolio—the core emotional intelligence capacities—so that you can immediately begin to get dividends.

Next, you diversify your emotional intelligence into your staff and client relationships. You can then begin to integrate emotional intelligence skills in to your daily work activities.

Finally, you keep your emotional intelligence on a roll through compliance—adhering to the rules that help you maintain your status as an emotionally intelligent financial advisor.

The bell is about to ring.

I would like to thank my investment team, which has helped me soar.

John Maurello has mentored me through the financial service industry. Much more than being supportive, John has taken every opportunity to help me get into the market. Best of all, he has become a friend.

Horsesmouth.com has been a terrific organization and I am proud to be associated with it. Steve Carchedi and Mary Anne Jones are great to work with and their enthusiasm and belief in my work is greatly appreciated

Elaine Berman has been a big fan of the material and her writing input is an acknowledgment I am happy to make.

Linda Andrews has been great in helping me make my work more accessible to financial advisors, and her contributions can only be realized by noting the references.

It has been a great experience to be associated with The Wharton School's executive education program. Joe Ryan, Katie Wiesel, Judy McHugh, Rob Cannon, Solveig Andres, Kimberly Whitby, and others have all provided me with opportunities to speak in the best executive education programs in the world.

Stewart Lee and Ed Alves have been great fun to work with, and listening to them has deepened my knowledge of financial advisors.

Dearborn Trade Publishing, especially my editor, Mary Good, has been a pleasure to work with, as well as open and trusting of my ideas.

Thanks to poet, Meredith Kaffel, for taking time to add poetry to my poem.

My mother, for as long as I can remember, provides me with irrational exuberance even when my bubble is bursting.

Lorie keeps me on my toes—she can be a bull, a bear, but is mostly a dear.

My children, Briana and Daniel, are my most valuable assets, and they are always bullish on me, even when I am a bear.

Finally, my personal bankers—Steve Gold, Mel Kinder, Kenny Cinnamon, Ron Podell, Dick Kowal, Lee Sachs, Alan Dreifuss, and Richard Greene—all keep me from crashing. They provide me with an unlimited reservoir of emotional intelligence on which I can draw carte blanche.

Investment team, thank you.

1

GROWING YOUR EMOTIONAL INTELLIGENCE PORTFOLIO

It is a seminar for financial advisors and I begin by asking, "How well do you manage anger? Can you concentrate when you're anxious? Is it easy for you to bounce back from setbacks? Do you get defensive when a client criticizes your performance? Do you feel down when the Dow goes down? Would you say that you are productive each day?"

Answers vary, but the responses I hear indicate that the overwhelming majority of the several hundred people there in the room better get their emotional intelligence going if they want to be successful. My first message surfaces quickly. Becoming an emotionally intelligent financial advisor (EIFA) begins with investing in yourself—specifically by getting your portfolio of emotional intelligence (EI) assets to work for you. Becoming aware of your emotions, learning to manage them, and learning how to harness emotions into motivational energy is the plan and result of growing your emotional intelligent portfolio.

YOUR EI PORTFOLIO

High self-awareness, emotional management, and *self-motivation* are the three core assets in your EI portfolio. They are your core assets because their value depends on nobody else, only you. The fact that you can be totally in control of these assets is what makes them so valuable. Developing your core assets is how you begin to make your emotional intelligence pay off.

The first step in growing your EI portfolio is to increase your awareness to your emotions and how they impact your daily results. Thus, the bell rings with self-awareness.

HIGH SELF-AWARENESS:
YOUR FIRST CORE EI ASSET

High self-awareness is your *ability to tune in to your thoughts, feelings, senses, actions, and intentions so that you can use the wealth of information these factors provide to enhance your results in life.* High self-awareness is your most singular important emotional intelligence asset. It is the seed that gives birth to all other emotional intelligence competencies and skills. For example, you cannot manage anger if you are not aware that you are angry; you cannot productively respond to anxious clients if you are not aware of their anxiety. You cannot self-motivate if you do not know what direction you want to take.

When you have high self-awareness, you can monitor yourself, observe yourself in action, and influence your actions so that they can work to your benefit. By being aware, for example, that your voice is getting louder and you are becoming increasingly angry at a client, and recognizing that you want to retain this client in your practice, you might lower our voice, defuse your anger, and respond to the client respectfully. Raising your self-awareness will give you more compass points to help you successfully navigate your life.

High self-awareness is a skill that anyone can cultivate by following these five steps:

1. Examine how you make appraisals.
2. Tune in to your senses.
3. Get in touch with your feelings.

4. Learn what your intentions are.

5. Pay attention to your actions.

These five steps will help you:

- Develop new ways of observing and processing the experiences that influence your thoughts, so that you can be more aware of those thoughts and see how they are formed.
- Become more tuned in to what your senses tell you, so that you can develop greater awareness of what is going on around you.
- Become more aware of what you are feeling, so you can develop a better understanding of your own emotions.
- Get a clearer picture of the short-term and long-term intentions that influence your actions, so you can stay keenly aware of what you want to accomplish.
- Pay careful attention to your actions, so that they will stay in sync with your intentions and make you more effective in business and in your personal life.

Let's look at how each step helps boost your self-awareness to your advantage.

Examine How You Make Appraisals—Becoming Aware of *How* You Think

Appraisals are your interpretations of events that help you define what is happening to or around you. Their roots lie in special qualities and circumstances—family background, natural talents, physical appearance, systems of belief—that help shape your personality. These combine to form the basis for the unique way you appraise the situations you encounter in daily life. Through your appraisals, you generate the self-statements and expectations that help guide your behavior.

A philosopher said 2,000 years ago, "Man is not troubled by things themselves, but by their thoughts about them." Psychologists today agree—it is the meaning we assign to events that gives them the power to affect us for good or ill.

For example, let's say the market goes down 200 points. If you make the appraisal, "This is really bad. I am going to lose more clients," you can be sure that your mood will be fear and anxiety. On the other hand, if you appraise the same event as, "Here is a great opportunity to get some good buys for some clients," your mood is likely to be enthusiastic.

In other words, it's not the event that causes you to feel good or bad, rather it's how you appraise the event that determines your emotional reaction. By becoming more aware of your appraisals—how you interpret the events around you, your inner dialogues, your expectations—you can learn how they affect your feelings, actions, and reactions. Armed with this information, you can work to change any self-defeating thought patterns.

Let's say you realize that you tend to see yourself in a negative light. You make this conclusion because you "hear" your self-statements: "This client thinks I'm small potatoes, and my presentation is bound to underwhelm him." If your lack of confidence causes you to act as if you don't have full command of the facts, this kind of self-appraisal can easily become a self-fulfilling prophecy. Once you recognize this tendency, you can start trying to put a more realistic and positive spin on your thoughts: "This client plays with the big guys and he wouldn't be here if he wasn't interested in what I have to say." Such thinking, in turn, can help you relax and behave in a way that exudes greater confidence and competence.

Here are some tips for leveraging your appraisals so that your stock in yourself increases.

- *Listen to how you "talk to yourself."* Pick a regular time of day to talk to yourself, and watch for patterns in your inner dialogue. Stay alert to self-destructive thought patterns, such as *all-or-nothing thinking* ("If my track record isn't perfect, I'm a total failure."), *catastrophizing* ("If I goof up, it will be a huge disaster for my career."), *discounting the positive* ("I landed this client, but it was just a fluke."), and *jumping to conclusions* ("I'm sure this client won't like me, even though we've never met."). Of course, some negative thoughts are perfectly reasonable and appropriate, but many aren't. With practice, you can learn to replace these thoughts with more rational ones ("Nobody is perfect," "One little foul-up isn't going to sink my career," "I landed this client because of my hard work and skill," and "Most of my clients seem to like me, so this one probably will, too.").

- *Use "I think" statements.* Have an inner dialogue using assertions that begin with "I think," such as, "I think I'm in over my head here," "I think this client is out of my league." These kinds of statements help you clarify what you're thinking, thus making it possible for you to examine the truth-value of what you are saying. At the same time, they help you see that you alone determine your perception of events.

- *Seek input from others.* There are several sides to every story, so it always pays to ask others for their take on events. Let's say you're required to attend a daylong workshop on raising self-awareness. You think the whole idea of emotional intelligence is a crock, and you view the workshop as a giant waste of time. But talking to your officemates at lunch, you realize they see things differently. They think they're gaining valuable information, and they back this up with examples of instances when greater self-awareness might have led to a better outcome. Their examples remind you of similar experiences of your own, and you head into the afternoon with a different mindset. Asking others for their appraisals can help you gauge when your own are dead-on accurate, way off target, or somewhere in between.

- *Focus on the appraisal-reaction link.* Remember that your appraisals—not someone else's actions (a client liquidating his account) or outside events (the Dow drops 200 points)—lead to your emotional and behavioral responses. This gives you power over your own reactions. Suppose the Big Prospect takes a phone call in the middle of your meeting. You might perceive this as negative, a sign that he's not really paying attention. If you accept this interpretation, you may give up and lose the business. On the other hand, you might see it as a welcome chance to collect your thoughts before the next part of our presentation. The choice—and the reaction that results—are all yours.

Awareness to your appraisals helps you, then, because it makes your thinking accurate, sound, and perceptive, thus increasing the likelihood that you make decisions and choose actions that are in your best interest. It also gives you the ability to modify your appraisals from those that have a discouraging impact on your performance to those that can help you improve it.

Tune In to Your Senses

Your senses—seeing, hearing, smelling, tasting, and touching—are the sources of all your data about the world. It is through your senses that you pick up information about yourself, other people, and situations you are in. But a funny thing often happens to your senses: the information they gather is filtered and transformed by your appraisals. The higher your self-awareness, the greater your ability to take the filtering process into account and distinguish between *sensory data* and appraisals.

For example, if you see a person frowning, chin down, you could make an appraisal that she feels sad. That could be a misinterpretation. Maybe she is simply concentrating. To make an accurate appraisal, you need more data. You can get more data through tuning in to your senses, which let you check, clarify, and alter your appraisals when needed.

Imagine your first meeting with a prospect who has never dealt with a financial advisor before. You expect him to be relatively unsophisticated, so you launch into a very basic overview of his financial options— a "Financial Planning for Dimwits" explanation. You're so sure of your expectations that you don't hear the client say he has considerable experience investing on his own. You don't see him shifting in his seat, or notice his eyes wandering during your spiel. And you don't realize until it's too late that you've lost the client's attention by underestimating his savvy.

You could have avoided this mistake by having greater *sensory awareness,* tuning in to the information that your senses provide. By increasing your awareness to the sensory data—eyes wandering, shifting in his seat— you could have made the tentative appraisal that you were losing your client's interest and adjusted your actions to pique him. Your lack of awareness to sensory information derailed you from success.

However, awareness to sensory data is only the first step. You must also make sure that you interpret the data accurately.

Let's say you begin a meeting with a client and after a few minutes, you notice he is frowning (sensory data). You make the interpretation that he is not very interested, and as a result you lose some of your enthusiasm. Next, you see him looking at his watch (sensory data) and appraise it to mean that he can't wait for the meeting to be over. Because these appraisals generate self-statements along the lines of "I am wasting my time; I might as well leave," you cut your presentation short, and leave without offering your card or a follow up phone call. You leave feeling dejected and a negative spell is cast on the rest of your day.

Reality check: Your client frowned because his wife was in the hospital. He looked at his watch to see if it was time to call the doctor. In other words, his reaction had nothing to do with you or your pitch; your reactions were based on misappraisals of the sensory data.

Both of these examples illustrate how a lack or a misreading of sensory information can affect your performance and emotional well being. In the first example, greater awareness to sensory information could have told you that it was time to switch gears. In the second example, a misreading of the sensory data was the culprit for negative feelings.

To make sensory information work for you, you must be able to do two things: first, *increase your perception of sensory data*, and, second, *distinguish between raw sensory information and your analysis of it*. Here are some tips for leveraging sensory information.

- *Take your brain through its paces.* For at least a week, practice sharpening your awareness to sensory data. Let's say you're at your desk first thing in the morning. Pay close attention to the sounds around you, particularly those you usually tune out: a phone ringing in another office, a door closing down the hall, traffic going past your building. Next, focus on the sights, especially those you usually wouldn't bother to register: the book that's out of place, the ding on the edge of your desk, a single brown leaf on your plant. When you go outside, pay attention to the smells in the air. Challenge yourself to see if you can tell the types of food being served as you walk past a block of restaurants. The idea behind this practice is to become more perceptive to the information that your senses provide. With this additional data, you can conduct yourself more effectively. For instance, instead of being blind to your client's fidgeting in her chair or deaf to her comments, your increased awareness to this data now allows you to adjust your appraisals and speed up your presentation.
- *Learn to tell sense from nonsense.* You get a lot of information from your senses, but in order to make sense out of the data, you have to interpret it. "You look nervous" is a subjective appraisal of an-

other person's appearance. It's opinion, not fact. In contrast, "I hear a tremor in your voice," "I see a tic over our right eye," and "I feel sweat on your palm when we shake hands" are examples of objective sensory data. Likewise, "I think you're bored" is an appraisal. "I hear your pen tapping on the desk," "I see you staring out the window," and "I feel the vibrations from your foot shaking" are sensory statements.

Making the distinction between sensory data and your interpretations will help you more accurately read the situation and, many times, save you from unwarranted emotional distress. Interpreting the sensory data of a client looking at his watch to mean he has to call the hospital is sure to lead to different feelings than interpreting the same sensory data as boredom.

O n   t h e   S t r e e t

Here's an easy exercise to practice differentiating sensory data from your appraisals. Sit down and observe your surroundings through your senses. As you make your perceptions, preface them with the appropriate sensory channel. For example, I *see* people moving quickly, I *hear* people speaking loudly, I *smell* Chinese food. Next, for every sensory statement you make, appraise it three different ways: *I see people talking to each other.* This means people are friendly; this means people are wasting time; this means people have nothing to do. Next, *I hear car horns outside.* This means people are jaywalking; this means there is an accident slowing traffic; this means someone has a flat tire. Do this for each of the sensory statements that you make. Gradually, you will become more and more adept at recognizing and differentiating sensory data from your interpretations. In so doing, you will begin to cut out many inaccurate appraisals of sensory data, thus saving yourself from unwarranted emotional distress and helping you choose your most productive actions.

Get In Touch with Your Feelings—And Their Messages

Your feelings are your spontaneous emotional responses to the interpretations you make and the expectations you have. Like sensory data, they provide important information that helps you understand why you do what you do. They alert you to your comfort level in a situation, and they help you understand your reactions.

Sometimes we're not comfortable with what we feel, and we pretend the feelings aren't there. The problem is that by ignoring or denying emotions, we deny ourselves the ability to work through them. Negative feelings can often fester, leaving us feeling worse that we would by tuning in to them.

Tuning in to our feelings is not something that comes easily to most of us. Part of the problem is that to tune in to feelings—especially distressful ones such as anger, sadness, and resentment—we must experience them. If we don't tune in, we are prevented from making use of the valuable information these feelings could give us and prevented from using our emotions intelligently.

What information do your feelings provide? Different emotions communicate different messages. For example:

- *Anger* communicates that something is wrong.
- *Anxiety* commutates uncertainty.
- *Fear* communicates a threat.
- *Depression* communicates feelings of hopelessness and helplessness.
- *Enthusiasm* communicates energy and excitement.

There are many other feelings, of course, but these five are basic aspects of emotional intelligence, and we will focus on them. The point for now is that becoming aware of your feelings allows you to respond to their messages in a way that helps you manage those feelings.

Take this example: An important client has just missed her second appointment this month without calling to cancel. You pretend to yourself that you're not angry, just happy to have an unexpectedly free hour. But when the client calls the next day to reschedule, you let your irritation show by being curt and sarcastic. You wind up losing a valued account.

Let's rewrite this story to give it a happy ending. Instead of denying your anger, let's say you recognize and acknowledge the feeling. This gives you the chance to use your feelings productively. You realize that anger communicates that something is wrong. In your mind, what is wrong is that the client cancelled without calling. You decide that the best thing to do is to speak to the client, otherwise the angry feelings will fester. When the client calls the next day, you offer to drop by her office. Once there, you calmly bring up the problem of missed appointments and suggest some practical solutions. You wind up agreeing to call the client the day before every appointment to confirm, and she'll give you at least 24 hours notice if she needs to cancel. The result is likely to be a stronger working relationship grounded in mutual respect.

To get dividends from your feelings, follow these two tips.

1. *Acknowledge your feelings.* Some feelings are harder to acknowledge than others. It's a lot easier, for example, to acknowledge that we feel happy than that we feel sad. Positive feelings are pleasant; negative ones may hurt us. Begin to think about which feelings are easy for you to acknowledge and which ones are difficult to confront. Thinking about it will make it easier to acknowledge all feelings. Think about the last meeting you had with a client and recount what you felt.

2. *Do not confuse your feelings with your appraisals.* "I feel it wasn't right that you didn't call me." How can that be? How can we feel "It wasn't right"? Right is not a feeling. It is an evaluative thought. We frequently express our feelings the way we would thoughts because we don't know exactly how to describe them when we experience them. Feelings expressed like thoughts are known as I-feel-thinking statements rather than as I-feel-emotion statements. A good rule for whether you are making an I-feel-thinking statement is to replace "I feel" with "I think." If the statement makes sense, then it's probably a thinking statement rather than a feeling, emotional one. For example, "I *think* it wasn't right that you didn't call me" makes sense. Using I feel emotion statements—"I feel angry that you didn't call me"—forces you to acknowledge your feelings, and thus become aware of the information they provide.

Following these two tips will help you become more comfortable with your feelings, thus making it easier for you to acknowledge them and use the information they provide.

On the Street

Keep a *feeling journal.* At the end of the day, or at different times of the day, make a note of what feelings you have experienced in the preceding hours. You might even rate them on a scale of 1 (little) to 9 (high) in regards to their intensity. For example, 1 (low anger) to 9 (very angry); 1 (low enthusiasm) to 9 (high enthusiasm). Doing this daily will increase your awareness of how and what you feel each day. After a week, ask yourself the following questions:

- What feelings do I experience the most?
- What feelings do I experience the least?
- What do my feelings tell me about myself and my workday?

Pay attention to the physical sensations you have every day. We touch thousands of things daily, yet it would be hard for you right now to get a good "feel" for each and every thing. For instance, what does your desk feel like? Can you get a good feel for its texture? Can you remember the feel of the fabric of yesterday's clothes? These sensations often escape us, even when we are directly experiencing them. Just because we're touching does not mean we're feeling. Studies show that as physical sensitivity increases, so does psychological sensitivity. Give yourself assignments of touching something smooth, soft, hard, and so on. The exercise will increase your ability to identify your feelings.

Learn What Your Intentions Are

Intentions often reflect your immediate desires—what you would like to accomplish today, in a specific situation, or, perhaps, in the coming week. Intentions can also refer to long-term desires—what you would like to get done by the end of the year or over the course of your lifetime.

The value in becoming fully aware of your intentions is that you can use the information to help you develop a strategy for your course of action.

Consider: You've been given a ticket to a high-profile charity event this evening. You know this is a golden opportunity to mingle with the rich and famous, but what do you *really* want to accomplish tonight?

A. Make a good impression, so that someone might call you later or recommend you to a friend.
B. Introduce yourself around, and maybe even set up a meeting or two later this week as a result.
C. Have a good time; it's free food, after all.

To make the most of this opportunity you must tailor your actions at the event to your intentions.

- If your answer is A, you might focus on circulating, chatting, and, of course, casually handing out your card when the occasion arises.
- If your answer is B, you might take a more direct approach to introducing yourself, describing what you do, and suggesting a meeting.
- If your answer is C, you might decide to take the night off from thinking about business, because everyone deserves a break now and then.

Learning what your intentions are helps you develop a strategy for action.

Being aware of your intentions can also help you rid yourself of counterproductive behavior. For example, you might want to yell at your assistant because she forgot to give you an important message, and you are furious. You also want her to feel comfortable working with you, which she wouldn't if you were to yell at her. If you recognize that your true intention is to have a good working relationship with your assistant, then you are more likely to manage your anger and less likely to yell when she errs.

If you're like most people, it's the short-term intentions that cause you the most headaches. Often, the problem is figuring out what you really desire, as opposed to what you think you want or what other people say you should want. As confusing as it can be to sort out your true intentions, it is well worth the effort.

Take the three intentions for the charity event cited above, for example. While all are perfectly valid, each implies a different course of action to reach the goal. In other words, *the more aware you are of our intentions, the better you can ensure that your actions are in sync with your wishes.*

Of course, you wouldn't consciously try to sabotage your own wish fulfillment. Yet that's exactly what can happen when your intentions and actions operate at cross-purposes, often without you even realizing it. Sometimes, this is because you have a hidden agenda. Perhaps your apparent intention is simply to make more money. However, your secret desire is to win the admiration of colleagues. So, recognizing your true intention doesn't mean abandoning your financial goals, but it does suggest that you might need to spend more time networking with other advisors.

A bigger problem arises when two intentions are in direct conflict. Let's say your goal is to build your business, but you also want to pursue personal hobbies during work hours. This second desire might get in the way of spending enough time on prospecting for new clients, which certainly will make it harder for you to achieve your first desire. In this case, it's important to clarify your true intentions. If your top priority really is to bring in new clients, then you need to find ways to stay more focused on professional responsibilities during the workday.

How can use discern your true intentions so you can profit from them? Follow these tips.

- *Identify your intentions at the start of each day.* Make yourself aware of your intentions each day before work starts by making a list of what you want to accomplish—build relationships with clients, prospect, and review client portfolios. Keep the list on your desk and, by frequently gazing at it, you will remain self-aware to your daily intentions. You then can decide what behaviors you must adopt to realize your intentions.
- *Tune in to your behavior.* In general, when you do something, it's because you want to do it, or at least because you stand to gain something by it. As a result, your actions are good clues to your

intentions. Let's say you're headed out the door at 5:00 to meet some friends for dinner when a client calls and asks if he can drop by in an hour. You can hardly believe it when you hear yourself agreeing. What were you thinking? Based on your behavior, probably that impressing this client is more important than having dinner with your friends. Later that night, you tell your friends that you really wanted to be with them, but the fact is, your behavior shows otherwise—it was really more important to impress your clients.

- *Use your feelings to surface your intentions.* When you follow your intentions, you feel good because you are doing what you want to do. When you do not act in accordance with your true intentions, you experience psychological distress, as you have put yourself in a setting that you would rather avoid. When you feel bored at a meeting or impatient with a client on the phone, these feelings tell you that you want to escape the situation —you want to leave the meeting or to end the call. On the other hand, if you feel good, you are probably where you want to be or doing what you want to be doing.

Consider this example: Your manager refers a client to you. Usually this makes you happy, but this time, you recognize that every meeting with this client leaves you uncomfortable and stressed out. You aren't sure why until you think about these feelings. You realize that the client takes up a lot of your time and rarely does any business with you. You feel angry and think you're wasting your time. You conclude that you really don't want to have this individual as a client. With your manager, you do some shuffling, get rid of the client, and guess what? You end up feeling better. You also have freed up time to do what you want to do— find better clients.

Thus, awareness of your intentions increases your productivity, because it tells you what you really want to be doing and helps you guide your behavior to get what you want. At the same time, you become more aware of those situations that you want to avoid.

Pay Attention to Your Actions

How do you act with your staff? How do you act with your clients? What actions cause you to waste time, and what actions help you be productive and get the results you want? The degree to which you can provide the answers to these questions is an indication of how aware you are to your behavior, the fifth component of your self-awareness.

In contrast to your appraisals, senses, feelings, and intentions, which are internal processes, your actions are external—they're out there for everyone, including yourself, to see. By tuning in to your behavior, you can begin to deduce important information that will help you become more productive. For example, you can begin to cut your time-wasting habits. You can begin to generate behaviors that are more productive to client relationships. You can also begin to delete your personal behaviors that others find distracting and annoying, and you can gain a greater awareness to your feelings.

You're probably already aware of the way you act generally (talking to an employee, for example), but you may be less cognizant of the finer nuances coloring your actions (speaking loudly). Other people undoubtedly notice these things, however, and use them to draw conclusions about your attitudes and feelings. If you speak loudly, your assistant may think you are angry and become defensive or angry in return, when in truth you are just excited about the plans you're discussing. By becoming aware of your actions (raising your voice when excited), you can learn to control them and communicate more accurately.

Are you aware of which of your actions turn off prospects and lose you clients? Consider your first meeting with a potential client referred to you by a friend. Neither of you has a lot of time, and the client has lots of questions, many of which you have heard before. In fact, before she can even finish her questions, you give the answers. The meeting ends and she tells you that maybe she will get back to you. Of course, she never does. A week later, when you mention her to your friend, you hear, "Yes, she told me she met with you but she felt you weren't listening to her." If you had been more aware to your "interrupting style," you could have let her finish her questions and perhaps she would have been interested in doing business with you.

Are you aware of what you do the first two hours of work? If your intention is to make money, you better make sure your morning actions are taking you in that direction. By being aware of your behavior, you can begin to identify those behaviors that help you improve your business and focus on doing them, rather than engaging in numerous activities that may be interesting and enjoyable (like reading the *Journal* and schmoozing with fellow advisors) but provide little to your bottom line.

Being aware of your behavior also gives you important insight into your emotional landscape. Let's say your manager frequently invites you to give presentations to potential clients. You note that you always turn down the invitations with reasons ranging from "not enough time" to "I have something else scheduled." You begin to think about your "refusal" behavior, and as you do, you become aware that giving presentations makes you feel anxious because you don't think you have the appropriate expertise to pull off a good one. Armed with this awareness, you begin a series of actions—gathering research, mentally practicing the presentation, anticipating questions, and preparing responses. After a while you feel confident, and when your boss again invites you to present, you not only jump at the chance, but also give a wow showing—and pick up a few clients!

How do you increase your awareness to your behavior? How do you maximize the value of this information? Use these tips.

- *Practice observing your behavior.* Choose an activity that you perform often, such as sitting down with a client. Then monitor your behavior on several different occasions to look for patterns. Do you sit up straight or slouch? Lean toward the client or away? Sit still or fidget? Tap your pen, make notes, or doodle? Once you identify habitual actions, think about what they imply. Sitting up straight, for example, might indicate that you're paying attention, while fidgeting might suggest a lack of interest. Leaning toward the client might indicate that you're listening carefully, while tapping your pen might suggest that you're distracted. The goal is to promote actions that work for you (sitting up straight, learning toward the client) while eliminating those that work against you (fidgeting, tapping your pen).

- *Observe how your actions affect others.* Select one action, and then perform it in several situations to observe others' reactions. Let's say you choose smiling. Make an effort to smile more often at clients during conferences, at coworkers during meetings, and at people from other offices as you pass in the hall. Do people smile back and make eye contact? Do they strike up conversations or invite you to socialize outside work? Do clients seem more motivated than on previous occasions? Do they vow to tell their friends about you? By observing your actions through the lens of others' reactions, you can learn to engage in constructive behaviors and eliminate destructive ones.

O *n the* **S** *t r e e t*

Analyze your day. For one week, play close attention to your work schedule, starting with the minute you walk into your office and ending when you leave work. Be tuned in to how you spend your time. Which actions help you take care of business and which ones deter you. Is your behavior productive in the morning or in the afternoon? How come? What behaviors do you avoid? Why? What actions do you need to do more of to enhance your business? The end result will be greater awareness to specific actions that can make you more productive.

As you become more aware of your behavior and the information it provides, you will find yourself generating actions that give you positive results.

Putting It All Together

Naturally, the ultimate goal of high self-awareness is to increase those actions that get you where you really want to be, while decreasing counterproductive thoughts, emotions, and behaviors. To achieve this goal, you must tune in to your own appraisals, senses, feelings, intentions, and actions.

Self-awareness is your core EI asset. Simply put, developing your self-awareness immediately increases the value of your EI portfolio.

The bell has rung!

O *n* *the* **S** *treet*

To put all the elements of self-awareness together, try these two exercises.

Review your self-awareness in play. At the end of a workday, write down a brief description of one of your activities. Then look at how each of the five components of self-awareness came into play. Here's an example: An important client calls to explain that your assistant was rude on the phone yesterday. You want to reassure the client of your professionalism and let her know that her business is important to you (intention). Then you notice your voice rising (sense), and realize you are embarrassed by your employee's lapse (feeling). Instead of becoming defensive, you tell yourself (via self-statements) that you can't control someone else's behavior, but you appraise the incident as an opportunity to show what a good and considerate advisor you are. You deliver a gracious apology (action). When you get off the phone, you congratulate yourself on handling the situation so well—and on being such as self-aware professional. Thinking about your awareness in play helps reinforce the importance of each self-awareness component by showing you how they affect your everyday outcomes. As you see how these factors influence you on a daily basis, you become much more likely to heighten your ability to use them advantageously.

The high self-awareness question. Several times a day, ask yourself these high self-awareness questions. Your answers will serve the dual purpose of developing your self-awareness and keeping you on the track of success.

- How am I thinking? Positively or negatively? Are my thoughts helping me make the day productive? How did I appraise my day when I woke up? Did this appraisal put me in a good mood?
- What am I tuning in to right now? How am I interpreting the data I sense?
- How am I feeling? What is the basis for these feelings?

- What do I want? Am I clear on my immediate goals?
- How am I acting? Are my actions matching my intentions? Am I engaging in productive behaviors?

The more you do these exercises, the more you will develop your self-awareness.

MANAGING YOUR EMOTIONS— YOUR SECOND CORE ASSET

You know the scene: A financial advisor is enthusiastically presenting his idea to his manager. The response is a barrage of critical comments. The advisor tries again, but this time, he is thwarted by booming interruptions. Throwing up his hands, he leaves feeling bitter, angry, and resentful toward his manager, whom he believes is an obstacle to his success.

So what does managing your emotions really mean? It means understanding your emotions and using that understanding to turn situations to your benefit. It's also making sure that you never let your emotions trigger behavior that is counterproductive to your intentions.

When we hear "get control of your emotions" or "chill out," we often take it to mean "stifle your emotions," and a lot of us try to do that. The problem is that suppressing emotions doesn't solve anything. It certainly doesn't make the emotions go away; it can let them fester, and that can cause problems.

Managing your emotions means something quite different from stifling them. It means using your thoughts to make good choices about your behavior. It means having the capacity to soothe yourself and shake off anxiety, gloom, irritability, and even irrational exuberance. Managing your emotions essentially means that you can maintain your emotional perspective.

What about the angry, frustrated advisor in the previous scene? What might be a more emotionally intelligent way for him to deal with his situation? Say he first *becomes aware that he is feeling anger* and uses it as a cue that *something is wrong*. What's wrong is that his manager is not listening to a good idea.

Then he tunes in to his own thoughts: "He's a pig! I could strangle him!" This advisor begins to have a constructive inner dialogue, and says to himself: "He's being unreasonable, but I will not let the situation get out of hand. I know my idea is a good one." Then he tunes in to the physiological changes—fast breathing, pounding heart—that he is experiencing, and he practices some relaxation techniques. He looks at his anger actions—clenching his jaw, making a fist—and stops doing them. Then he gives himself a time-out by going to get a drink of water. Finally, he resolves to have a meeting later to seek a solution to the problem.

This part of your EI portfolio shows you ways to manage your emotions. You will see and learn how taking charge of your thoughts, your visceral responses, and your actions helps you deal with your emotions in ways that can greatly increase your productivity.

Your Emotional Operating System

Three separate components of your emotional system are involved in recognizing and managing emotions.

1. Your thoughts, or cognitive processes
2. Your physiological changes, or arousal actions
3. Your behaviors, or action tendencies

Emotions are produced by an interaction of these three components in response to external events. Each component influences the others—think angry thoughts and your blood pressure and heartbeat are bound to increase. Take a deep breath and relax, and your angry thoughts are sure to diminish. Find yourself yelling and you can count on your thoughts being loaded with anger. In other words, the three components operate as a system—each affects the other.

A good way to think of your emotional operating system is as a triangle with your thoughts at one point, your emotional arousal at the second point, and the way you behave at the third. Managing your emotions requires that you take charge of these three components of your emotional operating system. It is your thoughts, physiological changes, and behavior that drive your emotional responses, not someone else's actions or external events.

In the case of the boss who rejects your idea (external event), it is your thoughts ("He's a pig"), your physiological action (heartbeat increasing), and your actions (clenched fist, sarcastic comments) that cause you to experience anger. When you understand this, you recognize that the power to manage your anger and other emotions rests with you, not with your boss, client, or anyone else.

Emotional Management Tools

Because emotions are so powerful, managing them requires potent techniques. Here are four.

1. Take charge of your thoughts.
2. Use relaxation to decrease your physiological arousal.
3. Take control of and generate effective behavior patterns.
4. Take time out to calm down, and even have a laugh.

These four techniques will help you:

- Recognize that your own thoughts, physiological changes, and behaviors drive your emotional responses, and that you can take charge of them to be sure that your behavior is in harmony with your intentions.
- Diminish anxiety, anger, and fear so that you can respond to clients in considered, emotionally intelligent ways.
- Recognize when behavioral patterns aren't working for you and find ways to change them, so you can move toward your goals with full effectiveness.
- Learn when to walk away from tense situations and calm down, perhaps with some good laughs, to restore your equilibrium and trigger positive feelings.

In other words, these four emotional management tools help you leverage your emotions into assets that enhance your bottom line.

Managing Your Emotions by Taking Charge of Your Thoughts

Among the many ways that our thoughts influence how we feel is through the things we say to ourselves. Our internal conversations, private speech, thought-talk, or self-statements are the mechanisms that allow us to bring to life the appraisals we make and the expectations we have. The statements that we make to ourselves precede, accompany, or follow the things we feel.

In emotional situations, self-statements play an important part in defining and shaping your emotions. For example: "I'm going to tell this client to shove it. I'm not going to take this crap anymore," or "Jeez, she's a real pain in the ass. I'm going to fix her good." Such self-statements add fuel to the fire and prolong distressful emotions long after an incident is over. The goal in taking charge of your thoughts is to be able to use your self-statements in a way that will enhance your results rather than derail you from the success track. There are two steps to take to reach this goal. First, you take charge of your *automatic thoughts* and minimize your *cognitive distortions*—appraisals that make the situation worse. Then, you use your thoughts in the form of *constructive internal dialogues* and *instructional self-statements*.

How your thoughts think.   Thoughts that spontaneously pop out and repeat (I could kill him; he never listens to me!) are what we call *automatic thoughts*. They are called automatic thoughts because they seem to occur without any prior reasoning or reflection.

Being aware of your automatic thoughts is important because it gives you practice paying attention to the specific self-statements you make when you are emotionally distressed or going into a potentially emotionally taxing situation. This awareness then becomes a cue that you need to talk to yourself differently—in a way that helps you manage your emotions, rather than your emotions hijacking you. Being aware to your automatic thoughts will also help you avoid *distorted thinking*—appraisals that you make that are misperceptions of reality and make the situation more distressful than warranted.

Automatic thoughts have the following characteristics:

- *They are private.* Most people talk to themselves differently from the way they talk to others. When we talk to others, we tend to describe our life events in a rational manner. When we talk to ourselves, we are frequently irrational and use horrifying overgeneralizations, such as, "I'm a failure. Nobody will ever love me."
- *We almost always believe them.* Despite their irrationality, automatic thoughts are unquestioningly accepted. They seem plausible be-

cause they are hardly noticed. We don't question them or challenge them, nor are their implications logically analyzed.

- *They are discrete and specific messages.* They give us a direct and distinct message about some event, such as "The client thinks I am a fool."
- *They usually appear in brief form.* Automatic thoughts are frequently abbreviated to one word or a transient visual image. For example, an advisor may say, "Zip" to tell herself that she will be left with no clients after a market nosedive.
- *They are learned.* Since we were born, people have been telling us what to think. Our family, friends, teachers, and even the media condition us to appraise events in specific ways.
- *They tend to be catastrophic.* Automatic thoughts tend to act as cues for other thoughts. One depressing thought may trigger a whole chain of depressing thoughts.
- *They are hard to turn off.* Because automatic thoughts go unnoticed, they seem to come and go as they wish.

Here is an example of an automatic thought that typically happens when a client is expressing anger or disappointment about your performance: The automatic thought, "That's it!" really means, "I am finished. He is pulling his account. My other clients will do the same. I will not have a job. I will have no money. Everyone will leave me. What's the point of living?"

Distorted thinking.   Automatic thoughts often lead to *distorted thinking.* Distorted thinking occurs when we make appraisals that are not tuned in to the reality of the situation. You might be five minutes late to an important meeting, but that is a far cry from telling yourself, "This client will think I am totally irresponsible." *Cognitive distortions* tend to make the situation much more emotionally intense than the situation warrants, and thus interfere with making intelligent decisions. This even applies to enthusiastic automatic thinking, because many a less-than-great financial decision can be tied to out-of-control enthusiasm.

Watch out for these common cognitive distortions.

- *Overgeneralizing.* This involves viewing a specific event as evidence of a general rule, when it's actually not. Yes, you forgot your notes for a crucial meeting this morning, but that doesn't mean that you always screw up. Such overgeneralization just sabotages your self-esteem. To spot such thoughts, be aware of using the words *always* or *never*. Ask yourself whether you might more accurately substitute a less global term: "I *occasionally* forget something, but *usually* I'm quite reliable."

- *Destructive labeling.* This is similar to overgeneralizing, except that, jumping from a narrow event, you apply an overly broad label to someone else. Let's say your receptionist neglects to tell you about a call. Okay, she made a mistake, but that doesn't mean she's an idiot. Such labeling just creates the false impression that the situation is irrevocably bad—that there's nothing you can do to make it better. On the other hand, if you focus on the missed call, you can look for ways to prevent the error from happening again.

- *Mind reading.* Many of us assume that we know what another person is thinking, feeling, or intending when we actually don't. If a client cancels two appointments in a row, for example, don't necessarily assume that he's planning to jump ship. Perhaps he's just tied up at work or has a family member in the hospital. You may never know what's actually going on unless you ask, "I noticed that you missed your last two appointments, and I'm concerned. Is everything all right?"

- *Shoulds and oughts.* This involves having rules for how other people ought to act, which just sets you up for disappointment and anger when they don't behave the way you want them to. Let's say you think a good financial advisor should put work before play. You're disillusioned to hear your mentor say she takes off early three afternoons a week to go to the gym. Your inflexible attitude keeps you from seeing her point of view and possibly learning something. Maybe the energy boost she gets from working out and the contacts she makes at the gym more than compensate for the time away from the office. Keeping an open mind about other people's behavior pays off.

- *Magnification.* Blowing the small stuff out of proportion is common. Suppose you sent a mass e-mail to several clients before realizing your PC had a virus. If you tell yourself that the situation is a disaster—all your clients will hate you and your career will be over—you may be too overwhelmed to act productively. If you manage to hang on to your emotional perspective, though, you can see that this as a bad situation, but one that can be fixed. At worst, you'll have to spend the afternoon calling the recipients to warm them not to open your e-mail. When you catch yourself thinking in terms such as *disaster* and *catastrophe,* be aware that you may be exaggerating the importance of an event.

Obviously, learning to avoid distorted thinking is critical. These tips are worth taking.

- *Don't overgeneralize.* Okay, your boss isn't listening to you today, but it isn't true that he never listens to you.
- *Stay away from destructive labeling.* Well, yes, she's being a bit of a jerk today, but she's not always a jerk, and you know it.
- *Avoid mind reading.* Don't guess what another person's motives, thoughts, and feelings are. If you really want to know, consider asking, "You seem dissatisfied with my performance. Are you?"
- *Don't have rules about how others should act.* Recognize that people are different and have their own sets of rules. Don't set yourself up for disappointment and anger when they don't behave as you want them to. Stay away from such words as *ought, should,* and *must.*
- *Don't inflate the significance of an event.* Everyone is entitled to a mistake now and then; don't let the small stuff trigger negative automatic thinking about other people or yourself.

O*n the* **S***treet*

For the rest of today and tomorrow, try to catch yourself having automatic thoughts. You will learn a lot about how you talk to yourself, and that's an important thing to know. Don't write anything down—just pay attention. Listen to what you are thinking and you will gain some insight into your automatic thoughts. See whether you overgeneralize, engage in destructive labeling, indulge in mind reading, have rules about how others should act, or inflate the significance of events.

After you have spent some time "hearing" your thoughts, look at the following pairs of sentences. From each, select the one that better describes what you "heard" when you paid attention to your automatic thinking.

- I heard myself overgeneralizing about a colleague or friend.
- I didn't overgeneralize.

- I heard myself giving someone a destructive label because I was angry.
- I didn't give anyone a destructive label.

- I caught myself having rules about how others should act.
- I wasn't thinking of rules about how others should act.

- I caught myself inflating the significance of an event.
- I didn't inflate the significance of any event.

- I heard myself having automatic thoughts triggered by enthusiasm.
- I didn't have automatic thoughts triggered by enthusiasm.

Repeating this for a few days will help you rid yourself of distorted thinking and the problems it creates.

Constructive internal dialogue and instructional self-statements. Combating distorted automatic thinking and replacing it with constructive inner dialogue is a great way to take charge of your thoughts. You can do this by a method I call *Checking Things Out.*

I've asked many advisors, "What makes you angry?" A popular response is, "When you have a good idea and your boss won't listen." A lively discussion follows focusing on their emotional responses in such a situation I sum it up this way: "The boss doesn't accept your prospecting idea and tells you to go away. Your automatic thoughts are, 'He's an idiot. He never listens to me! He hates my ideas! He doesn't respect me.' You feel belittled, maybe even dejected. You leave angry. The rest of your day is bad."

Everyone agrees that this is an accurate description of the scene, and everyone also agrees that if the incident occurs in the morning, the rest of the day becomes spoiled.

I tell them, "Over the years, I have developed a four-step process that can help you in situations you have to deal with that typically create emotional distress, preventing you from doing your best. The basic strategy is to rid yourself of the distorted, automatic thoughts such situations typically provoke, and then help yourself by having a constructive internal dialogue. I will show you how it works using the same example:

"He's an idiot. He never listens to me! He hates my ideas! He doesn't respect me."

First, acknowledge the emotion: "I'm really angry at George!" Then knock out distorted statements by challenging their truth-value and re-phrasing them to the specific situation.

- "George is an idiot" (destructive labeling) becomes "George is no idiot. I'm just angry that he's not doing what I want."
- "He never listens to me!" (overgeneralization) becomes "Is this really true? Just the other week he spent a good half hour listening to my concerns about a new client."
- "He doesn't respect my ideas" (mind reading) becomes "In the past, he's been supportive to many of my ideas. I wonder why he isn't sold on this one. I need to find this out. Maybe I'm missing something or maybe more dialogue will make it a better idea, one he will support."

After some more discussion, I summarize the useful procedure this way: "Checking things out is a four-step process for avoiding automatic thinking and developing constructive inner dialogue. The four steps are:

1. Acknowledge the emotion.
2. Check your thoughts for the distorted thinking styles and self-statements that evoke the emotion.
3. Restate the distorted statements so that they are reality accurate.
4. Reinterpret the event free of cognitive distortion.

To make sure the process is clear, I do it as a soliloquy:

George is such an idiot. He makes me so angry. I feel as though he never listens to me or to any new ideas from anyone, and he doesn't respect me. Wait a second, get a hold. Is what you're telling yourself really true? Well, not exactly. Okay, he

gave me credit for a new idea last week in front of everyone—
and thanked me. So it's this one he thinks is harebrained, not
all my ideas. Is that a guy who doesn't respect me? But he called
this one a harebrained idea! He always . . . . Nah, last week he
respected me. It's just this one idea he thinks is harebrained. I
wonder why. I never asked him. Maybe I'd better go talk with
him.

Bottom line is, I'm angry, better yet frustrated, that I cannot get George to go for this idea. But he is a smart guy and I
will talk to him again about it, and maybe we can come up with
something he will support.

And yes, there is applause!

Instructional self-statements.   A second and powerful way to get
away from the automatic thoughts that can work against you is arming
yourself with *instructional self-statements* that help guide you through
emotionally stressful situations. They are particularly useful when you
know you are entering a situation that can be emotionally charged or a
situation in which you must be at your emotionally best. Instructional
self-statements will reassure you and suggest the course you should
follow.

In these tough situations, your automatic thoughts might not match
your intentions. Instructional self-statements will help you stay focused,
so you can achieve what you intend to achieve, and avoid derailing yourself. Here's how to you use instructional self-statements.

1. Cut off negative automatic thoughts that don't match your intentions.
2. Replace the negative automatic thoughts with instructional self-
   statements—constructive thoughts—that will help you behave in a
   way that is beneficial to you.

Here are some examples of instructional self-statements.

- "I don't need to get defensive."
- "The branch manager knows I had no control over the problem."
- "I will pay attention to the positive things the client says, not just
  the negative ones."

- "I am fully prepared for this meeting."
- "I know that my planning is sound."
- "I am sure that my idea is good."
- "I will acknowledge and handle the client's concerns."
- "I will ask a question when something is unclear."
- "I will ask how we might resolve the situation together."

Here's a reliable tip: Use *emotional distress* as a signal that it's time to use your instructional self-statements and to have a constructive internal dialogue that challenges the validity of your automatic thoughts. Doing so will immediately allow you to begin the process of managing your emotions.

On the Street

1. Identify an upcoming situation, such as a presentation or a difficult client meeting, that might trigger negative automatic thoughts for you. Imagine the emotions that might be involved, such as anxiety or anger. Write them on an index card.
2. Next, think of three instructional self-statements that would cut off your negative automatic thoughts in that situation and help you manage your emotions, and write the statements on the index card. Read the sample self-statements above for inspiration and ideas. Use any instructional self-statements that apply to your situation and/or create your own. Remember to make them very specific—instead of "Relax," make it "Breathe slower."
3. Keep the index card in visible sight so that it will be a constant reminder of how to talk to yourself when you encounter the situation.
4. Create a card for as many emotionally arousing situations you can think of. Doing so will help you replace your old, automatic, counterproductive thoughts with productive self-statements. Inevitably, it will become second nature to use them. When this happens, your productivity will soar!

Managing Emotions by Regulating Your Physiological Arousal

All jokes aside, cavemen and advisors do share some traits.

Imagine that you're living in the Stone Age, and that you're out hunting for a nice juicy mastodon for dinner. Suddenly, you happen across a saber-toothed tiger and you immediately turn tail and flee. Later that day, you run into a member of a rival clan that is challenging your clan for territory. This time, you stand your ground and fight. Your outward reaction is different, but in both cases, your inward responses are the same—as your body swings into high gear, you experience an increase in your heart rate, blood pressure, breathing rate, muscle tension, and perspiration.

Now imagine that you're a 21st-century financial advisor. The market is down, calls from worried clients are up, and a new kid on the block is offering financial advice for cut-rate fees. As tempting as it might seem, you know you shouldn't run away from the phone or punch out your competitor. But when one of your clients mentions meeting him, your body automatically reacts to the perceived threat with the preprogrammed fight-or-flight response. Your heart pounds, your breathing speeds up, your jaw clenches, and you even start to sweat.

These kinds of physiological changes serve as important indicators that your emotional perspective is changing. In other words, they're signs that you have moved from a calm state to one of heightened arousal. By noticing these signs, you take an important step toward calming yourself. This, in turn, helps you think clearly and behave in a way that helps you match your behavior to your intentions.

Think of yourself as the thermostat for your own physiological arousal. First, you need to register any changes that occur, much as a thermometer registers a change in room temperature. You do this by becoming more aware of your own heartbeat, breathing, and perspiration. Then you control those changes, just as a thermostat can be used to adjust the heat.

The most effective way to control your physiological changes is to learn to reduce stress. By doing so, you reverse the physiological changes that occur with arousal. Your heart rate, blood pressure, breathing rate, and muscle tension decreases, and perspiration returns to normal. At the same time, you slow down your emotional arousal. This gives you a chance to think things through and make productive choices about how to behave, whether it's beginning an important presentation, or responding to an angry client.

Arousal indicators. Feelings tend to be associated with specific physical sensations—nervousness with a jittery stomach, anger with warm cheeks, for example. We refer to the physiological changes behind the sensations as *arousal indicators*. Before you can learn to relax in the heat of the moment, you must first be able to recognize your arousal indicators, for these are the cues that tell you it's time to relax. The faster you recognize your arousal indicators are changing, the faster you can begin to manage your emotions.

O *n the* **S** *treet*

For a day or two, pay close attention to changes in your physiological arousal level, especially your heart rate, breathing rate, and perspiration level. Get to know how your own arousal responses work—how you experience this arousal and what sets off your responses. Some helpful questions to accomplish the task include:

- In what situations do you feel most aroused?
- What do your arousal indicators feel like when you are tired?
- What do they feel like when you are stressed?
- What do they feel like when you are happy?
- What do they feel like when you are anxious?
- What do they feel like when you are dejected?
- What do they feel like when you are angry?

Compare your arousal indicators across different situations. The more you do this, the easier it will become to recognize when you need to relax and clarify your thoughts and intentions.

Developing your relaxation response. Your *relaxation response* (RR) is a protective mechanism to counter the harmful physical and mental effects of emotional distress. Specifically, learning to use your RR helps you short-circuit emotional arousal before it becomes too intense, and allows you to appraise the situation accurately, something you cannot do during intense emotional arousal. The ability to think clearly when you are emotionally aroused allows you to handle the situation productively.

Let's say you are doing paperwork and a high net-worth client calls and says, "I've been talking with another advisor." You feel your heart beating faster as she continues, "I'm considering making a change." You feel your breath coming more quickly and you might even begin perspiring. Your arousal level has gone from a calm state to a heightened one.

The best way to manage emotional arousal that doesn't support your intentions is to diminish the arousal as soon as you become aware of it. If you can instantly note the physiological changes, you have a cue that it is time to calm yourself and thus diminish exaggerated anxiety and fear. Then instead of responding impulsively, you can respond to the client in a considered, emotionally intelligent way. That response could make the difference between keeping and losing the client.

There are numerous techniques that you can use to develop your RR, such as Transcendental Meditation, Zen, yoga, progressive relaxation, self-hypnosis, autogenic training, and biofeedback. There are, however, four essential components that, irrespective of method, are thought to be necessary to develop your RR.

1. *A quiet environment.* When developing your RR, choose a quiet, calm environment without distractions. This will make it easier to avoid interfering stimuli while you focus on your RR images or statements.

2. *A mental device.* Having a mental device—a sound, word, image, statement, fixed gaze—helps you shift your mind from being externally oriented to being internally oriented. This is important because it enables you to focus on what is happening in your body. Having a constant word or image also helps you overcome a major problem in developing your RR—mind wandering. The word or image *breaks* your distracting thoughts. It is very important to remember to use the same image, word, sound, or other mental device each time you practice your RR. This consistency will strengthen the association between your thoughts and the desired level of physiological arousal, inevitably leading you to the point where using your mental device automatically elicits feelings of relaxation—Pavlov's dogs, if you like.

3. *A passive attitude.* Passivity is probably the most important component in developing your RR. Distracting thoughts will occur. Don't worry when this happens, just return to your mental device. If you worry about how well you are doing, you may prevent the RR from occurring. Adapt a "let it happen" attitude. Distracting thoughts do not mean that you're doing something incorrectly. Expect them.

4. *A comfortable position.* When you practice your RR, it is important to be in a comfortable position so there is no undue muscular tension. If a position gets uncomfortable, it is a signal that tension is increasing. Switch to a position that makes you feel more comfortable.

The following relaxation exercise is brief and it covers all the essentials for developing RR. It takes approximately fifteen minutes. Read it a few times so you can do it on your own. You will first exaggerate muscle tensions before relaxing them. Complete the following steps one at a time:

1. Clench your fist . . . tighter, tighter . . . relax.
2. Suck in your stomach; try to make it touch your back . . . hold it . . . relax.
3. Clench your teeth; lock your jaws . . . firmer . . . firmer . . . relax.
4. Close your eyelids tightly. Force them together more and more . . . release.
5. Push your head and neck into our shoulders . . . release.
6. Inhale . . . hold it as long as you can . . . release.
7. Stretch out your arms and legs . . . stiffer . . . stiffer . . . release.
8. Now do all seven steps together. Release and let a warm, soft, wave flow over your body, relaxing each part in turn as it slowly moves from your head down, around, over, and into every muscle. Especially let it loosen the tension around your eyes, forehead, mouth, neck, and back. Tension out, relaxation in. Let the wave of gentle relaxation dissolve all muscle tension. As you enjoy the feeling, visualize your favorite setting, or say a phrase like, "calm down." Use the same image or phrase every time you practice the exercise.

O n   t h e   S t r e e t

Once you've conditioned yourself to relax at will, you can use your relaxation response to counteract any change in arousal. Here's how:

1. *Imagine a distressing situation.* For example, you might think about making a cold call, dealing with a disgruntled client, or talking to your branch manager about a problem in your office. In your mind, go through the steps you would take, and try to make them seem as real as possible by using all of your senses. In the case of a cold call, you might imagine feeling the paper as you run your finger down a long list of phone numbers, looking at a specific number, lifting the phone receiver, hearing the dial tone, and then hearing the tones as you punch in the number. After that, you might imagine hearing someone's voice answering, then hearing your own voice introducing yourself and asking to speak with the prospect. Does this situation typically fill you with anxiety? Then focus on the arousal indicators you might notice as well, such as a racing heart, fast breathing, sweaty palms, or a shaking voice.

2. *Introduce your mental construct into the imaginary scene.* As you run through each of the steps in your scenario and the arousal indicators that ensue, imagine using the construct to keep your arousal under control. Let's say your voice starts to quiver as soon as you begin introducing yourself. You might silently say "peace, peace, peace" a few times until you're feeling calmer. Repeat this whole process once a day for several days, always using the same situation and emotion. When you can shift almost instantly from the first signs of arousal to your relaxation construct, then you know you've learned to associate the construct with the scenario.

3. *Introduce your mental construct into a real-life situation.* Make an actual cold call, and focus on your chosen thought or images at the first hint of heightened arousal. The ultimate goal is to have your construct kick in just before your arousal shoots up. If you encounter difficulty, go back to practicing the imaginary scenario until you can use the technique effectively in real life.

People differ in how long it takes them to develop their RR, but if you practice ten to fifteen minutes a day, you will feel the benefit of your investment.

Managing Emotions by Generating Effective Responses

There are many times when taking charge of your thoughts and being able to relax will help you manage your emotions. There are also times when these tools will be necessary, but not enough to alleviate the emotional distress of the situation—distress that is keeping you from doing your best. For example, the anxiety you feel about a client not responding to your call can be managed by focusing on other tasks or by keeping your thoughts positive, but these are only temporary solutions, as the anxiety will inevitably get to you. Your instructional self-statements may help when a client is yelling at you, but they are of little help in managing the anger that festers long after the incident is past. You might tell yourself that it's hard to get clients right now and that will change, but the motivational self-statements will lose their power when the results aren't increased but your dejection is.

In such situations, the key to managing your emotions is to be able to generate an effective behavioral response—a response that helps deal with the emotional distress by a *change in your actions.*

If you've been practicing what you have been reading, you are probably becoming more self-aware. No doubt, developing your self-awareness—especially to your arousal indicators—is helping you recognize when your emotions are derailing you from success. Also, taking charge of your thoughts in the form of instructional self-statements is probably helping you handle yourself professionally. These are important emotional intelligence skills and are necessary, but not sufficient to deal with the above-mentioned examples. To generate an effective behavioral response, you also have to *understand the message of the emotion,* because it is the emotion's message that creates the emotional distress.

Recall that all emotions communicate different messages.

- Anger communicates that something is wrong.
- Anxiety communicates uncertainty.
- Fear communicates a threat.
- Depression communicates feelings of hopelessness and helplessness.
- Enthusiasm communicates energy and excitement.

To generate an effective behavioral response, you must *act in a way that responds to the message of the emotion.* When you do this, you are using your emotions to make intelligent choices—you are applying your emotional intelligence.

For example, take the advisor who experiences anxiety because he hasn't heard back from an important client. He can choose how to respond. If he is overwhelmed by the anxiety, he will probably sit at his desk and do nothing but worry, which actually increases the anxiety of the situation. He could also try to distract himself by putting energy into other tasks. This could be productive, but in all probability, the anxiety will still seep through. Or, he could use his emotions intelligently by recognizing that anxiety communicates uncertainty. What is he uncertain about? In this case, the uncertainty focuses around whether the client likes his most recent proposal and wants to continue to do business. To act with emotional intelligence, the advisor must generate a response that reduces the uncertainty. So, the advisor might decide to call the client and ask for some thoughts. Either way, the advisor clarifies the client's interest. If the client isn't interested, the advisor can move on. If there is interest, it can be pursued. Either way, the advisor can move on and release the anxiety.

What about the advisor who is angry with her branch manager? Instead of developing an ulcer or reliving the incident in living color, or avoiding her manager or blowing up, she is much better off to respond to the message the anger communicates: Something is wrong! There is an injustice! The advisor can ask, "What is wrong?" Assuming there are no cognitive distortions, what is wrong is that the advisor believes she is not being treated fairly by her branch manager. To act with emotional intelligence, she should devise a plan for opening up a dialogue with her boss to express that she believes she is being treated unfairly. When this is implemented and accomplished, the advisor will find that her anger has dissipated, as her response has corrected the wrongfulness of the situation. Her response—the choice to have a discussion about what is anger provoking—allows her to move on.

What about our dejected advisor? Sitting around in mourning is sure to keep him on a downward spiral. But if he remembers that dejection communicates hopelessness, then he can ask himself, "What am I feeling hopeless about?" His next step is to generate a behavior that will put him in the process of finding new clients. Doing so creates feelings of empowerment, and he can move on rather than ruminating about how bleak the future is.

In all of these situations, acting with emotional intelligence helps the advisor alleviate the emotional distress of the situation and allows the advisor to move on to doing his or her best.

To generate effective behavioral responses, you must:

- Recognize the emotion and manage its arousal indicators.
- Understand what the emotion is communicating and act in a way that responds to the message of the emotion.

O n   t h e   S t r e e t

Identify a situation that creates emotional distress.

- What emotion do you experience—anger, anxiety, dejection, fear?
- What is the emotion communicating to you?
- What is the best way to respond to the emotion's message?

After a while, it will become second nature to respond to the messages of your emotions. When this occurs you will be applying your emotional intelligence, and you will find yourself becoming much more productive.

Managing Your Emotions by Taking Time Out and Having a Laugh

Granted that many of the aforementioned emotional management techniques require an investment of time and energy. In the meantime, to keep you covered on a daily basis, use these crash-proof tips to avoid getting emotionally derailed from the track of success.

- *Take time out.* In a volatile situation, get a drink of water, go to the bathroom, or go for a walk outside or around your floor. However you do it, get away from the situation, so you can calm yourself.

- *Take deep breaths.* Deep breathing slows you down, and you can use it as a method to get control.
- *Redirect your emotional energy.* Clean up your desk, sharpen pencils, wash your socks, or play oldies on the radio. Do any simple activity that will distract you from your anxiety or anger, and at the same time help you get something done.
- *Have a laugh.* We all know that laughter is life's best painkiller. A moment of respite can be quite useful for giving you pause to reappraise things and to get in control of yourself and your situation.

Putting It All Together

Here's a good activity that will enhance your capacity to use your emotional operating system advantageously.

Write down a description of a recent emotionally charged situation that you did not handle well, one in which you regretted the outcome. Provide the following information:

- What were you feeling?
- What do you suppose you were thinking?
- On a scale of 1 (low) to 9 (high), how strong was your physiological reaction?
- How did you act?

Look at your responses. Did they help you manage the situation productively? *Note the relationship between your thoughts, arousal, and actions.*

Now imagine you will encounter the same situation. What would you do differently to ensure better results? To help you answer, provide the following information:

- What is the message of the feeling you will experience?
- What do you want to say to yourself?
- How will you keep your arousal in check?
- What is the best way to respond?

Now compare your responses and you will see why and how the desired emotional operating system is more effective, and how the components of the system work to help you get better results.

O n   t h e   **S** t r e e t

Identify an emotionally charged or distressing situation that you are likely to encounter. Prepare an effective emotional operating system sheet. Keep it on your desk as a reminder of how you want your emotional operating system to function when you encounter the situation. If you do this, it will become second nature to keep your emotional operating system tuned for high performance.

Once you can manage your emotions, you can begin to develop your third EI portfolio asset—self-motivation.

SELF MOTIVATION: YOUR THIRD CORE EI ASSET

Think of an advisor whose career has stalled—maybe even your own. Chances are, he or she is suffering from a serious motivational deficiency. Such people tend to fall prey to wasted time, unfocused work habits, and lackluster performance. Their lack of enthusiasm is contagious, and they don't inspire much confidence in others.

Now think of the most successful financial advisor you know. Chances are, he or she is a high-energy person. Such people have the drive to make calls, meet clients, do research, and give presentations. They also have the tenacity to stick to a project and see it through. Other folks naturally are drawn to their go-go attitude. Colleagues find them inspiring and clients trust that they'll get the job done. Self-motivation pays off.

Technically, being self-motivated means you can use your emotions to propel yourself into action for a desired purpose. This is not an easy task, as even the most successful advisors at times feel unmotivated to take on the next challenge.

To leverage your ability to self-motivate, you must be able to turn the four sources of motivation into motivational forces; then you can take care of business and overcome adversity at its worse.

Your Sources of Motivation

There are four main sources of motivation.

1. First and foremost, you can motivate yourself with your emotional operating system—your own thoughts, actions, and physiological arousal.
2. Supportive friends, family, and colleagues may offer a much-needed push at times.
3. An emotional mentor can help jump-start your enthusiasm. A mentor can be an ordinary person you know and admire, or can be an inspirational hero, dead, alive, or even fictitious.
4. You can also use your surroundings to help you power-up.

Motivating Your Emotional Operating System

You've learned how to use your thoughts, arousal indicators, and behavior to help you manage your emotions. Here are some ways to use those same three components to get yourself to "Do it!"

Motivational self-statements.   Different individuals are motivated by different things. However, there are five key traits that all highly self-motivated individuals share.

1. Confidence
2. Optimism
3. Tenacity
4. Enthusiasm
5. Resiliency

These are the qualities you need to believe you can do a job, hope for a good result, stay on task until you achieve it, enjoy the process of accomplishing it, and bounce back if things don't turn out quite as well as expected.

One of the best ways to nurture these traits in yourself is by motivational self-speaking. Whenever you notice yourself having irrationally negative thoughts ("I'll never get this report done."), you can learn to replace them with more realistically motivational self-statements ("I can write this report. I know the material backward and forward. No one understands it better than I do. I'll finish the report today, and I'll do a good job.").

At first, you may feel a bit awkward playing the role of cheerleader to yourself. With a little practice, though, it will start to come more naturally.

O n   t h e   S t r e e t

Give yourself a motivational self-statement each morning as you first sit down to your desk. For example, "I'm going to have a productive day." Then, each time you begin a new task, give yourself another mini-pep talk: "I'm going to finish my calls this morning. I'm good on the phone. I can do this well. I'm going to stick with it until I make it through the prospect list." You can even write your most powerful statements on index cards and post them by your desk: I've got what it takes to be a great financial advisor. Nothing can stop me when I try.

Meaningful goals. Continuously setting meaningful goals is another way to keep your motivation high. A meaningful goal is a specific objective that fires up your desire. This arousal can then be transformed into the energy you need to achieve your objective. The trick is to pick a goal that's attainable, yet challenging. Aim too low and you may get bored. Aim too high and you run the risk of getting discouraged and giving up.

When you have a big meaningful goal—doubling your business within three years, for example—*break it down into smaller chunks.* This lets you acknowledge the progress you make en route to your final destination. Then set subgoals, such as increasing business by 10 percent over the same quarter last year. When you reach this milestone, you'll see that you are indeed progressing toward your ultimate objective, and this positive movement can spur you to keep pushing ahead. You become more confident and optimistic.

If you're a glass-half-empty type, you might be tempted to focus only on how far you have left to go. Instead, try to shift perspectives by concentrating on how far you've come. Even if you're only a quarter of the way toward your final goal, tell yourself you're 25 percent there. Don't worry about being 75 percent away from your objective, as that will most likely create thoughts that are demotivating.

Also, remember that the key is to set goals that are meaningful to you.

Visualize to energize. You can rev up your engine with *mental arousal.* With a little practice, you can learn to intentionally use your thoughts to mobilize your motivation. It's the old power-of-positive thinking philosophy updated for your workplace. To see how easy and effective this can be, try this simple visualization exercise.

1. Close your eyes. Take a few long, deep breaths to relax.
2. Imagine yourself performing the task that you're unmotivated to do. Let's say it's calling a list of clients you haven't heard from lately. Focus on the sensations you would actually feel in this situation—the sight of the list, the smell of a cup of coffee sitting on your desk, the feel of the phone receiver you lift in one hand, the sound of the dial tone, the movement of your other hand as you press the keys, and so on.
3. Imagine yourself struggling with the task and becoming frustrated. Say you call one number after another. The first number is disconnected, you don't get an answer at the second, and you get the runaround from a secretary at the third. Maybe you begin to tap our foot impatiently or slouch dejectedly in your chair.
4. Then, imagine yourself regaining your composure. You sit up straight but comfortably in your chair, and you feel calm and in control. See yourself picking up the phone receiver and dialing the next number with cool efficiency.
5. Next, imagine yourself successfully completing the task. See yourself working your way down the list in a swift and systematic manner. You stay calm when you don't reach a client, and you're pleasantly professional when you do.

6. Finally, imagine yourself feeling good about your success. You've remained focused and made all the calls in record time. You're happy to have this chore out of the way, and you're glad to have touched base with some valued clients.

You'll notice that this mental rehearsal carries over into real-life performance. The explanation is simple: The exercise helps you see a seemingly insurmountable task as manageable after all. By visualizing yourself through it step by step, you increase your confidence that you are up to the challenge. This, in turn, may spur you to tackle the task in reality.

Playing mind games to win.   Another way to kick your career into high gear is with *mind games.* Such games are based on the premise that mental fantasies can guide you to a more upbeat train of thought, which not only helps keep pessimism at bay, but also the arousal generated becomes fuel for enthusiasm. Here's how to play a mental game called *Day One.*

Let's say you've been asked to make a presentation about retirement planning. You've given dozens of similar presentations before. You know it needs to be done but you see it more as a chore than a turn-on, so you're have trouble getting fired up for this one. Imagine that you're a brand-new advisor instead, and this will be your debut presentation— your first day on the job.

Approach the chore as you would if this really were your first day (take a minute to remember how you felt). You probably would be filled with enthusiasm and eagerness to get started. By putting yourself in a new frame of mind, you can see the task ahead as a fresh challenge, rather than a familiar drudgery. This, in turn, will help you view it with renewed enthusiasm.

O n   t h e   **S** t r e e t

Reprogram your motivation using the Day One game. Post a sign saying "Day One" in your office or set up your computer to flash the words on the screen when you turn it on. Whenever you see the words, say them out loud several times in a forceful voice, and imagine those first-day feelings of eager anticipation and excitement. Eventually, you will condition yourself to experience these feelings just by looking at the signs.

Motivation in motion. A particularly successful financial advisor told me that before every one of his presentations, he goes in his office, does five minutes of the Ali shuffle, and comes out hot—ready to go.

That's another way to jump-start your productivity—simply by moving around. In its purest form, motivation is really just physiological arousal that incites you to action. You can learn to consciously crank up this arousal to keep your energy high.

Imagine you're having trouble staying awake as you try to read another coma-inducing prospectus. All you may need to do is get up and move around a bit. Try walking down the hall to get supplies or take a quick stroll around the building. If it's a lunch hour and you can take a longer walk or go the gym, even better. You may be surprised by how alert you feel.

There's a good physiological explanation for why this works: When you exercise, your blood pumps faster so that more nutrients can be brought to your muscles and organs. At the same time, our breathing becomes quicker so that more oxygen can be delivered to your cells.

When you return to your desk after a walk or workout, your body and brain have received the nutrients they need to be replenished. The drowsiness, which probably was caused by the lack of enough oxygen getting to our brain, has been banished as well. All of this makes you feel more wide-awake and alert and helps your brain function better.

O *n   t h e*   **S** *t r e e t*

To fit more movement into your day, try walking whenever you can. Take the stairs instead of the elevator, or park your car in a spot far away from the building. If you want to talk to Gloria on the second floor, go to her office instead of picking up the phone.

Do some simple stretches even while sitting at your desk. Move your head in a semicircle. Raise each arm in turn over our head and reach for the opposite wall, or lift each leg in turn and hold it parallel to the floor for a few seconds. If your office is private, you can even do some more vigorous moves, such as jumping jacks or running in place— anything that leaves you feeling refreshed and invigorated.

Locked-in interest. You can revive your energy by setting aside time and space to redirect your thoughts and behavior. Two techniques, called *Time Lock* and *Focal Lock,* can help.

In Time Lock, you block off a period of time—anywhere from a few minutes to several hours—for doing intense work. Tell other people in your office that you don't want to be disturbed and to hold your calls. Once you've made such a big deal about your intention, you'll feel as if you must put the time to good use. One word of warning, though: Don't make the time period any longer than you need. Otherwise, you risk starting to feel as you're spinning your wheels again.

In Focal Lock, you prepare to make the best possible use of your Time Lock period. Write down a list of all the tasks to be accomplished during this time. Let's say you set aside an hour. You might designate it for making five phone calls and researching a new mutual fund. This ensures that you don't waste your valuable block of time. As you cross off the tasks, it also reinforces your belief that you can be very productive when you set your mind to it. This, in turn, may help inspire you to be more focused and effective the rest of the time.

Before long, you'll probably notice that your energy and motivation are spiraling upward. After all, at the end of the day, nothing is more motivating than success.

All of the aforementioned self-motivational techniques are examples of how to use the components of your emotional operating system to get you to take care of business.

Your Mutual Motivation Fund

No advisor is an island, and sometimes it helps to get a little motivational push from friends, family, and coworkers. You can develop a network of friends, family members, and colleagues to help you overcome setbacks or crises of confidence.

The players on your personal support team need to meet three basic criteria. They must be:

1. *People you trust.* Otherwise you won't feel comfortable turning to them for help.
2. *Available.* They can't help you if they're not around.
3. *Suitable.* Otherwise they won't be able to help, even if they want to.

The characteristics of a suitable motivator vary with your needs. Sometimes what you really need is a good listener, while other times you need someone who spoons up a Mom-like dose of praise: "You're the smartest person in the office, and the hardest-working too."

One of the main functions of your support team is helping you keep your emotional perspective when times are tough. Maybe you've just lost an important client and are feeling dejected. Your supporters can remind you that it was just one individual and you still have more clients this year than last. Once you hear how other people see the situation, you might view it less emotionally and more rationally. In addition, you may regain your motivation to seek solutions to the problem. Share your ideas and ask for input from your supporters. Soon you may realize that there really is a way out of your predicament. For instance, you might come up with ideas to attract enough new clients to more than replace the business you've just lost.

Keep in mind that any good relationship is a two-way street. Let your supporters know that the willingness to help is mutual. Show your friends and coworkers that you aren't merely a foul-weather friend. Call or visit when you don't have problems too, just to say hello and ask how they're doing.

On the Street

Think of four people whom you trust and who are fairly available to you. Put their names on an index card and keep it on your desk. When you need a motivational push or support about a particular situation, give them a call. It will help.

Motivators Wanted: Dead or Alive

You can seek motivation from people you don't actually know but still admire. Your personal motivator can be alive or dead, real or fictional. You might pick a famous entrepreneur, a sports star, a figure from history, or a character from your favorite novel. Ask yourself what that person would do in your situation, or seek the person's advice in an imaginary conversation.

You may also think of specific moments in your hero's life that you found particularly motivating. Most likely, the thought of it will psych you up. One advisor told me that every time he needed to get himself pumped up, he thought of a World Series in which his team came back from the brink of disaster. "I think of myself as part of that team and it gets me going," he told me.

Rah-Rah Office Space

A third way to jump start your productivity is to cultivate an environment that is conducive to success in the context of emotional intelligence—using outside stimuli to evoke motivation. Here's how to turn your workplace into a place that makes you more productive.

- *Breathe clean air.* Nothing will get you yawing and nodding off faster than stale air depleted of oxygen. If you suspect that your office has a faulty ventilation system, contact your building management. Crack a window, if you can, or buy yourself a desktop air purifier. Then step outside during breaks for frequent infusions of fresh air.
- *Inhale the sweet smell of success.* Studies have shown that scents such as peppermint and citrus can enhance your energy and focus. Try plugging air fresheners into a nearby electrical outlet, or keep a little bowl filled with dried peppermint leaves or dried lemon rind on your desk.
- *Listen to soothing sounds.* Sound carries emotion. By emphasizing the right sounds and minimizing the wrong ones, you can decrease stress and increase motivation. If lively music works like a shot of adrenaline for you, try listening through your headphones while you read or do paperwork. On the other hand, if you spend your days listening to phones ringing, horns honking, and construction work on the floor below, try closing the door and using earplugs when you can. You can also try mediating to help tune out noise.
- *Work in good lighting.* Psychologists have found that some people lose their drive and become depressed when they don't get enough of the ultraviolet (UV) rays found in sunlight. Take advantage of natural light, letting the sunshine in during times of day when it

doesn't blind you or create glare on your computer screen. If you don't have a window, try installing a UV bulb in your lamp or overhead lighting fixture.

- *Gather support objects.* Surround yourself with items that spark your enthusiasm—a photo of your child, an inspirational quote from your business idol, or your Financial Advisor of the Year trophy, for example. You can also jot down inspirational quotations or notes on Post-Its to keep yourself on track.
- *Clear off that clutter.* If you have trouble finding forms or phone numbers because they're buried under a mountain of paperwork, you'll probably find your energy waning. Vow that you won't go home until all those papers are in their proper files, those phone numbers are logged into the right database, and the top of your desk is in full view. Then keep things neat and user-friendly.

One last reminder: You can draw strength from supportive friends, inspirational heroes, and an energizing environment, but ultimately, it's up to you to make the best use of these resources. When it comes to your own motivation, you're always the one with the final control.

Turning Setbacks into Comebacks

Unfortunately, even the best-laid plans don't always pan out. You may seem to be going along just fine, when suddenly—wham!—a setback sends you veering off course. Your forward movement comes to a grinding halt and your motivation plummets. At such times, your self-esteem may crash as well, leaving you waylaid by feelings of fear, doubt, and hopelessness.

People respond to career setbacks differently. Most, however, experience a setback as some type of loss—whether of direction, motivation, self-esteem, confidence, or pleasure in their job. Most also tend to go through the same stages in coming to grips with loss—disbelief, anger, wanting to turn back time, depression, acceptance, hope, and positive activity.

To regain your momentum, you must fully experience and move through each of these stages. You might experience several stages at once, or you might return briefly to a stage you've already passed. The only requirement is that you thoroughly work through each stage. This is where your *comeback toolkit* comes into play.

The tools you'll need. It's not easy to deal with setbacks—they are emotionally arousing, draining, and taxing. The good news, though, is, you already have learned the skills that will help you turn a setback into a comeback. The key is to remember to use them.

- Tuning in to feelings and thoughts
- Using motivational self-statements and constructive internal dialogue
- Keeping a sense of humor
- Practicing relaxation techniques
- Engaging in physical activity
- Using problem-solving methods
- Drawing from a support team
- Reassessing goals and setting new ones

Honing these skills gives you tried-and-true tools that really work—making up your essential comeback toolkit.

Here's how the skills in your toolkit can help you move smoothly through each of the stages that characterize the setback process.

- *Disbelief.* The most common response to setbacks is along the lines of, "I can't believe it," or "This isn't happening." At crisis points, however, denial serves a valuable buffer function by giving you time to compose yourself before the onset of powerful emotions. Eventually, of course, you'll need to tune in to your feelings and appraise your situation. But you can ease into this process gradually. Let's say, for example, that you've just learned that your top client is leaving. You might tell yourself, "I'm going to have to work extra-hard to find new clients to take up the slack. It's scary, because it's a tough time for business." When such thoughts become too threatening, however, try pulling a Scarlet O'Hara: "I'll think about that tomorrow." That way, you'll experience negative feelings, but protect yourself from being swamped by them.
- *Anger.* The next stage is usually resentment and hostility. You might find yourself thinking, "This is so unfair," or "That client always had it out for me." These thoughts can kick off a self-defeating cycle—you feel bitter and complain, which pushes people away, which just makes you feel more bitter and angry. Treat this

kind of anger as a cue that something is wrong—that you need to rethink your situation to determine where you got off track. In the process, you'll often wind up reassessing old goals and setting new ones. You can also burn off some anger with physical activity or reduce your level of ire by using your relaxation techniques.

- *Yearning to turn back time.* At this point, you probably find yourself pining for the good old days, thinking: "If only I hadn't missed that call," or "If only September 11 had never happened." The best way to deal with a counterproductive nostalgia attack is to engage in a *constructive inner dialogue.* Ask yourself, "So what do I do now? How do I shift myself back into high gear?" Maybe you need to consider some fresh prospecting or marketing tactics. A little yearning for the past can prompt you to explore your options for moving forward in the future.

- *Depression.* This stage might be your toughest hurdle, since depression can create an overwhelming sense of hopelessness and inertia. The good news is that once you've made it through this phase, you'll find yourself over the hump and well on your way to a successful recovery. To help banish your blues, draw on your *support networks*—friends, family, and colleagues who can help boost your motivation levels and keep you focused and positive. You might also try using motivational self-statements such as, "I can do this," or "I'm a great financial advisor, and I can convey that to clients."

- *Acceptance.* Reaching this phase means that you've made it over the hump. Your confidence is returning, and you know you've weathered the worst of the storm. Self-awareness can help you get in touch with your intentions. This, in turn, can help you focus on your new goals and plan a strategy for achieving them. If you want to attract new clients, for example, set your goal—say, developing a persuasive marketing letter—and then go for it.

- *Hope.* At this point, you're feeling downright optimistic. You've made it through the hard part without losing your sense of humor. You have a goal in mind, and you know the steps you'll need to take to achieve it. Your self-esteem is revitalized. This rush of hope gives rise to a burst of energy, which you can harness to carry into the next and final stage.

- *Positive activity.* Finally! You feel enthusiastic and ready to tackle whatever it takes to get back on track. Your motivation has returned full force. To convert your energy into effective action, try breaking down your goals into mini-tasks. You might write a first draft of your letter, ask colleagues to critique it, write a revised draft, and so on. This is also the time to use your problem-solving skills to devise effective solutions for any snags that may occur.

Encountering a stumbling block can often fuel a dreaded catch-22: suffering a setback temporarily snaps your motivation—motivation that, ironically, is precisely what you need to overcome the setback. If you find yourself stuck in this cycle, reach into that comeback toolkit. Drawing on these tools helps you mobilize your feelings, thoughts, and arousal to fight your way back, restoring your energy, confidence, and all-important drive to succeed. If you have been making the necessary investment, it is safe to say that your emotional intelligence portfolio is beginning to grow and pay dividends. The next step in becoming an emotionally intelligent financial advisor is to learn how to diversify your emotional intelligence into your relationships with your colleagues, assistants, and of course, your clients.

2

INCREASING YOUR BOTTOM LINE BY DIVERSIFYING YOUR EMOTIONAL INTELLIGENCE

Diversifying your emotional intelligence means investing it in the work relationships that impact your bottom line. For just about every advisor, this means applying emotional intelligence in relationships with managers, team/colleagues, and of course, clients.

You can leverage your emotional intelligence in these bottom-line relationships in many ways, but to do so, you must remember to use what you have already learned.

For example, if your manager or a client criticizes you, to take advantage of their thoughts you must manage your emotions so that you can make accurate appraisals and respond productively instead of defensively. If you are dealing with an emotionally aroused client, not only will you have to manage your emotions—perhaps by breathing slowly—you must also remember to respond to the message of the emotion so that you can respond effectively and bring rationality to the encounter. If you want to tune in to your colleagues and team members, you will have to remember to practice your sensory awareness, and especially refrain from making appraisals without getting them documented. In other words, your intrapersonal emotional intelligence supplies you with many skills that affect your work relationships. Now, we can diversify your emotional intelligence (EI) portfolio by developing your *interpersonal expertise.*

INTERPERSONAL EXPERTISE

Interpersonal expertise refers to your ability to relate well to others. Building consensus, managing conflict, dealing with those who are emotionally charged, giving and taking criticism, and making meetings productive are all skills that are seeded and bloomed by your interpersonal expertise.

Interpersonal expertise boils down to two main factors.

1. The ability to analyze a relationship so you can understand its goals and boundaries
2. The ability to communicate so you can exchange information effectively with another person

You can be the smartest, most knowledgeable, and hardest working advisor in your office, but if your interpersonal expertise falls short, so will your bottom line.

Can You Relate?

Before you can even start honing your interpersonal emotional intelligence skills, you must be aware of and understand three factors that impact all relationships: *needs, time,* and *communication.*

Relationship needs. People enter into relationships, first and foremost, to meet their needs. Ideally, a relationship is a mutually beneficial arrangement. Your relationship with a client, for instance, helps you make money and maintain your position at work, while it helps your client make sound financial decisions.

Emotionally intelligent financial advisors (EIFAs) are keenly aware of what they need from each of their work relationships. Armed with this information, they can begin to develop strategies on how to meet their needs.

EIFAs are also keenly aware of what others need from the working relationship. Armed with this information, they can begin to generate the actions that will meet the needs of others. Meeting the needs of others (and having yours met) promotes relationship longevity. With clients, it turns into trust and loyalty.

On the Street

Think of your relationships at work—your relationship with a particular client, a specific colleague, your assistant, your manager. Ask yourself (you may want to write it out):

- What are my needs for each work relationship?
- Which relationships are meeting my needs and which aren't?
- How can I get my needs met from my work relationships
- What are the needs of my manager, client, and colleagues?
- How am I doing in meeting their needs?
- How can I better meet the needs of my working relationships?

Relationship time. A relationship involves *ongoing* contact over time. If you see a client only every couple of years or so, the two of you are likely to remain acquaintances. If you see a particular client once a month, however, you'll have the opportunity to develop an actual relationship. By interacting with this client at different times and in a variety of circumstances, you'll gradually pick up clues about what makes him or her tick. As you build a rapport, you'll eventually see sides of the client's personality that were hidden from you before. Each meeting will provide fresh insights, which you can ultimately use to make future encounters as productive as possible.

Emotionally intelligent financial advisors are tuned in to the fact that they can improve their relationships by having *quality work relationship time,* if you will. When you have quality work relationship time—whether with your boss, clients, or assistant—you increase the chances of both parties having their needs met, thus perpetuating a productive relationship. This is because you communicate at a meaningful level, one in which both parties are free to express their *thoughts, ideas, and feelings.* Doing so promotes openness, genuineness, authenticity, trust, and a host of other factors that we all know make up the cornerstone of every good relationship.

Of course, it's impossible to communicate on a meaningful level if you don't spend time with the particular individual. This is why emotionally intelligent financial advisors are very high on "interaction"—they know that it's in their best interest to interact with those who influence their success. Thus, it's a good idea to think of ways you can spend more time with those who affect your success, as a prelude to promoting the quality of the relationship. As the quality of the relationship improves, you will find that your needs are being met.

O *n   t h e* **S** *t r e e t*

- *Increase your calls to clients.* Besides updating them, throw in a joke and ask how they are doing. Add a minute or two to your conversations.
- *Spend a little more time with your assistant.* Ask about his or her goals, what he or she would like to do more of, what gives him or her trouble, how you can be helpful.
- *Always acknowledge your boss.* At every encounter, even if it's for a minute, say more than just a hello.

Communication.   Communication is essential in any relationship. Broadly yet accurately defined, communication is *an exchange of information.* For example, you wouldn't say you have a relationship with the cashier who checks out your groceries at the supermarket once a week, unless you start trading gossip and news about your personal lives. Of course, negotiating this territory can be tricky when clients are involved, but the more emotionally aware you are, the better you can predict how a given statement about your feelings and thoughts may affect a particular client or colleague. This helps you share information in a way that is likely to serve your relationship well.

A crucial point is that there are many levels of information exchange. Indeed, when people say they are not communicating, it is often because they are using different levels of information exchange—one is on AM, the other FM.

To communicate effectively, you'll need to identify the various levels at which others are operating. Think of a team meeting where one person is exchanging pleasantries ("Nice weather, isn't it?"), another is stating facts ("Our profit margin is shrinking."), and a third is expressing feelings ("I'm really hurt by your attitude."). If team members continue to function at such different levels, they will be hard-pressed to accomplish much. To avoid a Babelesque scenario—one where coworkers are essentially speaking different languages—learn to recognize the current level of discussion and tweak it accordingly.

The four most common levels of communication are:

1. *Niceties.* These are the automatic pleasantries you exchange with friends, acquaintances, and strangers alike. "How's it going?" for example. Niceties are valuable as social lubricants, but the connections they forge are typically fairly flimsy. They tend to elicit such rote responses as, "Oh, fine. You?" Keep an ear out for the occasional, more meaningful reaction, such as, "Actually, I'm having a rotten day." This is your cue to ratchet up the level of discussion and talk about what's really going on.

2. *Factual information.* Whether you're reporting the latest sales figures, charting the Nasdaq, or teaching colleagues a new computer program, you're often in the position of articulating cold, hard facts. Remember that facts can provoke dramatic emotional responses. Think about the heights of happiness or the depths of despair prompted by a sharp rise or dip in the stock market. At your next team meeting, notice the impact of facts on our coworkers. Suppose you're reporting to your team on a decline in profits. If you observe beads of sweat forming on one advisor's brow or fidgeting in his seat, you can fairly conclude that the news is causing him significant anxiety. (Of course, he might also be ill.) Use this insight to help him put his fears in perspective. For example, you might point out the trends suggesting a turn-around next quarter.

3. *Thoughts and ideas.* Sharing opinions and beliefs means taking a risk. Unlike facts, your thoughts and ideas are not right or wrong. As a result, expressing them requires that you make yourself vulnerable to, perhaps, an out of hand rejection or harsh criticism. Most people become defensive and experience bruised self-esteem when rejected or harshly criticized, so it is safer for them to stick to the facts and discussions about the weather. Unfortunately, this often causes their business to stall. Emotionally intelligent financial advisors are willing to make themselves vulnerable because they believe that one of the ways they create their success is by expressing their thoughts and their ideas to their managers and colleagues, and certainly to their clients.

4. *Feelings.* When people share feelings, they feel even more emotionally vulnerable than when they share thoughts. Talking about feelings is precisely the path leading to the closest and longest-lasting relationships. The trick is to identify which feelings are appropriate to reveal and when. Some feelings are best kept out of the workplace—your sexual attraction to a colleague, for example. Others may be more acceptable, but only under the right circumstances. Talking about feelings might be quite helpful, for example, when your goal is to build trust or consensus within your team, or when you are trying to work out conflict or dealing with a dejected client.

Once you learn to identify the different levels of communication, start using your knowledge to build stronger relationships. The key is to *know what you need from each encounter and what level of communication you must use to get the task accomplished so the need can be met.* For example, if you want to know how a client feels about working with you, you have to get him to disclose his feelings—a risky communication. If you want to know how you can be more effective with your assistant, you will have to get her to disclose her thoughts. If you want to help work out a conflict in your team, you have to get people to disclose their thoughts and feelings—otherwise, the root of the issue will not surface. If you are looking for how the team is performing, you want the facts, not comments about low morale. (Certainly, this information would be important, but at the moment, you want just the financial data.)

Many times, you'll want to shift from one level to another, either because others are operating at a different level, because the current level is causing someone discomfort, or because the flow of information would be better served by temporarily forgoing thoughts and feelings for facts. *Until you shift people to the appropriate level of information exchange, you will be unable to relate effectively, and unable to accomplish the task at hand.*

One way to facilitate this kind of shift is to craft *strategic questions.* These questions force the individual to respond at the appropriate level of information exchange.

Suppose a team member named Susan is talking about an upcoming presentation. She's giving a straightforward summary—who, what, when, where, why—but her uncharacteristically jerky movements and halting speech seem to signal unspoken misgivings. To guide the discussion into feeling territory, ask a strategic question: "How are you feeling about the presentation?" Listen to the response. Many times, the person will respond with a thought, not a feeling, such as, "I think it's okay." If this is the case, follow up with something like, "I know you think it's looking good; I'm wondering, though, how you are feeling about it—excited, anxious?" You might also offer a statement about your own feelings and impressions: "I sense [you can document if you see fit] that you may be feeling a bit anxious." When one member of a group (or conversation) opens up this way, others often follow suit.

Another useful tactic is to *solicit feelings and thoughts directly by stating your need.* To do this, try using the introductory phrase, "I'd like to hear," as in, "I'd like to hear how you're feeling about the presentation," or "I'd like to hear your thoughts on this." Bear in mind that, whatever approach you take, some people will resist your best efforts to shift communication to the thoughts or feelings level. In such cases, your best strategy may be to solicit thoughts and feelings about expressing thoughts and feelings, as in, "It seems like it's a little hard for you to share your feelings with me. Is it something I'm doing? How do you feel about my asking you this?"

Take a client who is recently divorced and having to plan a financial future alone for the first time. As the conversation goes on, the client clearly grows more and more anxious. You not only hear this in his words, ("I'm afraid to even think about what would happen if I lost my job.") but see it in his actions (faster breathing and nervous fidgeting).

At this point, the client's strong emotions threaten to swamp his ability to make good decisions. As a skillful communicator, you realize it's time to take the intensity down a notch or two. You move the conversation away from feelings to a discussion of thoughts, ideas, and facts, and by so doing, actually help the client perceive the situation more accurately with a sense of confidence that his situation is manageable, especially when there is little chance of a sudden job loss.

Every situation is different, but here are some other circumstances where you might want to shift to a new level of communication.

- *Move to the facts level if someone is very angry or anxious.* This helps defuse the situation and put the anger in perspective. Once the other person calms down, it's easier to deal with the situation effectively,
- *Move to the feelings level if someone seems sad or hopeless.* Sometimes the other person will only show such feelings nonverbally (not smiling, looking away). By eliciting discussion of these emotions, you could help the person find ways to alleviate them.
- *Stay in the facts or thoughts level if you want to solve a problem.* Intense feelings make it hard to think clearly.
- *Stay in the thoughts or feeling level if you want to build trust.* An open, honest exchange of thoughts, ideas, feelings, and attitudes can gain the other person's confidence and cooperation.

When both parties are on the appropriate level of information exchange to get their needs met or a task accomplished, then both are relating well. Your goal is to relate well in your work relationships.

Increasing your awareness to relational needs and identifying the appropriate level of information exchange to satisfy those needs will allow you to diversify your emotional intelligence into the three most important work encounters, all of which affect your bottom line. Indeed, it's a safe bet to say that whether you are in Los Angeles, New York, or Milwaukee, within the first hour of your day, you will interact with your team, your manager, and your clients, so it makes good sense to see how you can use your emotional intelligence to get greater benefits from these relationships by relating well.

On the Street

Before the next team meeting starts, observe the different levels of information exchange being used. Ask yourself:

- What is the goal of the meeting?
- What level of information exchange is needed to accomplish that goal?
- How do I get the team to shift to an appropriate level of information exchange?

Your answers will make the meeting much more productive.
Before your next client encounter, ask yourself:

- What is the goal of this encounter?
- What level of information exchange is needed to accomplish that goal?
- How do I get the client to shift to an appropriate level of information exchange?

Your answers will help make your next client encounter more productive.

USING EMOTIONAL INTELLIGENCE IN THE OFFICE

It doesn't take long to realize that while colleagues might not give you any dough to invest, they sure can make it easier for you to get to and deal effectively with those who do. It might be a solid referral from your manager, or a great idea from a team member, or even a message given quickly and accurately to you by your assistant. Whatever the case, if you don't have good relationships with these folks, then you might as well follow some Soprano advice: "Forget about it."

Over the years, I have found many ways for financial advisors to leverage emotional intelligence in their relationships with their colleagues, staff, and boss. Two of the more powerful are becoming an effective team communicator and giving and taking criticism. When you become a better team communicator, you can strategically influence the meeting for the betterment of all. When you give and take criticism positively, you motivate, educate, and develop others as well as yourself. Mastering both of these skills requires applying your interpersonal expertise.

Emotional Intelligence and Team Communication

You've been there: Some team meetings are absolutely electric. Everyone is charged up with ideas and enthusiasm, and the air is crackling with group energy. At the end, you leave feeling as if you and the other team members have come up with some creative and collaborative solutions to problems.

You've also been to team meetings that are more like experiments in sleep deprivation. You struggle to keep our eyes open as one person drones on endlessly, while everyone else is too lethargic or scared to say anything. You leave feeling frustrated, isolated, and unproductive.

The difference between the two scenarios is team communication. A little constructive give-and-take lets team members resolve stubborn problems, generate fresh ideas, and learn how to work together as a cooperative unit. If your institution is one of the many that are integrating the services they provide to their clients, it is likely that you will spend more and more of your time in team meetings. Good team communication skills are now essential to your job.

Emotionally intelligent financial advisors realize that they cannot control their team members, but they also realize they can positively influence the team meeting by applying their emotional intelligence in the context of team communication. Consequently, if you asked emotionally intelligent financial advisors how they leverage emotional intelligence to enhance team communication, they would say:

- *Be inclusive.* Talk to everyone when you speak. Don't keep your eyes locked on one particular person. Instead, seek input from everybody, occasionally asking different individuals, "What do you think?" The EIFA wants the team to *feel* like a team, and so looks to get everyone involved, thus maximizing group energy. The EIFA also recognizes that everybody has the *need* to be included—

being inclusive helps this need be met and produces better team relationships.

- *Discourage dominance.* Don't let one person hijack the discussion. The group will benefit from hearing everyone's ideas. If necessary, politely ask, "What do others have to say about this?" The EIFA knows that some folks have trouble asserting themselves in the face of a dominant personality. Thus, by asking for their thoughts and feelings, the EIFA helps team members *self disclose* and *assert* their thoughts and feelings.

- *Show support.* Keep morale high by giving out the verbal equivalent of gold stars. For example, "That's a great idea," or "You've obviously put a lot of work into this." The EIFA promotes *positive feelings* to enhance team communication. Giving praise publicly not only gives recognition to the individuals and builds their self-esteem, but encourages others to take the risk of expressing their ideas too. It is also important to show support when a team member is feeling down—to do this, you must be aware of the feelings of your team members.

- *Stay calm.* Some meetings have greater potential for emotional volatility than others. A routine agenda is not as likely to generate fireworks as one affecting people's job security or reviewing their work performance, for example. Aim to keep the emotional tenor low key, whatever the topic on the table. If things get tense, ask questions that lead the discussion into neutral territory for a while. If that doesn't work, suggest a break: "Hey, there is a lot of enthusiasm here; let's take ten and then we can pick it up again!" Note how the EIFA has taken advantage of the fact that both anger and enthusiasm share increased *physical arousal,* and thus frames the situation as people becoming enthusiastic rather than angry. By encouraging the team members to appraise the situation as enthusiastic rather than anger provoking, the EIFA can preserve rationality, and at the same time promote positive feelings.

- *Pay attention.* Notice how each person participates and responds in the meeting. Who is being left out, hogging the floor, or developing hurt feelings? You won't know if you don't keep your eyes and ears open. The EIFA uses *sensory awareness* to enhance team communication. While others often interpret sensory data inappropriately, the EIFA checks the accuracy of appraisals by either *documenting* comments, or, asking other team members to document their observations. By taking responsibility for this action, the EIFA ensures that the team communication will be much more accurate.

- *Invite disagreement.* A yes-man or yes-woman isn't very valuable as a team player. Don't fall into the habit of appearing to agree even when you don't, just because it's easier. Also, if only one side of an issue is being examined, it might pay occasionally to assume the role of devil's advocate. The EIFA takes advantage of the fact that different people *appraise* events differently, and by seeking out different appraisals—information exchange at the thought level—increases exposure to new ideas. Because these different perspectives have been invited, conflicts driven by ego and power struggles are minimized. Recognizing that people appraise situations differently exemplifies the practice of being aware to the needs of others.

- *Use self-disclosure.* This involves clearly stating what you personally think, feel, and believe. For example: "I think productivity might go up if we hired another secretary." "I feel uncomfortable with this approach." "I believe the market is ready to rebound." When you share this way in a group, you may inspire others to do likewise. If people still don't open up, try throwing out such questions as, "What do you think about this idea?" "How do you feel about this situation?" The EIFA knows the importance of exchanging thoughts, ideas, and feelings, and so models the behavior and knows how to ask *strategic questions* that gently force others to respond on the communication level needed to get the job done.

- *Listen dynamically.* This involves not only hearing what someone else is saying, but also understanding, acknowledging, and responding to the emotional subtext. When in doubt, restate the speaker's message in your own words as a way of double-checking that everyone is on the same page. If you think a team member is angry, deal with it by asking what is wrong and then guide the team to problem solve. If you think a team member or several are anxious, focus on what the uncertainties are and help the team prepare for them so confidence can be restored. The EIFA pays particular attention to all words, facial expressions, speech hesitations, tone—these factors accompany the verbal expression and give a glimpse into the emotional landscape of the speaker. Of particular importance, the EIFA listens to the message of the emotion. This allows him or her to surface the underlying emotional currents that cause the meeting to flow in particular directions.

- *Be assertive.* Let's say you have a different view from the others. It's important to state your position clearly and persuasively, but without denigrating anyone else's opinions. Likewise, when another person is expressing a minority viewpoint, try to make sure that person gets a fair hearing. The EIFA remembers that he or she is just expressing thoughts and feelings, and so begins comments with subjective phrases such as, "I think," "In my opinion," or "I feel," rather than expressing thoughts as fact, which would be more likely to cause arguments, conflicts, and power struggles. The EIFA remembers that the *intent* of assertiveness is to express feelings and needs in an appropriate manner, and thus communicates in accordance.

Using your emotional intelligence in the context of your teams' will help you profit—now and in the future!

O *n t h e* **S** *t r e e t*

During your next team meeting:

- Practice inclusion by soliciting thoughts from all team members.
- Build positive energy by publicly praising team members.
- Use self-disclosure to model expression of thoughts and feelings.
- Help the team communicate effectively by documenting and asking others to document their observations.

Positive Criticism

Giving and taking criticism is one of the hardest tasks financial advisors encounter. In fact, even when necessary, many of them shy away from giving it, especially if the criticism is directed to a client or to their branch manager. What about taking criticism? Again, most advisors handle criticism poorly, especially when being criticized by their manager or a client. This is unfortunate because counterproductive responses to criticism almost always come back to haunt you.

However, if you apply your emotional intelligence when giving and taking criticism, you can transform it from a negative event into a positive motivational experience that boosts self-esteem and productivity. In so doing, you enhance your effectiveness with those you work with and this inevitably improves your bottom line.

Here are some tips that will help you diversify your emotional intelligence into the everyday event of giving and taking criticism, whether it involves your manager, colleagues, or team members. Note how different aspects of emotional intelligence come into play.

Befriend criticism.   Making criticism positive begins by revisiting and managing your emotional operating system. How do you appraise criticism? If you appraise it as a negative, it's not surprising that you respond defensively or end up feeling dejected. In contrast, EIFAs appraise criticism as valuable information that increases their awareness about how they are doing and how they can do better. This appraisal helps them listen to the information being presented and to evaluate it on merit rather than emotional irrationality. Because EIFAs have a positive appraisal of criticism, they seek it out from their managers, colleagues, and clients. Befriending criticism helps the EIFA continually learn ways to become more effective. Befriending criticism increases your self-awareness.

O *n   the* **S** *t r e e t*
_____

- Write down a positive definition of criticism and put it on your desk. For example, "Criticism is information that can help me grow," or "Criticism is teaching appropriate skills and knowledge."
- Write down three instructional self-statements that will help you respond productively when you receive criticism, such as, "Here's an opportunity to learn how my manager/client thinks," or "They are telling me how to do my job better."

Positive intent. Many times, the criticism we give or receive is destructive for the simple reason that we lose our *awareness about our intent.* Lots of criticism comes out of buried resentment and so the intent becomes to express anger and make the person feel bad. Better to express your feelings of resentment and anger then hide them under the guise of constructive criticism. To give positive criticism, your intent has to be *improvement oriented*—to make a situation better. With this intent in mind, you can begin to generate the behaviors and style of criticism that demonstrate your desire to help. One way to make your criticism improvement-oriented is to move the behavior you are criticizing into the future by emphasizing the next time. For example, "Hey Bill, *the next time* Mr. Jackson calls, let me know because I want to take his calls." This phrasing of the criticism communicates many psychological subtleties, such as confidence in Bill (I trust you to do it better next time) and job security (if there is a next time, you know you are not getting fired).

Be timing oriented. There's a time and a place for everything, criticism included. Sometimes, the best time and place for criticism is your office, other times the neutral conference center, and sometimes, you can just weave it into the natural flow of the conversation. Key questions to ask yourself to help you become timing oriented include: Am I ready to give this criticism and is the person ready to hear it? Is this the best place and time to give the criticism? Would I want to be criticized in this environment? One unsuitable time to give criticism is when you are not managing your emotions, especially anger. Not only will your anger quickly turn the encounter into a negative event, your recipient is also likely to blow off your observations, thinking what you said was motivated by anger, not your rational thought.

Also, don't criticize a colleague or assistant who is angry—you will most likely be told, "I don't want to hear it."

Protect self-esteem. When criticism attacks the recipient's self-esteem, count on a defensive response. Putting a person down is hardly a way to make people receptive to your thoughts. Avoid destructive labels and phrases such as, "That was really a stupid thing to do? " or "You are so pig-headed." Also avoid making statements that are gross overgeneralizations: "You *never* give me my messages," or "You *always* interrupt me when I am with a client." Such statements are rarely true, so you can expect a defensive response when you use them. Try changing your *always* or *never* to *sometimes*. "Sometimes you interrupt me when I am with a client," stands a better chance of getting through because *sometimes* is true, whereas *always* or *never* isn't. Of course, if you manage your emotions, you will be less likely to use overgeneralizations and destructive labeling statements because you will have greater accuracy in your appraisals of the individual.

Put motivation into your criticism. "Hey John, I'd like you to work a little harder in developing clients so I can make more money," will probably do little to motivate your assistant or partner. Don't be naïve; people change for themselves, not for you. To produce results, the EIFA is clear on how responding to the criticism benefits the recipient. Sometimes the incentive is money, other times recognition, or it might be the opportunity to do something different. Practice motivational flexibility—if one incentive doesn't work, try another.

Criticize strategically. You have a financial strategy for each of your clients. Do you have a *criticism strategy*? What do you want your criticism to accomplish? What is your criticism goal? How will you get the person to be receptive to your thoughts? How might they get defensive and how will you overcome it? When and where is the best time to give the criticism? Ponder these questions before you give criticism. Take the time to formulate a strategy for what you want to say and how best to communicate it. Ask yourself: "How can I communicate this information so the person will be receptive? " "How can I communicate to my assistant that he needs better skills with clients who call?" "How can I communicate to my manager that she needs to be more open to my suggestions?" "How can I communicate to my fellow financial advisor that his behavior in team meetings causes team distress?" Your answers will help you in creating an effective criticism strategy, and at the same time, often prevent you from giving criticism destructively.

Acknowledge that your criticism is subjective. In its purest form, criticism is an evaluation, so remember any time you give criticism that it is your subjective evaluation. Instead of making your criticism sound as though it is fact, preface your criticisms with subjective phrases such as, "In my opinion," or "This is what I think." Subjective phrases set the stage for transforming criticism from a one-way negative monologue into a dialogue—an information exchange of thoughts and ideas where the goal is to improve a situation. When you acknowledge that your criticism is subjective, you let recipients know that you are open to hearing their appraisals of events, and they are more apt to share their thoughts, especially if you ask for them. "These are my thoughts and I would like to hear yours too."

Recognize when you are ineffective. Pay attention to emotional cues, such as facial expressions, body posture, or interruptions, that can tell you how your criticism is being received. If you note defensive behavior, rather than saying, "You're getting defensive," recognize that *you are being ineffective in your communication.* Take a deep breath and try another approach.

Follow up. Sometimes it is an hour later, others times a day or two, but EIFAs check back with the recipient of criticism to see how he or she is doing, to give support, to make sure that the criticism was experienced as a put up, not a put down.

The Art of Criticism

The art of criticism means specifically identifying the criticism you want to give, and then packaging it, individualizing it, and stylizing it to the particular encounter. This means being creative, clever, and, most importantly, remembering to be strategic.

Sometimes, the art of criticism can involve more than just verbal communication. One financial advisor told me that he couldn't stand the cigars that one of his high-net clients smoked when he came to visit.

Every time, he visited, which was fairly often, he would light up one of his big stinky cigars. The smell was terrible and it was always noticeable to the client who came to visit later in the day. Because he gave me so much business, I wanted him to be comfortable and didn't want to offend him by saying anything. So the next time he came, I removed all the ashtrays from my office. It worked—he didn't light up. I don't know how long I can go without having ashtrays in my office but it least it gives me some time to think of something else.

The point is that *you can give criticism in multiple ways, not just with your words.*

Other times, the art of criticism can take the form of a one-line statement. But whether it is behavioral, a one liner, or a process over several weeks, strategic thinking must be used. How might the art of criticism sound in different scenarios?

I have heard many "how to criticize" questions from advisors. Here are a few of the most common and difficult criticism situations they encounter—examples of how the art of criticism might be practiced on the first try with a just few lines, or even one line.

- *Situation:* Criticizing a client who continually requests meetings but then doesn't show up or cancels at the last minute?"
- *Goal:* To get client to give appropriate notice if canceling and/or to get client to come to meeting.
- *Phrasing:* At the time client schedules next meeting, say: "Yes, Jack I can see you tomorrow at 3:00. Do me a favor, please—call me an hour before, around 2:00, to let me know you are going to make it. I understand that sometimes you get sidetracked and have to cancel—that's okay, but if I don't hear from you by 2:00, *I will assume you are not coming.* Of course, if you come anyway, I will make some time for you, but I can't guarantee I can see you exactly at 3:00. I hope you can make it because I have some exciting ideas to present to you.

- *Situation:* Criticizing your branch manager for not being supportive.
- *Goal:* To get your boss to help you by showing or implying how being supportive to you will help his bottom line.
- *Phrasing:* It's best to work this into the flow of conversation rather than making it a stand-alone conversation. Say something like, "You know, John, I've been doing a lot of thinking about how I can improve my performance, and I think I could greatly improve my bottom line if you would help me out by giving me a little more information."

- *Situation:* Criticizing a team member for being abrasive at team meetings.
- *Goal:* To increase the team member's awareness of how she comes across so she can relate more effectively to the team.
- *Phrasing:* Right after the meeting in which the team member acted abrasively, approach her with subtlety: "You know Gail, you may want to rethink how you are coming across at meetings. It may not be the way you want people to perceive you. I know that you are not abrasive, but when others hear comments like the ones you just said to Jane, what are they to think of you? I thought you might want to think about that."

What if you don't get positive results? What if the situation becomes repetitive and inevitably emotionally distressful? After all, there is no right way to deliver criticism and there is no guarantee that the recipient will be open to what you are saying.

To generate more effective responses to repetitive and difficult criticism encounters, follow these five steps.

1. *What is the goal of your criticism?* Once you know what you want your criticism to accomplish, you can begin to strategize about the way to deliver it.
2. *What makes the criticism difficult?* Sometimes the barrier is the relationship, such as your relationship with your manager or an important client. Sometimes it is the content of the criticism, such as the personal hygiene of your assistant or team member. Other times, it is a specific attribute of the recipient. Once you know what makes it difficult, you can begin to figure out how to make it less difficult.
3. *What have you already tried?* Awareness of what you have already tried will prevent you from continuing to be ineffective. In fact, anytime you catch yourself saying, "I've spoken to you a dozen times about this," you know that you have been ineffective for a while.
4. *How would others handle the encounter?* If you don't know how to handle the encounter, ask someone else. Chances are great that one of your colleagues has had to deal with a similar situation.

That colleague can help you brainstorm to come up with new responses.

5. *How can I communicate this information so the person will be receptive?* The bottom line is always to be strategic, to figure out how you can communicate the information—whether it is through your words, your actions, or even using other sources to legitimize your point—in a way that will increase the likelihood that the recipient will be receptive to what you say and act on it.

On the **S**treet

Think of a criticism that you have to give to a client, team member, or assistant. Ask yourself:

- What do you want your criticism to accomplish?
- What specific information do you want to communicate?
- What is the benefit to the recipient?
- What is the best time to communicate the information?
- How can you communicate the information so that the recipient will be receptive to your message and act on it?

EMOTIONAL INTELLIGENCE AND CLIENT RELATIONSHIPS

Talking with Clients

Money may talk, but financial advisors are the ones who must communicate what it's saying. By using emotional intelligence when communicating with clients, you can observe the influence you're having on their feelings, thoughts, and behaviors, and adjust your message accordingly.

Imagine meeting with a client to discuss her financial priorities, suggest a particular investment, or listen to a complaint. The wrong word or a misunderstood meaning can sink your relationship with the client. Effective communication skills, on the other hand, can spark a personal connection and forge a lasting bond. Among the most important emotional intelligence communication skills to hone are *self-disclosure,* which involves clearly telling the other person what you think, feel, and believe; *assertiveness,* which involves sticking up for your ideas and opinions while respecting the other person; and *dynamic listening,* which involves hearing what the other person is really saying.

Exposing Yourself

Self-disclosure is the term psychologists use for expressing your own thoughts, feelings, and beliefs. Not surprisingly, self-disclosure statements often begin with certain key phrases: "I think this might be a good investment strategy for you." "I feel more comfortable with this approach." "I believe this is a solid financial plan." By tacking the little word *I* onto the front of these statements, you acknowledge that they are yours and yours alone. This lends some credence to your statements, because it shows that they are based on your personal experience. It also makes it clear that they are the opinions of just one person, leaving the door open for other, equally valid opinions, including those of the client.

Sometimes it's important to let the other person know not only what you think, feel, and believe, but also what action resulted. *Action statements* inform the person why you did, are doing, or will do something. Let's say you promise to call a client's office at 9:00, but no one answers at that time, or at 9:10 or 9:20. By the time your client's assistant finally answers the phone and puts you through, it's 10:00. If you don't explain what happened, the client may assume you're calling late because you're unreliable or careless. By saying, "I tried calling a few times around 9:00, but didn't get an answer," you can prevent this misperception.

Asserting Yourself

Assertiveness is another big piece of the communication pie. It involves defending your rights, ideas, and opinions without denigrating those of the other person. This sets it apart from aggressiveness, which involves ignoring the other person's needs, and passiveness, which involves ignoring your own. When you assert yourself, you strike a balance that benefits both of you.

Let's say one client has a bad habit of showing up without an appointment and expecting you to drop everything to talk to her. Here are some ways you could use assertiveness to keep this from continuing.

- *State your position.* Tell the client that you value her business, but she still needs to make an appointment to see you.
- *Say it again.* Underscore your position by repeating it a few times, if necessary. Be consistent about what you want.
- *Give your reasons.* Explain that you need time to research, fill out paperwork, return phone calls, and accomplish other tasks that are crucial to the service you provide all your clients, including her.
- *Recall relevant facts.* If you already explained this to the same client last week, remind her about that conversation.
- *Watch your body language.* Sit or stand near the client, but not so close that you seem aggressive. Convey your determination by sitting or standing up straight and maintaining direct eye contact.
- *Control your tone of voice.* Speak in calm, confident tones. Don't let your irritation with the client turn up the volume.
- *Acknowledge her viewpoint.* Let the client know you understand her position that she should have ready access to you.
- *Look for a compromise.* Suggest that the client use e-mail when she has a quick question that isn't highly time sensitive or confidential. This lets you respond whenever you have a few extra minutes.

Dynamic Duos

Dynamic listening is yet another key part of the emotional intelligent communication process. Listening with emotional intelligence is more than just hearing what the other person is saying. It involves understanding, acknowledging, and responding to the emotional subtext beneath the words. To do this, you must become aware of how the other person's statements are filtered through your own feelings, thoughts, beliefs, and attitudes.

Consider a client who calls and says, "Something has come up, so I have to cancel our appointment on Thursday, but I'd like to talk to you when I get back in town next week." Because you're naturally a glass-half-empty kind of person, you tend to register only the worst of what was said. And because this client was passed down to you by a second-rate predecessor, you have a tendency to regard him as a poor prospect anyway. All you hear the client saying is that the appointment is canceled. You don't hear him express his interest in talking to you when he can. As a result, you may miss a chance to follow up next week.

In this case, you might have heard the message more accurately if you had been more tuned in to your predilection to pessimism and your preconceived bias against the client.

Here are other ways to improve our listening skills.

- *Restate what you've heard.* Put the speaker's statements into your own words, and then repeat them back to him or her. This lets you check that the message you received is, in fact, the one the speaker meant to send.
- *Clarify feeling statements.* When someone expresses a feeling, it often helps to respond with an "I hear" statement, such as, "I hear that you're concerned about the risk of losing your investment." Such statements reassure the speaker that you understand and care about what he or she is feeling.
- *Use acknowledgment phrases.* Comments such as "I see," "I understand," and "That's interesting," let the speaker know you're awake, alert, and on the same page—vital feedback for the other person to have.
- *Use body language.* This makes the same point as acknowledgment phrases, but with nonverbal cues. To show you're listening and understanding, give appropriate eye contact and nod your head when you want to communicate agreement or encourage the speaker to continue to self-disclose.

Communication Lines

If you want clients to put their money where your mouth is, good communication skills are essential. The same advice that one client might see as a welcome soft sell, another might view as too wimpy and vague. The same approach that one client might see as reassuringly professional, another might view as formal and distant. Dynamic listening can help you dig beneath the client's words for the true feelings that underlie them. In a world where one size of advice doesn't fit all, this information can help you custom-tailor your message more effectively.

Nowhere is this more important, more essential to your success, than when responding to emotionally charged clients.

Emotionally Charged Clients

Emotionally charged clients call you when they experience an emotional reaction that causes them to question your performance, investment strategy, or general client service. Sometimes, it's to express anger and disappointment over your performance, other times it's out of anxiety and fear as they watch their portfolio plummet. Regardless of the emotion, the task of the financial advisor is to *emotionally mentor,* to respond in a way that helps the clients keep their emotions in perspective so that they can make the best decision, one that is driven by rationality rather than emotionality.

This is not to say that the clients' emotions and feelings are not appropriate. Indeed, most people we know would be angry and disappointed if their portfolio dropped endlessly. However, *your clients–like most people–often mismanage their emotions.* So the emotional perspective they use to call on you is typically filled with distorted thinking, blaming communications, and a tendency to make impulsive choices. While it might be true that a client is best served by liquidating an account with you, you want the decision to be based on thoughtfulness, not emotional impulsiveness.

How do we know if clients are emotionally charged? Sometimes they will tell you something like, "I'm angry that you didn't sell this stock." Other times, we must be aware of their emotional cues—tone of voice, facial expressions, rate of speech, body gestures—but these emotional cues only aid us in a face-to-face encounter. The fact is, most advisors hear the emotionally charged client on the telephone—the major means of communication between financial advisor and client. So the prime way you will be subjected to the emotionally charged client is by their spoken statements–statements that are filled with emotions that blame, challenge, and express disappointment *These statements encapsulate the emotions that the client is experiencing.*

Whatever the emotions expressed, these moments are defining client-relationship moments. If you apply your emotional intelligence, you can respond to the emotionally charged client in a way that builds trust and credibility, two factors necessary for developing and maintaining long-term client relationships. Responding ineffectively is a pretty good way to cause clients to take their business elsewhere.

Responding to Emotionally Charged Clients

The ability to respond effectively to the emotional states of clients is a hallmark of the emotionally intelligent financial advisor. It is not a daunting or stressful task if you follow the four steps below, all of which bring your emotional intelligence skills into action. The steps to help you *emotionally mentor* your clients are:

1. *Identify active emotions.* The prerequisite to responding effectively to emotionally charged clients is being aware of the emotions in play. Sometimes this is obvious, as when clients state their feelings. For those times when clients just launch into their verbosity, ask yourself, "How would I have to *feel* to say this to my advisor?" Your answer will help you tune in to the emotions being presented. As to your own emotions, depend on your self-awareness to identify how you feel when the client speaks to you. Usually, the emotions evoked in you by the client's statements are the same that are fueling the client to call

2. *Determine what these emotions signal and how you will manage them.* To respond effectively to emotionally charged clients, it is crucial to understand the message of the emotions—theirs and yours. Once you understand the message of the emotions, you can determine how to manage them in yourself and how to respond in a way that returns the client's emotional perspective to a state that is reality oriented. As a refresher, here are the most common emotions that prompt clients to call you and what they communicate:
   - *Anger* communicates that something is wrong.
   - *Anxiety* communicates uncertainty.
   - *Fear* communicates the perception of threat.
   - *Disappointment* communicates being let down.
   - *Enthusiasm* communicates excitement.

   For the most part, 1) *taking charge of your thoughts,* 2) *staying relaxed,* and 3) *dynamic listening* will be the most effective ways to keep your emotional perspective when your client is charging you. Keeping your own emotions in perspective will allow you to focus on your response strategy.

3. *Set up a strategy for responding.* What do you want your response to accomplish? For example, if you detect that the client is angry, part of your response strategy should be to minimize blame, as clients who are angry tend to blame their advisor. If you feel that your client is anxious, part of your response strategy should be to say something that reduces the client's feelings of uncertainty. Generate your response strategy by asking yourself, "What do I want to say that responds to the message of the emotion?" "How will I restore proper emotional perspective to the client?"

4. *Put into words an emotionally intelligent response.* What are the *exact words* you need to say that implement your strategy?

Like anything, mastering emotional mentoring takes a little time, but as your awareness grows, it will become easier and easier. Inevitably, your emotional operating system habituates the steps, causing automatic thinking that generates an emotionally intelligent response to an emotionally charged client—every time one calls—be they statements from the angry, anxious, disappointed, fearful, or irrationally exuberant.

Here are some examples of how emotional mentoring might work with the five most common emotional states that prompt clients to call and throw a few emotionally charged statements at you. Remember, there is no correct response, so think about how you can make the model responses even more effective for you.

The angry client.   When clients are angry, they believe they have been wronged. Their communication is filled with blaming accusations. Usually accompanying anger is fear. The clients not only believe they have been wronged, but also that there is a threat, in this case to their financial solvency. Emotional perspectives driven by anger and fear often cause the client to call and say: "You've lost me lots of money!"

- *Active emotions:* Anger, fear.
- *Information communicated:* Something is wrong; there is a threat.
- *Response strategy:* Validate the feelings of anger, reduce the perception of threat, minimize blame by building trust and cooperation, and help the client regain a perception of control to reduce the perception of threat.

- *Response implementation* (with explanatory analysis in parentheses):

Well, I'm angry too, and believe it or not, I'm even angrier that you've lost money. (*The words "angry too" validate the client's emotions by implying that you know the client is angry.*) Why? Because my job is to make you money, not lose you money. (*Clarifying and stating positive intentions reduces anger.*) Can you imagine if my intent was to lose you money? I think I could do very well! (*This statement could be effective because it uses humor to exaggerate that your intentions are not to lose the client money. However, its effectiveness will be a function of your style and the quality of your client relationship.*) All right, listen, how about if we take a look at where we are—sometimes a team loses and makes no changes—and see what actions we might take. (*The strategy behind this statement is to make the relationship cooperative, thus reducing the tendency to blame in the future. Promoting shared responsibility and a problem-solving-oriented relationship is the goal. Note the instruction to the client to listen.*) XX percent seems like a lot to be down, but it is still below industry average, so you might want to keep that in mind. (*This statement puts the performance in realistic perspective. Anger often creates exaggerated negative perceptions about the reality of the situation. By putting the performance in perspective, anger is dissipated and a realistic appraisal of the performance can be achieved, which still might be anger-provoking but manageable, because it is at a more appropriate level in the context of the situation.*) So let's get started and make some money! (*This positive, action-oriented statement creates motivation and helps make the client relationship productive.*)

The anxious client. Anxious clients call when they feel unsure whether their money is invested properly. Usually, the client calls for reassurance that everything is okay. Frequently, there are also underlying feelings of frustration, as the client feels uncertain whether the current investment strategy will be successful. The anxious client does not know what action to take, and so says to you: "What should I do?"

- *Active emotions:* Anxiety, frustration.
- *Information communicated:* Uncertainty of actions to take; not attaining goals.

- *Response strategy:* The goal is to reduce anxiety by making the client feel more certain that the investments in place are good ones. Because the client is coming to you with lots of uncertainty, the call is also an opportunity to build trust. Provide information so that the client can see the actions taken are appropriate, thus reducing the need to feel uncertain about the prescribed course of action.
- Response implementation:

Well, I am pleased that you trust me and respect my opinion. I know I always feel better when there is someone I can trust to help me. Let's look at some data to base our actions on so we can meet our goals. (*Data reduces anxiety, and note how you can take advantage of the client's asking what to do by reframing it as a belief and respect of your opinion. Disclosing to your client that you feel better when you believe your advice is trusted implies that the client trusts you–the advisor.*)

The disappointed client. Feeling as though you have let them down is the emotional perspective that drives disappointed clients to give you a call. However, disappointment typically blends into anger. After all, someone has to be blamed and it's not going to be the market–it's going to be you! Often, disappointed people avoid taking responsibility for their predicaments, thus causing them to feel victimized. What do people do when their disappointment is colored with anger? They look to take some action that will make things better, like getting a new financial advisor. This is why disappointed clients often say: "I really feel I should liquidate my account with you."

- *Active emotions:* Disappointment, some anger.
- *Information communicated:* Unmet expectations, let down, blame.
- *Response strategy:* Redirect "feeling" into a "cognitive assessment" of the situation that will put it into a realistic perspective, *as disappointment often stems from unmet expectations, which are often unrealistic.* (A client who expects 15 percent will be disappointed with 10 percent.) That's why it is important to remember to *constantly clarify client expectations.* Because the client is communicating on a feeling level, respond on a feeling level first, then shift the client to "think" about expectations, rather than "feel" about them, as the client will be less resistant on thinking level than on a feeling level.

- Response implementation:

Well, that would hurt, but that is your choice. (*Disappointment often causes feelings of helplessness. This statement restores a sense of empowerment by letting clients know that they are in control of the choices they make, thus subtly getting them to realize they are not a victim, and if they choose to liquidate, it's their choice and they are responsible for the consequences the liquidation brings.*) I'm disappointed too, and also frustrated—my goal is to make you money, not lose your money. (*Acknowledging that you too are disappointed conveys empathy, and the clarification of positive goals will help dissipate the client's tendency to blame you.*) I respect your feelings. (*Instead of telling the client, "you shouldn't feel that way," you are validating the client's feelings, thus alleviating the need to keep expressing that disappointment.*) What do you think is the best thing to do? (*This part of the response helps the client move to a cognitive assessment of what to do, rather than ruminating in disappointment.*) You can give the order now or you can think about it. If you want to liquidate, let's come up with a plan. I don't want to be impulsive. On the other hand, if you decide not to liquidate, then we should look at your portfolio and make sure that the investments we have stand a good chance of meeting your expectations. (*In the end, clients will do what they want, and you show them that the choice is entirely theirs. Telling them you don't want them to be impulsive communicates that you are looking out for their best interest. Reassessing their investments will give you a chance to clarify their expectations and make them more realistic, so that future bouts of disappointment in your performance can be minimized.*)

The irrationally exuberant client. These clients call you because their irrational exuberance colors their perceptions to the point that they think their investments are on a roll that will not end. Their exuberance makes them want more. While it's nice to have enthusiastic clients, they can be dangerous, especially when the bubble bursts, as their enthusiasm will turn to anger directed at you. The key to handling these clients is to return their perspective to reality, and at the same time, take advantage of their positive feelings by getting them to give you more referrals. You have the opportunity to do this when they call and say: "You're doing a great job! I want to increase my position with this stock!"

- *Active emotions:* Enthusiasm, pleasure.
- *Information communicated:* Excited, trusting, expectations exceeded.
- *Response strategy:* Take advantage of their "positive affect" by asking for referrals and more business. It can also be a smart move to tone down client enthusiasm by pointing out that there are always market conditions, independent of your abilities, that affect performance, and right now, these conditions are favorable. What would be the rationale for this response, which is best said after you get referrals?
- Response implementation:

Thank you. I appreciate you telling me! It really makes me feel good. (*Praising clients for praising you is sure to increase the chances that they will praise you in the future. You are also exchanging information on the feeling level and this helps solidify trust.*) You know, you wouldn't believe how many clients that I've done well for never even thank me, so I really appreciate it. Also, I've been meaning to ask whether you have any friends that I might help too!" (*Telling the client that others do not praise you makes the client feel special. The fact that the client is thanking you for doing a great job becomes the perfect time for asking for more business.*) As to increasing your position, we can do that—if you want to—but you have to remember that nothing goes on forever. I would suggest that we review your portfolio, look at the risk, and then see if you still want to go ahead. Remember, my job is to be realistic about your investments. (*These statements remind the client to think things through realistically, and also make the client recognize that if you buy more, you are simply following their directive. Thus, if things sour, the client must accept some responsibility and not blame you.*)

The fearful client. Fearful clients come in all sizes of net worth. Whether they are high net clients or a young couple starting out, they have an emotional perspective that sees an investment as a possible loss of what they have already banked. Because anxiety is well connected to fear, their communications are marked by many investment questions and they are very slow to take action. Their fear keeps them stuck, which for you means a lack of business. Minimizing their fear so they can start to put some money on the table is the key. Fearful clients often tell you: "I do not want to lose money!"

- *Active emotions:* Anxiety, fear.
- *Information communicated:* Uncertainty, threat of loss, lack of trust.
- *Response strategy:* Label the emotions/feelings so you can help clients manage them. Validate their feelings, present data to reduce anxiety, clarify intentions, and minimize the threat of loss.
- Response implementation:

Listen, nobody wants to lose money, and everybody feels some concern about the prospects of their investments, whether it's buying a house, car, or even a new suit. (*This statement helps you reframe fear into concern, a more tolerable feeling, and also makes the point that concern comes with any investment. By mentioning a house, car, and suit, the statement also implies that the client has already made numerous investments.*) What I want to show you is how I can help you prosper with a risk level that you feel comfortable with and think is appropriate. (*This statement is useful because it communicates your positive intent to help them without taking them out of their comfort zone.*) As I said, nobody wants to lose money, but my fear is that you will lose money by not investing. (*This is an ingenious statement that takes advantage of the person's fear by pointing out that if they do not invest, their fear of losing money might become a reality.*) Let me give you some investment ideas that are little threat to your assets. (*This statement allows you to start the advising process, with the reiteration that there is no need to be fearful.*)

There are many other emotionally charged statements that encapsulate the same five emotions, so the idea is not to memorize a particular response, but rather, to focus on the strategies being used for a respective client emotional state. To make it easier for you to put your emotional intelligence into play with emotionally charged clients, study the summary chart on the next page showing how EIFAs respond to emotionally charged clients. It would be a good idea to make a copy of the chart and keep it on your desk to remind you of your response options when emotionally charged clients call.

Client's Emotional Perspective				Irrational	
Communicates	Anger	Anxiety	Fear	Exuberance	Disappointment
	Something Is Wrong	Uncertainty	Threat	Overly Enthused	Let Down
	Validate their feelings.	Give information to reduce uncertainty.	Remind client of previous investments.	Praise client for praising you and ask for referrals.	Be nondefensive by listening and acknowledging feelings of disappointment.
	Reflect and clarify expectations to minimize blaming communication.	Build trust by telling client you appreciate being asked for advice.	Give realistic expectations to put fear in a proper perspective.	Reiterate the importance of having realistic expectations.	State that you are disappointed too.
	Provide facts to help restore appropriate emotional perspective.	Remind client of short-term fluctuations but that investment is for the long run.	Point out risk for not investing.	Remind client of market conditions beyond your control that affect performance.	Acknowledge feelings of frustration in not meeting investment goals.
	Use humor, if you have a strong relationship.	Help client tolerate anxiety by explaining that it comes with any investment.	Present lots of data and be very patient in answering questions.	Review portfolio to assess if increased position is feasible.	Clarify expectations in context of current market.
	Problem solve with client by focusing on best actions to take.				If purely bad investment, problem solve with client to decide best action to take.

Advisor
Manages Own Emotions
Take charge of thoughts, relax, practice dynamic listening.

O n   t h e   S t r e e t

Think about statements you've heard that were driven by the emotional state of your clients—for example, anger, anxiety, dejection, or enthusiasm.

Your task is to walk through the process for reacting to this statement in an emotionally intelligent manner.

Emotionally charged statement: _____
  • Identify the emotions you feel on hearing this statement

_____

  • Determine how you will manage your emotions productively.

_____

  • Identify your client's emotions. _____

_____

  • Determine what these emotions signal. _____

_____

  • Determine a response strategy. _____

_____

  • Implement a response. _____

_____

A DAY IN THE LIFE
OF AN EIFA

It's the night before Monday,
And no one's awake
Except for the EIFA
Who wants dawn to break,
Wants Monday morning
(Just a hours from now),
Waits for that big opening
To make his big wow!
With that in mind
And not too tense,
Falls right to sleep
(Bulls jumping the fence).
So the stage is now set
For the EIFA to begin.
He'll take over now
And give you his spin.

Ring! Ring! Ring!
Don't yell to get me up.
I'm an EIFA
And I will not get stuck.
Thoughts in my mind
Run, run around,
But I'm in charge.
They don't bring me down.
I love my work
It's fun to do.
Singing Do WA ditty,
Ditty dum ditty Do!
Now that's a game
I love to play,
It gets me ready
For another big day.
Off to the train now
Down to the street,
I prospect when
I take this beat.
It's not always pleasant
But I keep in mind
That I am one special FA,
One of a kind.
Before the bell rings,
There is no torment.
I'm an EIFA—
I know my intent.
Calls, calls galore,
Then research due,
I'll lock myself in
And complete these two.
Later when I hear
The market is down,
I just tell myself
That it will rebound.
A meeting now,
With an angry man,

I see color change
(Not from a tan).
Anger, anger
Lose your spell!
How it does when
I relate to him well.
A presentation
Coming up,
High net worth
Says "Batter up!"
And though I'm nervous
(Just for a bit),
I figure I'm A-Rod—
I'll get a hit.
Market closes,
More calls to make.
I want my clients
To know I'm awake.
Before going home,
I review my day.
See once again
I've earned my pay.
Heading home
It's a little rest.
I'm relaxed, happy;
I've done my best!
Well, there you have it,
So goes the day.
When you do it
The EIFA way.

4

COMPLIANCE

What the Emotionally Intelligent Financial Advisor Always Remembers

Call it a summary if you want. To be an emotionally intelligent financial advisor (EIFA) for the long haul, there are four points that you must always comply to, and if you do, you will always be applying your emotional intelligence. The four compliances that emotionally intelligent financial advisors rigidly adhere to are:

1. *Awareness to intent.* The EIFA comes to work each day keenly aware that his intent is to be productive. As a result, he automatically begins using his thoughts as a motivating tool and to guide his behavior for achieving his results.
2. *Awareness to actions.* The EIFA is always paying attention to her actions so she can "keep an eye on herself," ensuring that her actions match her intent to be productive and, at the same time, ridding herself of behaviors that could block her success.
3. *Using emotions as cues for gauging their day.* The EIFA is adept at using his feelings—be they anger, stress, anxiety, enthusiasm—as

a cue to how he is experiencing his day. If it's emotional distress, he knows it's time to examine his self-talk for negative messages, take a breather to regroup, realize he must generate a more effective response, or as a reminder that an important issue that is affecting them must be confronted. If he is enthusiastic and feeling productive, he reminds himself what he is doing and thinking that is making him feel great.

4. *Staying proactive.* The EIFA recognizes that success requires proactivity. This belief becomes her impetus for self-motivation, turning setbacks into comebacks, problem solving, and going after new business opportunities.

When you are in compliance with these four points—Congratulations! You are an emotionally intelligent financial advisor!

Blueprint for Applying Your Emotional Intelligence

The blueprint for applying your emotional intelligence is a tool designed to help you integrate emotional intelligence into your daily functioning. The more you follow the blueprint, the more adept you will become in using your emotional intelligence. Doing it every day will yield results in a short time. For the blueprint to be effective, *all of the steps are mandatory and must be implemented as prescribed.*

EI PREPARATION BEFORE WORK

The following tasks are to be done *the night before* you go to work.

- *First thoughts.* On an index card, write down three statements that will help you start out the day on a positive note. Give the card high visibility on your night table and on your desk.
- *Practice relaxation for ten minutes.* When you practice relaxation, make sure that you conjecture up a relaxing image and associate it with a key phrase.
- *Intentions for day.* Write down three intentions that you have for the next day, such as calling certain clients, researching an invest-

ment, or setting up a presentation. Prioritize them with the first being most important.

- *Behaviors to do.* Make a list of behaviors that you need to do to accomplish the intentions you have identified. Put them on an index card, take the index card to work, and put it on your desk so you can see it all day.
- *Time lock.* Identify several periods for doing the specific behaviors that will help you accomplish your intentions. Let people know you are time locking.
- *Focal lock.* Identify the necessary behaviors to do for each of your time locks.
- *Anticipate setbacks.* List three possible setbacks that you might encounter, such as a client leaving you, a cancelled meeting with a hot prospect, a barrage of negative thinking, or interruptions to your time locks. Take a few minutes and mentally rehearse how you would deal with each setback. Also be aware of what emotions setbacks evoke in you and how you can manage these emotions.
- *Gather emotional information.* Make a list of emotions—anger, anxiety, fear, disappointment, enthusiasm—on an index card. Next to each, make a notation of how you will best manage that emotion when experiencing it. Put the card on your desk. Several times a day, ask yourself what emotions, at that moment, you are experiencing. Check your immediate thoughts and examine your behavior to see if you are acting productively. If you are feeling anxious, for example, are you mentally paralyzed or are you engaged in activities that help manage the anxiety? If the former, check your card.
- *Anticipate interpersonal encounters, phone calls, and meetings.* Make a list of each interpersonal encounter you are likely to have the next day and write down your intentions for each anticipated encounter. Mentally rehearse how you will conduct yourself so that you best might make the encounter productive and achieve your desired results. Also, be sure to mentally rehearse how to conduct yourself and manage your emotions in interpersonal scenarios that are emotionally charged, such as your branch manager criticizing you at a staff meeting. Make sure you mentally rehearse effective responses in these situations.

APPLICATION AT WORK

- *Follow the blueprint.* Follow your blueprint exactly as you have planned it. Each day you follow it, it becomes easier to build your emotional intelligence.
- *Identify your successes.* At the end of the day, identify your successes, whether it is completing your time lock and focal lock, or giving an effective presentation. Reflect on these successes and increase your awareness of how you conducted yourself to achieve your results. Be specific in your thoughts.

TROUBLESHOOTING: IF YOUR BLUEPRINT ISN'T WORKING

- It might be too hard for you to follow. Simply write down one intention instead of three; time lock once a day instead of twice.
- It may also be that you are not effectively implementing the content of each step. Perhaps your intentions are too general; maybe you are not fully aware of the actions that are derailing you. Skill development and increasing your awareness will help you construct and implement your blueprint, so reread the pages on these subjects.

Do the above every day for the next month. After that, you will have it imprinted into your emotional operating system.

Weisinger, H. *Anger at Work*. New York: William Morrow, 1995.

———. *Emotional Intelligence at Work*. San Francisco: Jossey Bass, 1998.

———. *The Power of Positive Criticism*. New York: AMACOM, 2001.

Weisinger, H. and L. Andrews. "Motivating Yourself When You're Stuck." Horsesmouth.com, 9/25/2001.

———. "Managing Your Emotions in Rocky Times." Horsesmouth.com, 10/18/2001.

———. "Staying Motivated for the Long Haul." Horsesmouth.com, 1/17/2002.

———. "5 Ways to Develop Self-Awareness." Horsesmouth.com, 1/24/2002.

———. "How a Skilled Communicator Talks and Listens." Horsesmouth.com, 1/24/2002.

———. "Fix Communication Breakdowns for Better Teams." Horsesmouth.com, 2/7/2002.

———. "Sharpen Interpersonal Skills to Reinforce Client Relationships." Horsesmouth.com, 3/19/2002.

———. "Reduce Stress and Stay Focused in Difficult Times." Horsesmouth.com, 4/2/2002.

———. "From Setback to Comeback in 7 Steps." Horsesmouth.com, 5/20/2002.

———. "Develop High Self-Awareness to Boost Productivity." Horsesmouth.com, 5/28/2002.

———. "When Every Work Counts: Talking with Clients." Horsesmouth.com, 5/29/2002.

———. "What Your 5 Senses Can Tell You about Clients." Horsesmouth.com, 6/4/2002.

———. "Taking Care of Your Behavior and Defusing Bad Habits." Horsesmouth.com, 6/9/2002.

———. "Good First Impressions: Your Intentions Need to Match Your Actions." Horsesmouth.com, 6/11/2002.

——— ."Speak Up and Get What You Want." Horsesmouth.com. 9/17/2002.

Dr. Hendrie Weisinger is world-renowned psychologist and a *New York Times* bestselling author. He has worked extensively during the past five years with financial institutions, including Merrill Lynch, Morgan Stanley, Legg Mason, Dain Rauscher, Robert W Baird, Prudential Securities, Bank of America, Scott & Stringfellow, JP Morgan Chase, and others. He has also spoken at many Security Industries Association events and is a regular speaker at the SIA/Wharton Branch Management Leadership Institute, SIA's Branch Manager Development Program, and the prestigious Wharton Securities Industry Institute. In addition, his work is featured on Horsesmouth.com, the leading online provider for the education and development of financial advisors and branch managers.

Dr. Weisinger is a leading authority on the application of emotional intelligence, an expert in anger management, and the originator of the highly regarded techniques of criticism training. He has consulted with, and conducted workshops for numerous Fortune 500 companies, such as IBM, AT&T, Intel, Control Data, Fireman's Fund, Digital, Hyatt, Hughes Aircraft, Warner Lambert, Pacific Bell, Sheraton, ARCO, TRW, Rockwell, Bristol Myers, AVON, Merck, Union Carbide, and United Technologies, to name just a few. His expertise has also been sought out by government agencies, including the U.S. Justice Department, the Secret Service, and the National Security Agency.

Dr. Weisinger is the author of several successful books. His first, *Nobody's Perfect,* reached the *New York Times* bestseller list. Dr. Weisinger's *Anger Workout Book,* published in 1985, is now in its 25th printing. *The Critical Edge,* published in 1989, is considered the definitive text on the subject of giving and taking criticism in the context of work. *Anger at Work,* a 1995 release, was hailed by the *Journal of the Library of Congress* as a book that "Managers at all levels will find useful. Highly recommended." *Emotional Intelligence at Work,* published by Jossey Bass, is his signature book and received critical acclaim from both the academic and business world. His latest book, *The Power of Positive Criti-*

cism, published by AMACOM, has already been translated into a dozen languages.

Dr. Weisinger has made over 500 appearances on major TV news, and informational programs, including the *Today Show, Oprah, Phil Donahue,* and *Good Morning America.* Recently, he was featured for five consecutive days on the *Today Show.* His work has been featured in numerous newspapers and national magazines, including *The New York Times* Sunday Business Section, *USA Today,* and *Business Week.* His article for *The Wall Street Journal,* "So You're Afraid to Criticize Your Boss," was selected as one of the 60 best articles to appear in the Manager's Column and is reprinted in the *Wall Street Journal on Management,* published by Dow Jones. His article for *TV Guide,* "Tutored by Television," is being read into the Congressional Record.

Dr. Weisinger has taught and currently teaches in a number of executive education and MBA programs, including UCLA, Wharton, MIT, Cornell, NYU, University of Washington, and Rensselaer Polytechnic Institute.

During the past five years, Dr. Weisinger has been helping financial institutions integrate the concept of emotional intelligence into their operations. *The Emotionally Intelligent Financial Advisor* is his first work on the subject. He is currently working on *The Emotionally Intelligent Branch Manager.*

You may contact Dr. Weisinger at HWeisinger@msn.com.

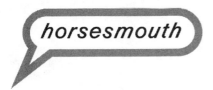

Share the message!

Bulk discounts
Discounts start at only 10 copies and range from 30% to 55% off retail price based on quantity.

Custom publishing
Private label a cover with your organization's name and logo. Or, tailor information to your needs with a custom pamphlet that highlights specific chapters.

Ancillaries
Workshop outlines, videos, and other products are available on select titles.

Dynamic speakers
Engaging authors are available to share their expertise and insight at your event.

Call Dearborn Trade Special Sales at 1-800-621-9621, ext. **4444**, or e-mail trade@dearborn.com.

Dearborn™
Trade Publishing
A **Kaplan Professional** Company

Praise for
On Thin Ice

"In a new book, *On Thin Ice*, Beck documents a group of churches that not only have a radical left agenda, but employ half-truths, deception and intellectual dishonesty. His revelations are those of an insider who took extensive notes."

Cal Thomas
Los Angeles Times Syndicate

"Beck writes about his experiences with almost childlike candor. He seems truly shocked to find churchpeople motivated by less than a Christlike spirit of justice and compassion."

Diane Winston
Dallas Times-Herald

"It is a classic. I would be surprised if it doesn't get referenced in investigative journalism classes. Would that some of the bureaucrats he exposed had been as tenacious in digging out the details of a situation as he had been."

Judy Weidman
Inside the American Religious Scene

"*On Thin Ice* is an extraordinarily compelling and painfully honest account of how the Christian establishment in America has lost its moral power, and how it reacted when Beck chronicled that loss in article after article."

Fred Barnes
Christianity Today

"Beck's book is more than a dreary compilation of the failings of the church. Like the Ozark storyteller he is, he weaves a captivating tale which reader after reader tells me 'can't be put down.'"

"In the end, however, the book is not about politics; it is about integrity. And its conclusions are profoundly disturbing."

Diane Knippers
Religion and Democracy

"Roy Howard Beck, a Methodist layman and working newspaperman, can appreciate the subtlety of the ancient Chinese curse: 'May you live in interesting times.'"

Larry Witham
The Washington Times

"When . . . the history of 20th-century religious journalism is written, *The United Methodist Reporter* will have to be included. Roy Howard Beck may be worth a chapter in his own right."

John Lovelace
The United Methodist Reporter

"Most of Beck's book gives detailed documentation of the most controversial political and racial issues he wrote about during his tenure as a Methodist reporter, including investigations in which he concluded that actions of the National Council of Churches were tilted to the political left."

Ray Waddle
Gannett News Service

". . . You are missing an utterly fascinating read if you don't get it."

Richard John Neuhaus
Religion and Society Report

On Thin Ice

A
Religion
Reporter's
Memoir

ROY HOWARD BECK

**BRISTOL
BOOKS**
WILMORE, KENTUCKY 40390

ON THIN ICE:
A Religion Reporter's Memoir
© 1988 by Roy Howard Beck
Published by Bristol Books

First Edition, March 1988
Second Printing, August 1988

Scripture quotations indicated (NASB) are from the New American Standard Bible, © 1977 by the Lockman Foundation. Used by permission.

Scripture quotations indicated (RSV) are from the Revised Standard Bible © 1946, 1952, 1971 by the Division of Christian Education of the National Council of the Church of Christ in the U.S.A. Used by permission.

Scripture quotations indicated (NEB) are from the New English Bible, © by the delegates of the Oxford University Press and the Syndics of the Cambridge University Press, 1970. Used by permission.

Library of Congress Card Number: 88-70211
ISBN: 0-917851-12-9
Suggested Subject Headings:
    1. Beck, Roy Howard
    2. Journalist, American--Correspondence, reminiscence, etc.
Recommended Dewey Decimal Classification--070.92'4

BRISTOL BOOKS
An imprint of The Forum for Scriptural Christianity, Inc.
308 East Main Street, Wilmore, Kentucky 40390

To Shirley, who models integrity

78265

Contents

Introduction

My call came at 11:30 p.m. in late August 1980 without warning or expectation.

The rest of the family was asleep when the phone rang. I answered it in the kitchen and eventually settled to the floor when I realized the laconic Texas voice on the other end was in no hurry.

I did not know the man. But he had something of a life-turning question: Would I be interested in leaving the Cincinnati *Enquirer* after a decade with various daily newspapers to cover the world of religion for the *United Methodist Reporter*?

The voice belonged to Spurgeon Dunnam III, the editor. I was only vaguely aware of the *Reporter*, although I would learn it was the largest-circulation weekly religious paper in the world. The fact that a man would place a midnight call to a stranger and be so direct, tenacious and lengthy served as fair warning for the special kind of work environment I would. . .shall I say. . .*enjoy* the next six and a half years. I found that a call from God could come at any time, but from Spurgeon, it usually was late at night.

Jumping from "pure journalism" into a specialty publication was not an easy decision. But the church was a familiar place.

I was a lifelong, regular churchgoer. And I had found journalism and the church had many similarities in their imperfect pursuits of truth. While reporting on cops and robbers, politicians and government bureaucrats, corporations and citizen activists over the past decade, I often wrote stories that posed questions about social dilemmas, human suffering, injustice and the conflict between good and evil. I found my participation in churches confronted me with the same questions.

By 1980 when the tales included in this book began, I had grown increasingly interested in how Christian faith might relate to every aspect of modern life in America.

I wondered about the ancient message of the carpenter from Nazareth. Does it have power mainly to transform individuals in their private lives? Or does it also provide strength, compassion and wisdom to help Christians play important roles in transforming society? I wasn't looking for a "Christian nation" the way the New Religious Right was envisioning it. But I did feel the gospel of Jesus Christ was relevant to the headlines in the newspapers I worked for.

For me, the old mainline Protestant denominations seemed to provide the most receptive and encouraging environment for such questions. When I and my family moved to Cincinnati, we joined Hyde Park Community United Methodist Church where I was particularly excited about the emphasis of John Wesley on reason as one of the pillars of the Christian faith, along with Scripture, personal experience and the collected wisdom of the 2,000-year tradition of the Christian church.

Shirley and I eventually started and taught a mixed singles and couples class that grew rapidly. We named it the Mainstream Class because we were individuals from lots of careers and social situations seeking to live according to Christian precepts in the mainstream of American society—living them through our work as well as through our personal relations.

Then came that late night call out of the blue, and I soon found myself with the *United Methodist Reporter* covering all kinds of people and church organizations worldwide dealing with the issues of our Mainstream Class. Their struggles—and mine—are the tales of this book.

The *Reporter*, based in Dallas, Texas, was serving more than a half-million households and reaching a million people each week. Soon after I got there, we started an interdenominational weekly called the *National Christian Reporter* and later took over the operation of the 50-year-old *Religious News Service* that provides daily interfaith wire coverage to public and church publications nationwide.

Besides operating with an obvious entrepreneurial flair, Spurgeon Dunnam over a decade had guided an editorial staff to an entrenched independent and feisty reputation. I soon felt at home. It was no stale house organ.

My stint with the *Reporter* afforded me an extraordinary observation post to witness the challenges, joys, tensions and pitfalls of some of the hottest Christian social action episodes of the '80s.

I was close enough to feel the heat. Enough heat that my reporting often became an issue in itself, leaving me feeling vulnerable and on thin ice with one group and another in the church.

But I wasn't the only one.

In a sense, all who venture to take a stand while claiming moral reasons are in danger of being on thin ice. Our footing on a social issue is only as solid as our own judgment and information. Even with the best of intentions, the foundation can be thin indeed without a high degree of intellectual integrity.

I selected the episodes in this book for their illustrative value on the importance of that integrity. But they are not unique. Dozens of other issues and hundreds of other people could have served the purpose. Lapses of intellectual integrity are endemic. And even to talk of lapses leaves me more vulnerable than I might wish, for my own intellect is bound to have failed in many instances and my integrity surely wavered during the period covered.

We'd like to think of our position on an issue in terms of steely cold correctness, like rock-solid ice that enables us to walk over water. But too much self-assurance can be dangerous, like a people walking onto a frozen pond so convinced of its solidity that they don't test it.

While God desires us to have the divine relationship of "On Christ the solid rock I stand," maybe when it comes to living the Christian life in this world, God wants us to exercise the caution, the self-criticism and the looking for help from others like when we're walking. . .on thin ice.

1

Groundhog Day
for Liberals

He didn't look like a CIA operative.

Actually when I saw him at the Louisville airport, I thought he was a Methodist. Why shouldn't I? I was in my new career as a religion journalist and enroute to my first national church agency meeting—not to some political den of international intrigue.

Not that I didn't think the assignment had its intriguing aspects. This was something of a low morale point for liberal Protestant social action agencies like this United Methodist Board of Church and Society.

It was February of 1981, only three months after Ronald Wilson Reagan was elected—despite these church leaders—as president of the United States.

February, a month of holidays celebrating presidents and groundhogs, was symbolic. This meeting turned out to have the feeling of a sort of Groundhog Day for progressive and liberal Protestants, remnants of past church crusades against racial segregation, the Vietnam War, etc. Underground since the political climate turned radically inhospitable in November, these past shapers of America's moral agenda were coming up in February to check their shadows.

But many national commentators were suggesting that they didn't cast much of a shadow at all anymore over American social and cultural thought. After decades as the preeminent religious voice, mainline Protestant leaders had become overshadowed by a new phenomenon called the Religious Right. It was being given credit for helping usher in a new conservative era.

A bit of a seige atmosphere was in evidence, both at the social action agency meeting and a gathering afterward of a couple of the church's most liberal caucuses.

The caucuses met in a budget-rate motel along a two-mile section of Louisville that had collapsed into the sewers after a recent series of chemical explosions. The scene dripped with symbolism. National Guardsmen patrolled the streets in jeeps as the liberals met behind barricades. Members, seeing each other for the first time since the 1980 elections, embraced in solemnity like survivors regrouping after being scattered by an attack. They saw themselves almost as an underground resistence to the Reagan Revolution.

"I'm Sure He's Not One Of Us"

I wasn't thinking about Reagan Revolution shadows when I arrived at the Louisville airport just before the meetings; I was looking for somebody who might be headed the same way as I. That's when I first spotted a tall, self-assured man walking from the terminal in front of me and toward the curb that was my destination.

Was he one of the progressive church leaders? I asked myself in a little game I'd concocted. I assumed some of the hundred or so people coming to the meeting from all over the country would be out front looking for the same shuttle bus as I. Anticipating too many hours spent in airports the next few years, I started a game to see if I could guess by looks and mannerisms which people were church leaders. The man on his way to the curb was, I decided.

"Going to the Methodist meeting at the Marriott Inn?"

"Yes," he answered.

Great, I thought, *he is a Methodist leader*. I obviously had a knack for religious observation.

As the man introduced himself as Constantine Menges, I watched a woman dragging luggage toward us. I couldn't decide whether she also was going to the same hotel. Should've gambled. She was an Arkansas director on the church board.

The three of us were the only van passengers on this shuttle run. Constantine and I entered into a spirited conversation, I being eager to learn as much about the Methodists and their social activism as possible before the meeting began. He was very knowledgeable, giving me much history and even mixing in some criticism about the agency's being out of touch with its grassroots.

As we approached the Ohio River bridge, our Arkansas traveler began contesting some of what the man was saying. Her tone was cold, like that of a person talking to a stranger who has ventured a bit too close.

At the hotel, Constantine grasped his bag and walked inside.

"Where's he from?" I asked the Arkansas woman.

"I have no idea. I've never seen him before."

"Isn't he a member of the board of directors?"

"I'm sure he's not one of us," she said.

What's this? I thought. *Is attendance at these church meetings so coveted that people will do impersonations to get in? Come to think of it, I guess the man had said only that he was attending the meeting. No need to make a conspiracy out of it.*

When the first business session began, Constantine was nowhere to be seen. The board of directors, I soon found, was a kind of mild debating society. Debate, I realized, could be no more than mild. There wasn't enough diversity of opinions—despite 50-state representation and a valiant effort at ethnic diversity—to sustain a lively exchange of ideas. Still, I personally felt comfortable with the moderate-to-liberal views that prevailed.

Boiled down simplistically, this national board wrote and approved resolutions. All the mainline Protestant denominations had boards like this one: the Presbyterians, United Church of Christ, Disciples of Christ, Episcopalians and Lutherans. The millions of members of the denominations were supposed to use the resolutions as educational guides for applying their faith to public issues.

When you saw a headline like "Presbyterians urge boycott of Nestle" or "United Church opposes MX missile," these kinds of boards likely initiated the action. Their voices, combined with that of the Catholic hierarchy, tended to sing in the same key on Capitol Hill, attempting to influence the formation of public policy.

Many people made fun of this process, deriding it as meaningless and a waste of time. In my first time of witnessing it, though, I was encouraged by the emphasis on Christian compassion and the wrestling with moral dimensions of peace and justice matters. America was full of think tanks weighing issues from all sorts of views. Why not think tanks from the view of Christian compassion and justice?

At this meeting the board passed a number of resolutions including ones calling on the Soviet Union to renounce the use of force in

Poland and asking Congress to urge all outside forces, including the U.S. government, to terminate military aid to El Salvador.

In an open letter to all United Methodists, the board said it recognized the "serious problem in our economy created by inflation," but it was concerned about President Reagan's proposed budget cuts. The letter asked laity and clergy to consider whether the cuts placed an increasingly heavy burden on the elderly, unemployed, single-parent families and persons with low incomes. It asked members to act in the interest of those people.

The expression warmed me. Those were concerns that seemed in danger of being lost in the immense national focus on other priorities such as tax cuts, social-program trimming, military buildup, inflation-fighting and unleashing the forces of free enterprise.

Resolutions Without Troops

This type of resolution exercise once had more impact. But the November elections had made startlingly clear what had been feared for some time: Members of mainline Protestant denominations were marching to a different tune than the one publicly sung by their leaders.

Ronald Reagan had overwhelmingly won the votes of mainline Protestant members. Yet on one issue after another, he had staked out positions far different from the ones church leaders and boards had suggested were the moral ones. Around dining tables and in the hallways during the board meeting, I found the Methodists deeply concerned about their inability to inspire more people in the pews.

The president of this agency, Bishop Leroy Hodapp of Illinois, was frank with me, "We have reached the point in Protestantism—and I think the Catholics are close to that point—where we speak to legislatures, but they know there are no troops behind the resolutions. We've got to rebuild a constituency."

I wondered at the time how the constituency had been lost. Through the next years I would gain insight in a very personal way.

The United Methodist Church was a good place to take the pulse of liberal Protestantism. Its 9.5 million members dwarfed the other denominations. Its institutions' actions tended to signal the style and direction of the whole of mainline Protestantism.

At the end of the first evening session, a conservative pastor from Kentucky, who rarely spoke, invited everyone to hear an "expert" he had invited to tell what really was going on in El Salvador.

I immediately noticed a nervous stir among the directors and staff. Who was this expert, they wanted to know.

I thought, *What's the big problem? Just let the guy talk and see what he has to say.*

But some of the people were becoming skilled in identifying efforts of the Reagan administration to undermine opponents.

A couple of the staff people were particularly adept at spotting what they believed to be conspiracies connected to a mind-boggling network of splintered ideological groups. I thought they were being a little melodramatic. After all, the liberality of hearing widely varying views helps people hone their own.

Finally, the decision was left to each director. Many weary social action leaders found their way to the door of the unofficial guest. Inside stood Constantine Menges who introduced himself as a professor. But out of earshot in low-volume murmuring, the question was asked, who is he really? On whose bidding has he come?

Constantine basically made a case for the Reagan administration's plans to beef up El Salvador's military to stamp out the rebellion there, a rebellion he acknowledged had roots in serious injustice in that tiny Central American nation.

Several directors made it clear they were not the professor's students by not taking seats, standing tenuously around the room. They angrily challenged him after his opening remarks and they indicated their horror at the virtual bloodbath that had begun in El Salvador. They feared that their government and their tax dollars were making things worse. They also feared Constantine. Hints of ulterior motives were made about his appearance.

I followed Constantine into the hallway. He suggested we slip into the hotel bar, presumably where we wouldn't be bothered by Methodists. That was a wrong assumption, despite the social action agency's roots in crusading for prohibition against evil liquor. I sipped a ginger ale as he gingerly answered my questions in the dark lounge.

Constantine said merely that the one board member had invited him and that he was an academic working for the Hudson Institute, a conservative think tank that was generally supportive of the new U.S. administration. He'd traveled widely, especially in Communist-governed nations. A Roman Catholic, he said he was concerned about well-meaning Christians being misled by slick propaganda supporting communist-backed movements.

"I think there probably are some people who fall into that," I said. "But I don't think that's a major problem."

"It's more of a problem than you think," he said mysteriously.

Nicaraguan Hot Links

It was funny how Constantine acted as if some of these church people were pawns of international leftist master plans and how some of the church people acted like the professor was a kind of CIA agent sent to fight liberals in a church agency. But it didn't seem funny at all several years later when I realized the serious potential repercussions of such suspicions and counter-suspicions.

In autumn of 1985, when church meetings had become old hat to me and I'd developed wide contacts in religious circles through constant travel domestically and abroad, I got a frantic call one evening at my office in Dallas. Similar calls continued over a four-day period.

The story: Several Nicaraguan evangelical ministers were being ripped from their homes and families in the middle of the night, thrown into the bowels of Nicaragua's state security prison, stripped, locked in refrigerated cells and subjected to psychological torture.

When asked to explain their actions, the Sandinista Party rulers gave a justification that involved a name I'd not heard since 1981— Constantine Menges.

I immediately thought of our 1981 encounter.

Between then and late 1985, I learned, Constantine had served a short time in the employ of none other than the U.S. Central Intelligence Agency. The Sandinistas used that fact and several other alleged links to determine that their move against evangelical leaders was necessary.

Nicaragua claimed Constantine was involved in a CIA plot to subvert religious groups to U.S. government purposes against the revolutionary Nicaraguan government. They didn't link him directly to the Nicaraguan pastors. Rather, the Sandinistas said Constantine was part of a small Washington, D.C.-based organization of dissident mainline Protestants, people who had been critical of their denominations' support for the Sandinistas. Further, the dissident group was accused of maintaining contacts with the Nicaraguan pastors.

Because of Constantine's CIA background, the Sandinistas reasoned, all those links made the Nicaraguan evangelical pastors prime suspects as CIA counter-revolutionary functionaries.

Several U.S. mainline Protestants quickly backed those claims and said the Nicaraguan pastors probably had deserved the Sandinistas' special attention. But Nicaragua's Marxist rulers failed to make a case against the pastors and released them. The pastors continued to report intimidation, however.

Constantine and the church dissidents group labeled the whole Sandinista explanation a fabrication. The group claimed it had not had contacts with the Nicaraguan pastors and that Constantine never had had a relationship with it. The group even petitioned Congress to investigate the Sandinista charges of CIA connections, and a congressional committee gave a clean bill of health to the group.

I was startled some time later to see documents revealing that the Sandinistas had not on their own come up with the charges against the conservative Nicaraguan pastors. Rather, information about all the alleged links had come from the United States—from people connected to the National Council of Churches.

Did those Nicaraguan pastors get caught in U.S. intra-church squabbles? I worried.

The episode certainly indicated that those church agency leaders in February 1981 were not paranoid but in fact had a reason to fear that the mystery professor might be on some kind of early mission of the Reagan administration to neutralize likely hotbeds of opposition. Is that what I happened onto?

Or was I indeed observing at that 1981 meeting a destructive paranoia, perhaps widespread through church circles, over the change in U.S. political climate? And did that paranoia lead to an over-reaction that unconscionably spilled over into Nicaragua in a way that endangered the lives of innocent victims five years later?

Those were questions that, back in 1981, I did not anticipate would be mine as a religion reporter. And to think, most reporters at the newspapers where I'd worked thought the religion beat was too tame!

I forget what the groundhogs saw in February of 1981, but I saw a lot of shadows.

2

Squaring Off With the Roundtable

Near midnight on Friday the 13th of that same February, a .38 caliber bullet pierced the plate glass window in the *United Methodist Reporter* reception area and smashed into the wall across the room. My office was on the other side of that wall. The slug lodged almost directly behind where I usually sat in my desk chair.

It was quite an item of conversation the next Monday among the more than 175 people who worked at the *Reporter's* Dallas publishing complex. Some of the production workers who knew of the angry letters I'd been getting in response to my first four months of stories did some teasing about right-wing crazies out to get me. Others of us thought the incident might have something to do with Dan Louis' recent articles warning about the rise of the Ku Klux Klan.

The editor, Spurgeon Dunnam, could've been the catalyst, too. He had symbolized, both through the paper and through TV news interviews, the continuing national presence of Christian moderation in the face of the much more visible New Religious Right.

These were tense times. That's why our imaginations ran wild after the shot and why we at least momentarily wondered if the shot was an act of religious extremism.

I had learned during my first four months with the paper that a publication full of nothing but religion news could get a lot of people quite worked up. Although we felt most comfortable in a kind of middle ground, we didn't discount the value of efforts and ideas from the left or right, theologically and politically. We tried to be responsive to and reflective of Christians with views as far to the ends of spectrums as possible. Editorially, we tended to ride the middle without being morally or theologically neutral.

The big glass window through which the bullet had come sort of illustrated the breadth of our view.

Window On Two Dallases

If you looked through the bullet hole slightly to the right, you stared squarely at Dallas' booming downtown a couple of miles away. Our building was on the side of a knoll in an industrial park and rewarded us with a clear view of the gleaming glass structures that reflected the sun by day and were outlined in white, red, amber and green lights by night. This was a view of progress and modernity. Of the monuments to free enterprise. Of the can-do spirit exemplified by the nation's new administration.

Enjoying the exciting view over a six-year period, I would witness through that window a skyline that more than doubled in the number of skyscrapers. Each Sunday when Shirley, the boys and I walked out of First United Methodist Church downtown, we marveled to look up and view a sky full of cranes.

Our newspaper wasn't left out of the boom. We saw that hard work and risk-taking could pay off. We were part of the Dallas entrepreneurial spunk. From merely a state Methodist paper a decade earlier, our publishing enterprise had grown into the largest circulation weekly religious newspaper in the world. We went into the homes of more than a million readers nationwide each week. All that without official endorsement or subsidy from the denomination.

But there was another view from the *Reporter* window. You had to look a bit to the left to see it. And a bullet hole was an appropriate vantage point.

Starting only a few blocks from us and extending over a large flat section were public housing projects full of dim pasts and hopeless futures.

It was the highest crime area in one of the nation's most violent cities. It provided a steady stream of thieves who stole from *Reporter* employees' cars, particularly targeting batteries.

"Someone's breaking into a car in the parking lot," the receptionist often would have to call over the intercom. A group of men, like volunteer policemen, would stream out the front door in response. Sometimes we chased the thieves off the lot empty-handed. One time my writing colleagues, Stephen Swecker and John Lovelace, cornered a young thief but were backed off by a menacing knife. Most of the time, though, the thieves made clean getaways to nearby fencing operations.

Only once did we catch a culprit. A young man named Moses got chased around the back of the building. He escaped by slipping in through the back door where he calmly applied for a job in the press room. A secretary back there became suspicious and called Dan Louis, a writer whose tough demeanor and experience as a Houston crime reporter made him a good choice for the job.

This was a view of the bottom side of America, a side that we feared might grow larger during the planned changes of the Reagan Revolution. We could see part of America's unfinished social agenda through our front window. It was a local reminder that not all was like the glistening boom of downtown. It reminded us of the suffering in the industrial Rust Belt and the pockets of poverty that were resistent to the economic upturn enjoyed by much of the nation.

This fit right into the middle of what a church's and a Christian's concerns ought to be, as defined by Christ's parable of the last judgment. But it also got awfully political.

In a way, everything since I arrived had seemed like a reaction to the fall election.

As an individual, I had some strong opinions. As a reporter, I had almost an obsession with staying open to all points of view. I tried to offer people a chance to make a persuasive case for even the most off-the-wall ideas. I attempted to give all ideas a chance in my stories so the readers could judge for themselves. My philosophy was right at home at the *Reporter*.

"You And Your Converts To Atheism"

Some people, though, didn't want others' views displayed.

Our mail was full of that attitude. It was as though the arch-conservative Methodists had spent most of their lives feeling far from the nation's power centers, and now that their time finally had arrived with President Ronald Reagan, they were extremely defensive about church leaders questioning any of his proposals.

A Montana woman was typical of the way some people talked on the edge of thinly veiled violence. She was provoked by stories I'd written about church leaders' concerns that conditions in El Salvador were growing increasingly more brutal, perhaps partly as a result of

U.S. policy.

"Anybody that reads anything but the garbage you print knows what is really going on down there," she wrote. Then she took off on a story I had written after John Lennon was gunned down. The story was about the long-standing United Methodist position against the sale and ownership of most handguns. She reacted, "May God help us to retain our guns so we can protect ourselves from people like you and your converts to atheism."

One woman laid most of the world's troubles at the feet of an international Jewish conspiracy and got in a jab at the church for supposedly giving money to "Leftist-Marxist Revolutionary groups in Central America and Africa." Like many ultra-conservative readers, she was convinced we were part of a conspiracy of silence about misdeeds of the Left.

A retired Air Force colonel in Arizona reacted to a story by warning that the church was encouraging blacks to be out of control.

A "Methodist for 48 years" in Oklahoma cancelled his subscription when I wrote about some United Methodist efforts aimed at "healing Iran-U.S. wounds" after the hostages were released. "How can you dignify Iran by publishing such rot?" he asked.

I sometimes found myself wanting to disdain all conservative critics of the church. *Racism, anti-semitism, idolatrous nationalism and irrationality seemed to substitute for Christian conviction with them,* I thought. Such letters, and my own reaction to them, helped me have sympathy through the years for how church leaders sometimes could treat the rank-and-file members with such contempt.

But I had to guard against generalizing. If you allow yourself to write off segments of critics, you forfeit the chance to influence people who could be influenced. And you lose the chance to be informed by their own parts of the truth.

Thinking About Gus

I tried to remember Gus Morgan.

Gus was a middle-aged businessman back in Cincinnati. I served with him on our congregation's Christian Social Concerns Commission. I saw him as an "aginner," always slowing things down and blocking the way for our commission to take some bold stands. He also was a Methodist charismatic with a "Praise the Lord" response to everything, a mannerism tending to grate on a mainstreamer.

Over time, though, Gus won me over. I didn't see the world with his political insight and not entirely with his theological view, but I saw that he, more than most of us more liberal types on the commission, was personally involved in Christian service. He was the one working nights at an inner city school and campaigning during the days with corporations to adopt what to him was a more Christian approach to workers.

If I could be as initially wrong about the basic goodness of Gus, I could be wrong about others too, I reasoned. So, I tried to correspond sincerely with all the nasty letter writers. That was a practice developed to a ministerial science by editor Spurgeon. He got piles of letters every day and answered each one personally.

So, to the Oklahoma man who would hear nothing about trying to reconcile with Iran (a tough act, to be sure), I wrote:

> Were you all that surprised that leaders in a denomination of Jesus Christ would follow his command to love our enemies? I find it a bit hard to love the Iranians right now. But I have to believe that's what Jesus meant.
>
> We as Christians can do our part to not add to any unchristian rancor that speaks to retaliation, vengeance or hate.
>
> I personally am proud that the voice heard from our denomination is one that rose above the kinds of feeling the world may be justified in having and reflected instead a much higher plane of thinking as advocated by our Lord and Savior.

That was the style we typically used in trying to address a concern as rationally, calmly and biblically as possible.

It was an approach I also attempted toward the Religious Right movement, despite my personal misgivings about so much of it. The movement was a fairly narrow one, not at all including the majority of Reagan supporters or conservative mainline Protestants. But its influence at that time appeared to be spreading over conservative Christians who traditionally were part of the broad middle of the church.

The movement had many admirable aspects. It had taught the responsibility of citizenship to several million fundamentalist Christians who formerly had treated politics as too dirty to participate in. It had helped force society as a whole to look more at problems in the breakdown of American families and traditional moral values.

The Religious Right also posed a dilemma for me. I believed strongly that the gospel gives special emphasis on the needs of the poor and the outcast. Well, a large number of Religious Right followers were the working poor and had spent their lives shunned as inferior by most of society. But being poor and an outcast did not necessarily make a person correct in all assertions.

Most of us at the *Reporter* felt many of the leaders and followers of the Religious Roundtable, Moral Majority, Christian Voice and an array of religious TV programs had less than the highest commitment to truth-telling. We especially were concerned about the way they married the Christian faith to the right wing of the Republican Party.

Protecting The Bible From Liberal Tinkerers

The week of the bullet-through-the-*Reporter*-window, a fund-raising letter from the Religious Roundtable also pierced our headquarters, tending to confirm for us some of our worst expectations of the Religious Right movement.

The four-page, fund-raising letter had pictures of president Edward E. McAteer and the angry young Baptist evangelist James Robison at the top. McAteer was the architect of the Religious Right, having put together an historical convocation in the late '70s that generally was credited with officially galvanizing the movement.

The letter, in part, read:

> Dear Christian friend,
>
> Do you have a few minutes to protest the removal of the words SON OF GOD from the Bible?
>
> Your name on the enclosed petition will build our chances to stop the National Council of Churches from completing and nationally promoting a very anti-Christian Bible.
>
> . . .This anti-Christian translation ignores God as our heavenly FATHER. It also ignores the father as the head of the family in our homes.
>
> . . .Imagine the consequences if a "Bible" like this was accepted for reading in schools.
>
> Disobedience and violence is already running wild in

our public schools.

Immorality, drug abuse, homosexuality are already far too common for many of America's boys and girls.

. . .It's no surprise to me that the first NCC conference to discuss the acceptance and national promotion of this anti-Christian translation is being held now after the election of President Reagan.

I believe the NCC liberals know they now must go on the offensive as never before. They know we Christians are beginning to make our voices heard across the land. But the NCC would like to keep us silent.

. . I'd like to invite you again to become a founding member of our national organizing committee. . .Gifts from founding members for $10, $20 and $100 are needed immediately. . . .

Talk about blurring religion with politics and drawing narrow lines, including some wild tangential ones! "We Christians," indeed!

Spurgeon Dunnam took the letter on as his personal project. He immediately began checking out the facts of the NCC project that had inspired Ed McAteer to write the letter. We seemed to have a prime opportunity for challenging the movement.

The letter obviously was referring to recent NCC discussions about avoiding male-only language in a translation of Scripture. NCC officials, though, told us no rewrite of the Bible using gender-inclusive language was planned by the committee currently revising the NCC's authoritative Revised Standard Version of the Bible.

The NCC, however, *had* authorized a separate panel to paraphrase some verses for a lectionary, a collection of passages for use in worship. The idea was primarily to use gender-inclusive words about people where the original writer obviously had not intended to exclude women.

But the flamboyant paraphrases in Roundtable mailings supposedly from a "rewritten Bible" obviously were bogus, since the members of the NCC panel hadn't even been chosen yet.

Some Christians might have legitimate concerns about what the NCC was planning, Spurgeon said, but questions should be based on the truth, not inflamed falsehoods.

Spurgeon lashed out with a stinging editorial headlined "Religious

Roundtable use of lies about NCC to raise funds: deplorable." It pointed out several glaring inaccuracies in the letter, which the editorial labeled "a spurious attack on the NCC" designed "to prey on pre-existing fears and prejudices, and thereby to produce dollars for the Roundtable's coffers."

Soap Salesman Comes To Call

On Monday, February 16, 1981, the day the paper with the editorial on the Religious Roundtable came off the presses, I began pressing to be allowed to pin down Ed McAteer.

"Let's find out why he thinks he can spread such false stuff and hold him accountable," I argued. By the end of Monday, I'd persuaded the others to turn me loose.

Spurgeon suggested I start with Herb Bowdoin, the only name on the Roundtable letterhead list of advisors that we recognized as being a United Methodist. Herb was an evangelist out of Florida, with TV and crusade work around the country. One of the things I liked about the United Methodist Church was that such evangelists couldn't just wing it any way they chose with no accountability to anybody. They were under appointment of a bishop and had an ongoing, organic relationship to other clergy and lay leaders in state-type conferences.

Spurgeon said he'd been on an overseas trip with a group that included Bowdoin and that he'd found the evangelist to be conservative but not at all mean-spirited like the Roundtable letter. Nonetheless, Bowdoin should be held accountable for anything he allowed his name to be placed on, we felt.

Tuesday I called Bowdoin and told him of the editorial. He was very nervous. He said he'd not seen the letter that included his name, Jerry Falwell's and many others. When told of the inaccuracies, he said he would call McAteer, who lived in Memphis and maintained an office in Virginia.

Herb's concerns got through to McAteer. Wednesday morning I awoke to the ringing of the phone. I crawled over Shirley, picked up the phone, pulled it back to my supine position and answered in my early morning bass, "Morning."

"Roy, this is Ed McAteer," came the response. It was a sharp-edged, carnival-barker kind of voice on the other end that sounded like it had been awake for hours.

Full of energy, McAteer made it clear he was acting as a result of

Bowdoin's phone call. "I wouldn't want to do anything to hurt my dear friend, Dr. Bowdoin. He's told me about your paper."

I put a few of my chief questions to him, and he said he would call me back.

Not much later at the office, I heard from McAteer again. He said he was going to be in Dallas later that very day to do some fund raising and would like to come by the *Reporter* offices. To be in Dallas that day seemed like quite a coincidence. But we *Reporter* staffers were exhilarated that we would meet the warrior of the Religious Right face to face.

Late Wednesday afternoon, Ed McAteer walked in our doors with a local Roundtable supporter. He was all smiles and pumping arms, exhibiting the style that made him a successful Colgate-Palmolive salesman, a career he had retired from. We traded a few jokes about the bullet hole in the window and my wall. Somebody couldn't resist a crack about how we tended to have high-caliber guests.

The two visitors walked with Spurgeon, managing editor Sharon Mielke and me to the windowless conference room in the back of our building. (I don't know if it was a conscious decision to avoid Spurgeon's office with the proudly displayed pictures of Spurgeon at the White House with President Carter.)

We gathered around a long table in the room. With sloping floor and wall about to fall off the foundation slab, it seemed designed for the *Reporter's* editorial policy. Anybody who chose to sit near the edge had to maintain a scrupulous balance, for the least bit of tilting in a chair in any direction on that downhill floor might send a person crashing.

McAteer's demeanor crashed as he read the editorial we handed him. He didn't appreciate being the butt of moralistic rhetoric like that he typically dished out. There was a lot of heat during the three-hour session. But Spurgeon had a method for such encounters. Basically, he simply wore people down. He just kept going over and over something until there was agreement on a point or a plan. I think he felt that he saw the true person after he wore them out.

I saw Spurgeon's renown—some said eccentric, others said driven—style in the way he answered critical letters with pages upon pages of detailed reaction. It was also there in the marathon job interviews that often ran past midnight and then went on for hours the next day without breaks. At least a couple of times each year, he delighted in keeping the staff working through a night and well into the next day to complete a major project. "If it doesn't hurt, you haven't done a good job," was the way long-time circulation executive Bill Strickland phrased the Dunnam philosophy.

McAteer was responsive to the wear-down method. He eventually appeared to believe that the three of us were Christians with many of the same values as he. And we began to understand more the common man behind the right-wing myth.

The idea for the Religious Right movements was spawned during years of business flights, he said. "I found that whenever I started asking people around me about certain issues, the majority agreed with me," he said. "I had thought I was alone. Yet the people in government weren't representing me, so I thought we needed to organize to get our voice heard," he explained.

We began to agree on some facts related to this supposed Bible rewrite. On several other details that I'd dug out during the week about what the NCC really was doing, McAteer was almost persuaded and said he would check them out with Roundtable executive Ed Rowe.

McAteer made no apology for the sensational tone of his letter, "I use shocking letters—stimulating letters. I'm appealing to instincts. There's nothing wrong with instincts." He talked a lot about his salesman background and said he considered himself more of a salesman of ideas than a theologian, "However, I don't want the letters to be dishonest."

It was beyond him why anybody would want to rephrase Scripture so that words like "man" and "he" wouldn't be taken by some women to exclude them. It was clear that he had not adapted to or even been touched by the sensitivities of language concerning women over the past two decades.

Risky Honey

Early in the afternoon, McAteer turned to Sharon Mielke and, in what I felt certain was not intended as an incendiary remark, called her "honey." I braced myself, not wanting to fall off the sloping slab as a result of Sharon's response, but she grimaced and maintained a professional facade.

Then he "honeyed" her several more times. Such syrupy terms of endearment for people outside my family had never passed my lips anyway. But a few months covering church meetings had taught me that a man never wants to use such terms on a mainline Protestant woman. McAteer was operating from a different world view. But our tough, church-battle-seasoned, skeptical managing editor continued to let the "honey" bounce off her and allowed the discussion to remain on an easier non-personal plane.

We tried to explain to the architect of the Religious Right how a large percentage of women felt excluded by male-only metaphors and pronouns previously intended to include both men and women. It's hard for a lot of women to feel invited by the language, "No man comes to the Father except by me." Why create that barrier when Jesus obviously intended for it to apply to women and men, we argued. The explanation sounded plausible, although a little silly to our guest.

He balked more when we described the reasons why some people feel exclusive use of male language about God is offensive. God, after all, is not a man, we said. God is God. Both men and women are made in God's image. Most of us acknowledged that as writers, though, it certainly was awkward to not be able to use a "He" every once in awhile. A valid reason to be updating the language to ensure inclusive hearing was to be certain nobody felt left out of the call to accept the good news of the gospel, we said.

I don't think any of us indicated that we thought the inclusive language issue was one of the more burning ones of the church, nor that it was one we wished to devote a lot of time to.

McAteer told us of his fondness for the Methodist Church because it was at a Methodist revival where he was saved. Mainly, he said, he was strategizing on bringing his adopted Southern Baptist Convention into the Religious Right fold. (I would have a chance a few years later to observe firsthand his political handiwork on his own denomination.) At the end of the afternoon, McAteer conceded that it sounded as though there might be some mistakes in his campaign and that he would do some more research.

As we stood to leave, Spurgeon suggested we gather in a circle for prayer. The moment was disarming for all of us. Everybody seemed to relax after that.

I worked late into the night writing the first draft of my story on the episode and then arose early the next day to fly out of Dallas-Fort Worth Airport at 7 a.m. to cover a meeting.

That Thursday night, McAteer met with his executive director, the Rev. Edward Rowe, in Virginia and over dinner discussed all the

Reporter's contentions. From my meeting, I kept talking back and forth with McAteer, trying to press him to say for sure if his letter had mistakes and, if so, what he proposed to do about it. Finally, I got a call Friday in my hotel room. McAteer admitted errors and pledged to compensate for them.

"We'll rewrite [the letter] and tell everyone who has received the mailing what the facts are," he told me. "To do otherwise would not be Christian. Nothing is more destructive and confusing than getting out false information." He said he continued to distrust the National Council of Church's intentions and would fight any effort to write a "de-sexed" Bible but that he had been convinced that his alarm had been at least premature.

I had to rip my story apart on deadline day and give it an entirely different approach. Instead of putting him on the journalistic rotisserie and applying the flames of truth, I had to present him as a man of reason convicted by facts. "Roundtable president to correct mail campaign errors" was the headline over my story the next week.

Spurgeon, never one to willingly miss an opportunity to raise the visibility of the *Reporter*, asked Sharon to put out a press release to all the nation's public religion writers about our story and previous editorial. A number of reporters, including the wire services, ran with it, giving our efforts a lot of secular exposure around the nation.

I felt good about the week-long ordeal. It seemed to show that there was at least some shared common ground between the religious faith of mainliners and Religious Righters.

New Paper After One-Month Gestation

Our work was not unnoticed by several large Presbyterian, Disciples of Christ, Assemblies of God, Lutheran and Baptist congregations who, at about that time, were contacting the *Reporter* about creating an ecumenical version of the *United Methodist Reporter*.

They said they'd admired the *Reporter's* integrity and broadmindedness for years. Some were enthusiastic about the lead the *Reporter* had been taking in challenging the Religious Right to truthfulness. They wanted to put their congregational news on the front page and send the paper to all members. They had been doing something similar for years with another publisher that was about to go out of business.

Spurgeon gathered the national writing staff and the heads of the local editions and conference editions departments in the back conference room to hear about the new challenge from him and Bill Strickland, circulation manager.

The key question, Spurgeon said, was what mission we would serve by creating a new paper? After all, he said, we weren't just a publishing enterprise that dealt with religious news. We were committed to religious communication out of a commitment to Christ's church. That was it, various people said. Our commitment was not just to the United Methodist Church but to the church universal.

We believed an interdenominational version would increase the possibilities of healthy interaction among different Christian groups by providing a common base of understanding. Our style of vigorously pursuing the truth no matter in which theological or ideological direction it led us was one well-grounded in the freedom of the Christian faith, we believed.

Before the meeting was even over, Sharon had begun scurrying in and out of the room, collecting recent back issues of the *Reporter*.

While Spurgeon and Strick talked postal regulations and costs, the rest of us began pasting down the stories that were the most ecumenical in scope. By the time Spurgeon went around the table asking each person whether she or he was willing to give the extra effort to see an ecumenical paper off the ground, Sharon had a good start on a prototype paper.

Within a couple of days we had printed a prototype *National Christian Reporter* in which we had done some rewriting of stories to de-emphasize the Methodist angle and add details from other denominations. We called it "demethodizing."

Strick, a physical giant of a guy, who wore loud sports coats and possesed a salesman's touch that had snared much of the *Reporter's* new circulation through the years, immediately took the papers to Oklahoma City. He sold the first edition there, guaranteeing the new paper at least a couple-of-thousand circulation.

The first issue was March 13, with my Religious Roundtable story from two weeks earlier anchoring the main page. The total gestation of the new paper from the first confidential phone call was less than a month.

I came into the office early on the day we made up the paper and hung pink crepe paper streamers around the composition shop and put up a big poster on the wall that proclaimed, "It's a girl! UMR has a sister—NCR." Within weeks, the circulation was approaching a broad audience of 30,000.

One of the members of the *Reporter's* executive board who had been asked to approve the new endeavor was Twila Roller of Albuquerque. She said, "As usual, I am impressed by the UMR staff's seeing how this could be done instead of finding reasons why it couldn't be done. Your non-bureaucratic approach is refreshing."

Indeed, things could move fast at the *Reporter*. I was thrilled and felt we were seeing commitment to truth-seeking rewarded.

There were many national religious publications on the market. But all were advocates from one side of a theological and political spectrum or another. Certainly, our editorials also were within the advocacy style. But I felt our editorial page tried harder than any other national religious publication to include letters and guest columns reflecting the full range of Christian perspectives. And our news pages were even more different from other religious journals. I was unaware of any religious publication, unless you count the general circulation *Christian Science Monitor*, dedicated so fully to the ideals of mainstream American journalism.

I realized that American journalism wasn't universally recognized in the religious community as having the highest of aspirations. Certainly, the practice fell short of the ideals, and I wouldn't want to hold "The Journalist's Creed" as an equal to the Apostles'. But I found much consistency with my understanding of Christian discipleship in "The Journalist's Creed" written by Walter Williams, who founded the world's first school of journalism in 1908 at my alma mater, the University of Missouri.

William's language didn't meet the newer ideas of sexually inclusive language, but the principles seemed targeted for the modern moment.

. . .I believe that a journalist should write only what he holds in his heart to be true.

I believe that suppression of the news, for any consideration other than the welfare of society, is indefensible.

. . .I believe that the journalism which succeeds best— and best deserves success—fears God and honors man; is stoutly independent, unmoved by pride of opinion or greed of power, constructive, tolerant but never careless, self-controlled, patient, always respectful of its readers but always unafraid, is quickly indignant at injustice; is unswayed by the appeal of privilege or the glamor of the mob; seeks to give every man a chance, and, as far as law and honest wage and recognition of human brotherhood can make it so, an equal chance; is profoundly patriotic while sincerely promoting international goodwill and cementing world-comradeship; is a journalism of humanity, of and for today's world.

Standing His Ground, After All

Within a week of the publication of our new ecumenical paper, I was jolted when I called Ed McAteer.

It had been three weeks since he had come to the Reporter's offices. He had promised to send correction letters to the 200,000 households that had received the first error-filled mailing. I wanted to check up on the promise. I also wanted to know whether he or Ed Rowe had met with NCC officials, as pledged, to be clear about what each other was planning.

"Well, Roy," McAteer said enthusiastically. "Good to hear your voice. I have some questions about some other people's motives, but I don't doubt that you are trying to do a good job. I don't doubt your sincerity one bit. I know you're a true Christian." But, he said, he had to tell me he was not persuaded by the previous conversations that his original letters had been wrong. He hadn't sent out the correction letters. And he didn't intend to.

I was flabbergasted. I'd heard the promise with my own ears three weeks earlier. There had been some misunderstanding, he said. He then read a three-page press release he'd just put out in response to heavy media questioning prompted by earlier stories and our own press release.

It was as if the meeting in our offices and our conversations by phone had never happened. In his new statement, he was stuck on Spurgeon's editorial that had run before all of that. The editorial's sting had immobilized him. I had the feeling that he read and re-read the editorial as if it had followed our meeting instead of preceded it. He seemed unable to move forward and instead was back with all his old mistrusts and hyperbole.

"The hysterical charges of Spurgeon Dunnam III that I lied and falsely stated the case against the evil scheme of the NCC to change the Word of God was only a smokescreen to veil the Council's shameful deeds," McAteer said.

As for dialogue with NCC officials to be certain he had the facts straight, he said he was too busy organizing state Roundtable chapters to bother with meeting with anybody from the NCC. Rowe said he had tried back in November to talk with NCC people and had gotten no results. That fulfilled the Roundtable's moral responsibility, he said.

I asked him, "What if the NCC sent you all minutes of its meetings so you could see whether a rewrite of the Bible is planned in the way you fear?

Rowe's answer was a classic in its distrustful logic, "People who would tamper with the Word of God would tamper with minutes."

I really felt left alone on thin ice. I'd been the one to push McAteer to make promises and the one to tell everybody they'd been made. His press release certainly was a challenge to my integrity, even if the writers said it wasn't aimed at me.

I resented what seemed to be a pattern of the Religious Right's use of distortions, half-truths and villifications in implying that those of us connected to mainline churches and with liberal political views weren't among "we Christians," as the Roundtable letter had put it.

Certainly, there ought to be boundaries that define a Christian. But what are the signs of a "real" Christian? Honesty and fairness surely are minimum standards, I thought. Scripture says Christians are to be transformed in *all* aspects of life, even when dealing with people believed to be enemies.

Paul, the first century missionary/writer, set a severely tough standard when he described Christian discipleship in a nutshell in the 12th chapter of his letter to the Romans:

> I implore you by God's mercy to offer your very selves to him: a living sacrifice, dedicated and fit for his acceptance, the worship offered by mind and heart. Adapt yourselves no longer to the pattern of this present world, but let your minds be remade and *your whole nature* thus transformed. Then you will be able to discern the will of God, and to know what is good, acceptable, and perfect (NEB).

I remember when my older son both learned and taught the all-important concept that being a Christian is far more than saying some words of belief. It happened one Advent season.

"Anybody Can Just Say It"

In a custom developed under the guidance of supposedly non-spiritual mainline churches, the Beck household has been committed to nightly devotions around the Advent wreath each year. In honesty, I have to say that "nightly" ended up being about four times a week. And the setting wasn't always along the Prince of Peace theme. We sometimes had to delay devotions until we settled a squabble over which boy had lit or blown out the candles the night before. Transformation into a sharing spirit wasn't yet complete. Nonetheless, the singing, reading, praying and talking in a dark room with only the candles flickering light on our creche created an atmosphere of great exploration of the foundations of the faith. We kept the little services open for questioning. A stack of commentaries and Bible dictionaries were kept handy to search out questions that arose, such as how many wise men really were involved.

The Advent when Jeremy was six, he pushed deeper and deeper into the nature of God and human relationships with God. In the middle of it I had to fly out of state for a couple of days on a story assignment. I called home the first night to learn that Jeremy had insisted on making a formal commitment to Christian discipleship.

"I was reading the church Advent booklet," Shirley told me over the phone, "about *peace within, the divine residing in each of us,* and Jeremy interrupted me." As soon as the boys had gone to bed, she'd written the conversation in the notebook she kept on the kids.

"What's the divine living in us?" Jeremy had said at the Advent wreath.

"That's Jesus living in our hearts," Shirley answered.

"I'm not sure if Jesus is inside me. I haven't asked him to come inside me, but sometimes he puts thoughts inside my head. Like when I got mad at Stephen at school today and I wanted to hit him, but Jesus told me not to."

"That's Jesus living inside of you when you listen to him," Shirley said.

"But I want to ask him to live in me all the time. How do I do that?"

"You just tell him that you love him and want him to live in your heart. But that's a very important decision and something that you really need to understand."

"I know that Jesus is God's son," he said, "and that he loves me and that he died for our sins. Why did he have to die for our sins?"

Shirley reached down deep to try to be as open and simple as possible. "God wanted people to listen to him and to know how much he loved them. But people started listening to themselves and forgot about God. So he sent his son Jesus to earth to live with people so they could understand God's love. Everyone does things that aren't right—called sin. Jesus took everyone's sins as his own and died for everyone so that their sins could be forgiven and people could turn to God when they believed in Jesus."

"I understand that Jesus wants to live in my heart, and I want him to," Jeremy said.

"That's great. But it's not that simple. It's a big responsibility and not easy. Mommy and Daddy have to work very hard at that and we still don't always do what is right. You don't always feel close to him and sometimes it's hard to tell what he wants you to do. It's very complicated and Daddy thinks you may need to be a little older to understand."

"I want to ask Jesus into my heart right now, and I want him to stay there," Jeremy persevered.

Shirley decided it wasn't her choice.

"How do I do it?" he asked. "How will I know he believes me? I mean anyone could just say it."

Anyone could just say it, I repeated to myself. That was the point we had been trying to make with him. He understood. With a first-grader's simplicity, he made it clear to us that he knew the world of difference between just *saying* you're a Christian and *being* one in the nooks and crannies of daily life.

Every time I read Shirley's account, that comment of Jeremy's just before he prayed his prayer of commitment has reminded me of the foundations of what it means for a person to choose to be a Christian.

In the spring of 1981, my experiences with the Religious Right had me feeling especially concerned about the need for Christians to tend to all areas of their lives, including ridding them of intellectual sloppiness and distortion. One bishop, perhaps intemperately, charged after the 1980 election that the Religious Right movement was driven by hate; which, by the way, is not a fruit of the Spirit. It seemed a reasonable comment now.

Intellectual sloppiness leads to such things as the so-called Christian Report Cards of the previous election. Members of Congress were given "Christian" ratings based on their votes. But the votes were on complicated measures such as weapons systems and taxes, as well as emotional favorites such as public school prayer, on which Christians of good will surely could disagree.

One result was travesties such as giving a 100 percent "Christian" rating to a congressman who had been censured for seducing a teenage congressional page and a zero rating to an active, committed, evangelical Christian like Republican Sen. Mark Hatfield.

Some conservatives told me the Religious Right wasn't doing anything the religious left hadn't been doing for two decades. Maybe so, I said, but I wasn't encountering such abuses at the time.

Religious Right Inroads Blocked

A week after Ed McAteer talked to me, Spurgeon took the Religious Roundtable on again in the editorial page. Across the top of the main news page, the headline on my story said, "Roundtable president denies all / Claims pledges to correct errors never were made." The national wire services and daily religion editors once again spread the story. And in a shaded box inside my primary story in that paper, I had an article about Herb Bowdoin that may have symbolized the Roundtable's defeat in the United Methodist Church.

When I had called Bowdoin about the latest turn of events, he was in Massilon, Ohio, conducting an interdenominational evangelistic crusade. With his flowing white hair, cherubic face and a strong drive to ingratiate himself, Bowdoin wasn't a person you'd expect to be in the middle of a public controversy.

He told me he was tired of the controversy and said he was going to call McAteer to remove his name from all Roundtable literature and to drop his membership in the Roundtable. "I'm not interested in being a part of an organization that every few months comes up with an issue. . .and I don't even know about it," he said. "I believe in being a positive element."

Bowdoin agreed with the Roundtable's concerns about returning traditional moral values to America, but "I didn't plan to be witch-hunting."

He said he'd been asked to serve on the Roundtable board because a United Methodist was needed. With him gone, the organization didn't have any United Methodist to broaden its appeal inside the denomination. That seemed to thwart the Religious Right's strategy for the United Methodist Church.

So Bowdoin, a low-key evangelist acting on his own and under the *Reporter's* spotlight, may have turned the course of history a bit the day he dropped out of the Religious Roundtable because of its error-filled material. He rang the bell of integrity with his simple statement, "I don't care if you're fighting the devil, you've got to fight with the truth. I don't want to be a party to anything that is dishonest."

The Roundtable, we learned later, had halted the mailing of the original material and did deal with most of our concerns before sending anything else out. Publicly, though, its leaders didn't want to give a hint of anything that might look like they had lost a battle.

I Felt I'd Been Had

There was no doubt in my mind that the Roundtable had errors to correct. That truth held through the years. But the NCC and its supporters turned out to be far from spotless themselves in the area of truthfulness, the kind that not only abstains from lies but is diligent to be certain no misunderstanding exists.

My 1981 stories carried assurances from several ecumenical leaders that an inclusive language lectionary would apply almost entirely to male-only words about people and male pronouns about God but not about Jesus. They said there was no way that such traditional and theology-laden terms as "the Son of God" would be changed. The idea was to do things like use "humankind" for "mankind," "men and women" for "men," and repeating the name "God" in many places where God is referred to as "he." Jesus, of course, was a man so would continue to be referred to with male words, they said.

In October 1983, I flew to New York City to go to the NCC headquarters for the unveiling of the first edition of *An Inclusive Language Lectionary*.

Imagine my surprise when I opened the collection of scriptural readings and found that, in fact, "Son of God" *had* been expunged from the text. The NCC committee had done away with several other traditional metaphors for Jesus. He no longer was called the "Son" but the "Child" so as not to place too much emphasis on his maleness. That was a change with vastly more negative theological significance to large segments of the Christian community than simply changing "mankind" to "humankind." Top Lutheran leaders were among many who cried foul. In addition, the NCC lectionary changed "Lord" to "Sovereign," and "Son of Man" became "the Human One," among other attempts to keep the Scripture from seeming to say that men have a special relationship to Jesus because of their maleness, the authors said.

While the lectionary committee's explanation for the changes deserved thoughtful consideration, I was left with the feeling I had been had in 1981. Some of the church leaders' pledges about what would and would not happen apparently were as transient as Ed McAteer's first promises to me.

I felt like I owed Ed something now. I tracked him down by phone, more than two years since our last conversation. When he heard my name, it was the same soap salesman on the other end of the phone, "Roy, Roy. Always good to hear from you!"

I told him what had happened and offered him a chance to say "I told you so." His faith in humanity was raised by the fact I would call him about that, he said. Then, Ed became uncharacteristically low-key. He acknowledged that he had nothing in 1981 that could back up the claims he was making in his literature and that I had been correct in saying he didn't. Some of the claims I had challenged him on never proved true, especially the wild suggestions about the breakdown of society if inclusive language were used in Scripture. But he had been right about some things. He said he just had a feeling in his bones that the NCC would do what it ended up doing.

In my imperfect career of pursuing the truth, I didn't know what else to do but run a story with his saying those things.

Back in the spring of 1981, though, there was nothing to detract from our feeling at the *Reporter* that we'd scored a direct hit for the cause of truth and moderation. Our efforts won us a lot of plaudits from Protestant leaders and institutions. The National Council of Churches, liberal church caucuses, women's organizations and many readers commended us for taking the initiative to confront distortions and falsehoods advanced by the Religious Right.

I reveled in the affirmation. But autumn would bring new challenges and a similar but very different story to write. To the affirmers of spring, my name by fall might as well have been Ed McAteer.

3

Out of the Subway

I came up out of the New York City subway at a time on Sunday morning when half of America generally was heading to church. But not on Broadway Avenue at 116th Street, I noticed. The European-feeling sidewalks and boulevard were drenched in autumn sunlight but dry of people that October 11, 1981.

I had no idea that I was about to walk in on something that would turn my world topsy turvy, with years of repercussions.

For the moment, all was tranquility. The tower of famous, cathedral-like Riverside Church rose behind some buildings about six blocks up the island. I was going to a different kind of church, though.

A conference on southern Africa, heavily supported by and identified with mainline Protestant denominational groups, was concluding at Columbia University, just up the sidewalk from the tunnel entrance where I stood. This was a conference to start mobilizing Americans behind efforts to bring down the apartheid system of racial dictatorship in South Africa and to drive that nation's army out of neighboring Namibia.

I had attended sessions of the three-day conference on Saturday in Riverside Church and found them rather dull, with little explicit sign of the sponsoring church groups. I questioned whether I had an angle for a story in my religious publication. Thus, I almost skipped this morning's meeting to take an early flight back home to Dallas.

What a difference that might have made in my life! It wasn't so much that what I would observe was so momentous or shocking. But when I chose to write about what I saw, the reaction was so volatile and widespread that my reputation would be stood on end. As a result, mainline church leaders from then on tended to greet me with suspicion; liberal activists tried to figure how I fit into conspiracy theories; conservative and right-wing political publications would feature me as a liberal who for once told the truth; numerous books, magazine articles and TV shows for years would include my story and me in text and footnotes—a one-shot claim on immortality.

All of that because I went to Upper Manhattan one Sunday and wrote one story about it.

"Warm And Fraternal Revolutionary Greetings"

I walked up the sidewalk to the side entrance of McMillin Hall, checked my program to be sure I had the right place, then pushed open the door.

The auditorium, full of several hundred people, was as dimly lit and dingy as the subway tunnels. The speech from the austere stage immediately reminded me of the tunnels as well. It had the ring of some of the political graffiti I'd just seen below. The crowd was cheering a harangue against "U.S. imperialism."

I listened a few minutes and realized the conference had begun adopting a lengthy *Recommendations for Programs of Action* that was to reflect the composite thinking of "this broad-based cross-section of people from across the country—the church, labor, entertainment, sports, international and more." It was hard to follow. People on the stage read a long list rapidly. Somebody from the audience quickly moved the adoption of a recommendation, and the vote was taken by applause. Somebody tried to offer an amendment but was told that was out of order. I scribbled rough quotes on my note pad to record the action.

"The conference authorizes efforts to counteract anti-Soviet propaganda," I heard from the stage. "Move its adoption." Applause. "It's adopted."

"All churches will be encouraged to establish monuments outside their buildings to the people's revolutionary struggles in southern Africa." Adopted.

"The traditional news sources of the UPI [United Press International] and Associated Press have failed to provide accurate, adequate information on apartheid. We oppose the U.S. act that doesn't allow the import of Cuban literature as alternate news sources." Adopted.

"Encourage providing broadcast facilities and publications to the African National Congress [ANC] and the South West African People's Organization [SWAPO]." Adopted.

I thumbed through my program to make certain I was in the right place. The subject was correct, but the style seemed strange for a conference with such heavy church identity.

The crowd really got to cheering when the former Marxist-Leninist prime minister of Guyana spoke. "I remember when we heard the United States say there will be no more Cubas in the Caribbean," he said at the end. "But now we are so happy to see Grenada and Nicaragua."

Sustained applause.

"The United States stopped us in Bolivia and the Dominican Republic. But they met their match in Vietnam!" the Guyanan screamed. The audience leaped to its feet with a thundering ovation. The people on the stage surrounded the speaker, embracing and kissing him.

"Hysteria," I wrote on my note pad. This was not dull. But I was growing increasingly bewildered about the church angle here.

Another standing ovation ensued when the moderator of the conference introduced a man from a "tiny island which refused to be intimidated or frightened by U.S. imperialism. They have said to the terror of this planet [the U.S.], 'Go to hell!'" Comrade Unison Whiteman, minister of foreign affairs of the new coup-created Marxist government of Grenada, moved to the microphone. "I bring you warm and fraternal revolutionary greetings."

In the hallway just off the stage, a scuffle began. Journalists from the *New York News World*, a conservative daily paper owned by the Unification Church, had offended the conference leaders. The managing editor told me later that he had been asking one of the conference leaders about funding for the event. Carl Bloice, the conference coordinator, ordered the managing editor away from the stage. When Bloice saw him near the stage later, he asked him to step into the lobby. Once there, the newsman asked Bloice if any speakers would be making any statements on behalf of the Afghan freedom fighters against the Soviet Union, since the conference had wholeheartedly endorsed the revolutionary movements in Africa and some other parts of the world.

That was the last-straw for Bloice. Two people blocked the door to keep the newsman from getting back into the auditorium.

The managing editor began to yell. The conference staff shoved him against the wall, grabbed his throat and banged his head repeatedly against the wall. A *News World* photographer began taking pictures, but Bloice's men pushed the camera into her face. They forced both journalists into the street.

A third *News World* journalist who had remained in the auditorium was forced out a short time later. When the photographer took pictures of that, the conference coordinator's men chased her up the sidewalk. The third journalist grabbed the arm of one of the attackers. Two men threw the newsman against a car, tore off his glasses and punched him in the face. One then chased down the photographer, threw her to the ground and tried to take her camera, pulling it with enough force to snap the leather strap around her neck.

Finally things cooled down outside. The *News World* journalists left, promising to seek retribution. (The New York Press Club later expressed outrage and filed a formal grievance.)

And this was a church-sponsored, bishop-endorsed conference!

Where Was The Church?

Back inside, I seemed to be the only reporter. I was shaking my head about how the churches had gotten so involved with a conference like this one. The church backing of the event was why I was assigned to cover it. I thumbed through the sheaf of pre-conference publicity and weekend materials to make certain I'd not gotten mixed up.

No, every piece of paper had the name "Conference in Solidarity with the Liberation Struggles of the Peoples of Southern Africa" and right under it, "c/o United Methodist Office for the UN." I later would find that the recommendations I heard adopted were printed on stationery with the United Methodist name on it.

The list of sponsors on the program I was looking at included 23 national leaders and clergy of the United Church of Christ, Roman Catholic Church, United Methodist Church, World Council of Churches, National Council of Churches and African Methodist Episcopal Church. I checked and found several thousand dollars of financial backing from the church groups for this conference that drew 1,200 to 1,500 participants.

But where was the church today? The only religious leader I saw on this third day of the event was a Baptist pastor from Harlem. He spoke during the morning and pointed out that there wasn't much sign of the church at today's event because most church people were at that moment in the "institutional church," too busy worrying about escaping hell after death instead of doing something about hell during life.

"What you are doing *is* the church," he shouted at the audience. "I commend you for taking the church from pew and pulpit to the problems of the world."

Standing ovation.

I knew I could be totally wrong, but my gut feeling about the people applauding was that not very many of them had been near pew or pulpit for some time, at least not in a worship environment.

By now, I realized that the conference leadership on the stage and the recommendations passed by the audience were committed to the support of the revolutionary ANC in South Africa and SWAPO with an army fighting South Africa's army for control of Namibia.

At the end, ANC and SWAPO representatives stood on the stage and sang what was introduced as their national anthem as most of the audience stood and raised clinched-fist salutes.

Puzzled By It All

I sat for a moment in a dark corner in the back, puzzled. I appreciated the fervor of the assembled people's convictions and certainly understood the extreme frustration and repression in southern Africa that apparently had driven the Africans on the stage to choose violent revolution. But I couldn't figure out the various mainline Protestant groups' strategy. Why lend the church name and then relinquish all control, allowing something like the journalist scrap to occur?

Various mainline Protestant leaders had grown alarmed during the first year of Ronald Reagan's presidency at what appeared to be a disregard for the suffering non-whites of South Africa. They had been looking for ways to begin to mobilize the millions of members in the pews into a praying, studying, political force for a more active, even radical, role on the part of the U.S. government and U.S. corporations. Supposedly, that was why some United Methodist agency people contributed money, office space, a phone, staff and the church's identity to this October conference as a part of the mobilization strategy.

But I couldn't figure out why they created an event like this, especially when the involved church agencies in other settings heavily pressed the preferential option of pacifism or non-violent resistence for Christians.

Although the first two days had a somewhat broader and more open feel, this final day seemed designed to repel American Christians and ensure they would not adopt the South Africa justice cause as their own.

I began to feel a little angry. Concerns and time constraints of family and job are ample reasons for the average American Christian not to be active on an important social issue. Why provide an ideological excuse likely to let most people's conscience off the hook for not becoming involved?

This event seemed counter-productive to me. I had found mainline Protestants tending to be warm-hearted moderate-conservatives, not people eager to rush out on any fringe. Various surveys showed them to be tolerant, compassionate but basically cautious.

Oh, the Presbyterians, Congregationalists and Methodists, for example, had been known to crusade at times—in the suffrage movement for women's voting rights, Prohibition and labor reforms of the industrial excesses early in this century. But the members of the predominantly-white, mainline Protestant denominations also had formed the backbone of the American middle class and the Republican party for decades. Ronald Reagan was able to depend on them for overwhelming personal support even though surveys showed them to disagree with him on a number of social issues.

The mainline Protestants weren't the president's most passionate supporters. That was hardly surprising; passion of any kind ceased to be a common mark of most of them a long time ago. Nonetheless, what most mainline Protestants lacked in passion they compensated for with reasonableness.

I loved them for that. I found that in the Presbyterian and Methodist Sunday school classes and forums I taught regularly, a person could make just about any kind of pitch—within reason—and the members would give a reasonable hearing.

To truly mobilize those masses, you needed to help them feel the problem and then reasonably examine several alternative routes that might be available to them. The route chosen probably would be one that fit some value they already held. But this conference chose the route before it began: support for the revolutionary movements. It gave the common church people few reasonable handles for the issues.

"Sadaat Was Assassinated"
Largely ignored were many other movements for peaceful change and reconciliation in South Africa: the assertive South African Coun-

cil of Churches, some other conservative but gradual-change black Christian denominations and tribes, free trade unions, etc.

Certainly, it made sense for any conference on southern Africa to include discussion of the ANC and SWAPO as two important players in the struggles. What didn't make sense was that the church would sponsor a conference committed exclusively to the ANC and SWAPO solutions.

Perhaps I was more on edge about this violence business because of what had happened a few days earlier.

Before I even had awakened the first day of the Board of Church and Society meeting that I attended here in New York just prior to this conference, I got a phone call from my managing editor, Sharon Mielke.

"Have you heard the news?" she asked.

"I haven't heard anything, I was sleeping."

"Anwar Sadaat was assassinated!" she said.

I felt a physical revulsion begin in my abdomen and immediately overwhelm me as I thought, *The cycles of violence. Who will end them? Another peacemaker gunned down.*

In the days since then, I couldn't shake a general, low-level depression. I was not in the most receptive mood for an appeal to support a violent revolution over all other recourses, even if the target was one of the most repressive governments in the world. *Shouldn't the church throw its primary weight behind non-violent solutions?*

It seemed like the attitude at this conference was not different from that of the new Reagan administration that appeared constantly to put its first faith in military answers to problems.

I had to find out more about how this conference got put together. Walking down to the front of the emptying auditorium, I approached a woman I had seen at the registration desk on Saturday.

"I'm a reporter from a United Methodist newspaper," I said. "I see the United Methodists listed on all this literature, but did they really help you on this?".

The woman, Laura Hosston, a lawyer at New York City College and a conference worker, told me of the "extraordinary generosity" of United Methodists whose work was integral to creating this special forum. "I wonder if this could have happened without the United Methodists who month after month were helping out," she said.

I asked for a list of the planning committee. She handed me several pages of names. It seemed like a perfunctory enough act but would prove pivotal to me later on and would draw an injured outcry from conference supporters.

I flew back to Dallas Sunday evening, thinking I probably did not have enough for a story. That thinking was influenced by the way the assignment had started. Sharon Mielke and I had decided I should cover the event because we had for some months been looking for an angle to begin educating our more than one million readers in a half-million households about the South Africa problems. We thought this event would do it.

With so little participation by church people and so few explicitly religious concerns raised in the actual proceedings, I thought it probably best just to skip telling about this one.

Dallas Luncheon Debriefing

I barely mentioned the conference during our weekly Monday morning editorial staff meeting the next day.

But my colleagues changed my mind over lunch.

Luncheon debriefings were very important at the *Reporter*. Seldom were all writers in Dallas the same week, since we were kept on a plane or on the phone most of the time to cover a national church. So we caught up on each other's experiences while eating in the old, traditional section of Dallas where the *Reporter* headquarters was located. On the "wrong side" of the river near downtown the choices for lunch generally came down to dark, grease-stained, hole-in-the-wall eateries specializing in Tex-Mex, barbecue, steak house or—in the case of Norma's Home Folks Cafe where a multi-ethnic working class crowd wore their own layers of grease and dirt—heaping plates of okra, black-eyed peas, chicken fried steak and corn bread.

This Monday, though, we chose a variation and crossed the Trinity River to eat at Cafe Cancun, a bright yuppie place with big windows and lots of plants in Dallas' premier gay neighborhood. The *Reporter* editorial staff took a long table in the corner where a brilliantly colored mural fairly engulfed diners.

Unwritten protocol allowed a just-returned writer to dominate the discussion for at least one and maybe two lunches back in Dallas. The rostrum was mine this Monday.

The Ozark mountain storyteller in me usually broke through in these circumstances. As I was wont to do, my arms became animated and my voice dramatic as I assumed the roles of the various revolutionary speakers for all in the restaurant to behold. My fellow writers were having a great time joking around with the material, as they were wont to do.

Eventually, as always happens when a reporter tells too good a story to colleagues, somebody drew the talk to a single point: "Are you going to write it?" I told why I'd decided against it. They all said it was much too interesting and significant a story to withhold.

But, I protested, Spurgeon insisted on each story having a strong church or personal Christian frame. I couldn't create a frame where there was none. The others argued back: Maybe that's the story, how the church turned up missing at a church event or how somebody else took over the show. Besides, don't the rank-and-file members deserve to know about the interesting kinds of people and ideas featured at the event carried on in their church's name?

I felt my news sense had been upbraided. Coming back and saying there was no story for lack of an explicit church mark on the event was like the journalism school example told of the cub reporter sent to cover a night city hall meeting and returning with no story because the city hall burned down. All my luncheon mates agreed I should talk to Spurgeon back at the office about the story.

Ordinarily, Spurgeon would have joined us for Mexican food, but this faire was too much like Mexico City's. Too light, healthy and free of the heavy Tex-Mex gravics. Spurgeon's eating habits included using tortilla chips like spoons to drink hot sauce, keeping jalapena peppers at his desk as snacks and drinking Dr. Pepper at all occasions. One of the joys of adulthood for Spurgeon was not having to eat most vegetables. Many of us felt that if it was true that you are what you eat, we had a pretty good start on understanding our editor/general manager.

Spurgeon's Grotto

After that Monday lunch, some of us gathered in Spurgeon's office. It was a dim, windowless, almost grotto-feeling room with an uncomfortable couch and chairs around the perimeter of his stacked-up desk. Because of a recurring health problem, Spurgeon said he needed to keep his office temperature a few degrees below the comfort-level for most visitors. As was the custom, he came out from behind his desk and slouched down into one of two, overstuffed, overused, swiveling, yellow chairs.

Not even 40 at the time, Spurgeon was one of those people difficult to pigeonhole in any generation. With full gray beard to match his hair and a somewhat stocky, medium-height build, he seemed like he'd always been at least 40. But sometimes, especially late at night at the office when he was trying to pull a joke on somebody, he could seem like a teenager.

His father told us a story from Spurgeon's boyhood when he had a job sweeping up for a rental vehicle company. He got so involved in observing all the details of the business, the kid sweeper soon was telling the owner how he could better run his business. That's basically what happened when he hired on parttime to sweep up at the *Texas Methodist* paper while going to seminary. By the time he graduated he'd learned every part of the operation, and he was so full of ideas on how the operation should be run the board of directors made him the editor. Texas wasn't big enough for him. He soon turned the state paper into a national publication. And the new *United Methodist Reporter* succeeded, financed by subscriptions, while some denomination-subsidized national publications had to fold from lack of interest.

My colleagues helped me tell my South Africa conference story to Spurgeon. Spurgeon winced. Then he began to try to list all the problems the story posed to the church and to the *Reporter*.

Making editorial decisions without fully assessing their impact was not the way Spurgeon had become what the *Washington Post* once called the most powerful person in United Methodism. The *Reporter's* news and editorial pages were a national pulpit reaching far more people on a regular basis than any bishop or national agency official.

Although the *Reporter* was not an official voice of the church, Spurgeon felt editorial decisions and, indeed, even word selections in a story ought to be made with the deliberation of a major church council. He also had a natural inclination to get involved in details and to correct people. For years he insisted on final approval of every staff-written word that went in the paper and commonly returned notes from staff with his editing marks on misspelled words and questionable grammar.

Spurgeon loved to be exhaustive. A chief tool was to be exhausting. He would call the staff into the office and ask for the opinions of each on an impending decision. Everyone would speak. Then he would assess what all had said and then ask for responses. The staff would go around and around for hours until we couldn't imagine any consequence or piece of logic or information that hadn't been analyzed.

Spouses knew that when they called at 6 or 7 p.m. and found a meeting was underway in Spurgeon's office, they very well might go to bed before they heard again from their mates. Often when I thought I might faint from hunger in a session long past meal time, I would create banners out of my note pad with words suggesting food or starvation. I'd hoist them on pencils and pica poles or tape them to the wall behind me to try, without interrupting the conversational flow, to shake Spurgeon from the meeting trance that held our human needs prisoner.

The session on my conference story was quite moderate in length by *Reporter* standards.

Publishing Would Make Innocent Victims

One of the first concerns expressed about running the story was that it might decrease support for efforts to bring about majority rule in South Africa. Why allow the concerns of millions of suffering people to be lost in an intra-church squabble about the appropriateness of agency and staff actions that very well might arise if we published the story? Another problem was the way this story would build on some previous scorchers written by the *Reporter* staff through the years. A vocal minority in the denomination already believes our East Coast agencies have a bunch of Marxists working there, Spurgeon said. Running this story will just add more information to be abused by those people in making far-out attacks. And most of our readers won't like their offerings and church name being associated with an event like the conference, Spurgeon predicted. In fact, a lot of them will be angry enough to make trouble in local congregations deciding how much to contribute to the national agencies, he said.

The timing is terrible, he said. "Most local congregations are in the midst of fall campaigns to raise their 1982 budgets." Members upset about something their denomination has done don't make cheerful givers. And that posed a direct threat to the *Reporter's* own financial interests.

Many of those local congregations had special editions of the *Reporter*. About half of our million readers got the *Reporter* through nearly 400 of what we called local-church editions. Local churches sent all their weekly newsletter material directly to us. Our Local Editions staff laid it out as the front of a broad-sheet newspaper. Our national news and editorial pages filled out the rest of the four and six-page papers. The local congregations paid to send that paper to every member.

If some of those congregations had trouble raising their budget because our paper made members angry in the middle of the pledge campaign, the churches might conveniently decide to cut costs by cutting out the *Reporter*. Other threats to our circulation base could arise through the 40 annual conferences (of 73 in the United States) that published editions with us.

Spurgeon remarked to us about how different reality is from what so many of our critics imagined. The *Reporter's* critics were no different from those of any other newspaper; they accused us of printing controversial information to sell more papers. Obviously, Spurgeon said, they don't understand a situation like this. Controversial stories cost you—at least in the short run. It took a lot of courage and willingness to suffer financially for a paper like the *Reporter* to publish highly controversial material.

Bound By Consistency

Having listed all the negatives, we turned to reasons why we *should* run the story. Spurgeon spoke for all of us. Our integrity as a newspaper was built on both journalism's and Christianity's value of the truth and information-sharing.

For nearly a year, the *Reporter* had been an outspoken critic of the self-righteous thundering from the Religious Right. A lively criticism developed from some readers who charged us with applying standards for mixing religion and politics only to conservatives.We retorted that we would use the same standards to expose any questionable use of religion by people on any part of the political spectrum.

That pledge remained untested, though, as only right-wing foibles popped up for us to examine.

It wasn't just the episode with the Religious Roundtable the previous winter and spring. We hit the daily newspaper headlines again in July when Spurgeon entered into a month of unsuccessfully challenging the Moral Majority's Jerry Falwell to a debate. Spurgeon felt somebody in mainline Protestantism needed to make it clear to the public that the Religious Right did not represent all of Christianity and to call into question some of the movement's shaky biblical assertions.

Where most journalists would fear to tread, Spurgeon rushed in. He had no compunction against being at once the news purveyor and the newsmaker. He eagerly sought such opportunities. He felt he could keep the two parts of himself separated so as to avoid conflicts of interest. His role as an actor in the church apart from his editor's chair was not wholly endorsed by his writing staff through the years and created not a small amount of underlying tension in the office.

Spurgeon, Dan Louis and John Lovelace wrote a long interpretive analysis that ran September 18, only three weeks before the South Africa conference. "Religion and politics: It's OK to mix but not merge them," read the headline. In it they laid out behavior from the Religious Right that they found unacceptable and at the same time said all religious activity in politics should be held to the same standard.

One of our biggest charges against the Religious Right was that it didn't leave room to hear a multiplicity of views on an issue. Certainly, that was a failure in New York City last weekend, we said.

There were lots of liberal critics of the Moral Majority taking public stances all across America. But Spurgeon felt it was the middle, the mainstream, of Christians that wasn't being heard from. He called for a "militant middle" that was defined not by straddling the fence but forcefully pleading the wisdom that often lay between extremes. If you're going to call yourself the middle, you've got to show your disagreements with those on either side of you when they occur.

I'd also had a nagging concern since last winter's Religious Roundtable episode. It was exhilarating to catch it in its faults, but I wondered if maybe it was a little too easy to be taking potshots at an outside group while essentially defending your own institutions. Jesus' Sermon on the Mount teaching about judging others was awfully strong that your priority should be on dealing with your own weaknesses ahead of others. *As mainline Protestant papers, our first obligation must be to provide the information that could help our own institutions be as righteous as possible,* I thought.

The conference I had treated as just an interesting event the day before was taking on much more important dimensions.

Sponsors List A Sham

That day in Spurgeon's office the staff agreed that I should try to write this South Africa story as straightforwardly as possible. Just tell what happened; but to make that work in this instance, perhaps I would do best to depart from normal practices at our paper and write this story as a first-person account.

I had quite a bit more research to do. I went into my office and picked up the phone. My ear was to it the rest of the week. It was a crash course in how special-interest events of all leanings tend to be put together.

Quickly I found that the "sponsors" list was something of a sham, if it was supposed to suggest that the people named had anything to do with the event. Conference organizers sent out the sponsors list with all promotional literature before the event and with the recommendations afterwards. The names obviously were meant to lend validity.

But my phone calls determined that most church leaders on the sponsors list had no part in planning the event and weren't present at it. They told me decisions about joining, financing and overseeing such conferences usually are left to agency staff persons. The staff work for the Methodists turned out to have been done by a junior member whose supervisor was gone during most of the conference planning.

Relatively quickly, I was quite certain that the one junior staff member of the United Methodist women's agency was the only person on the 31-member conference planning committee who represented a religious group. I was beginning to understand why the conference didn't have much of a religious orientation to the problems of U.S. policy toward South Africa. Somebody apparently had thought it would be helpful to put a religious front on the conference. But the church inadvertently or perhaps by design had no hands—except for one young, junior staffer—on the levers.

What I still needed to know was who the 30 non-church colleagues were on the planning committee.

What Do You Do With A Communist?

I called a few sources I'd known through the years and read the list of the "secretariat." The term "communist-type" kept coming up. The term startled me and gave me great discomfort. All of my adult life, I'd heard ideas that deserved consideration get dismissed with a flip labeling that they were pink, or commie-tinged, or Marxist, or radical leftist.

I'd been labeled and dismissed that way, myself. It had happened to me as a reporter in Grand Rapids, Michigan, and Columbia, Missouri, and Cincinnati, Ohio, when I wrote stories that carried challenges to conservative institutions and principles. It had happened to me as a student at the University of Missouri when I led efforts in religious groups to question the morality of the Vietnam War and participated in sit-ins related to the peace issue at the administration building.

My analyses and work during those times may have missed the mark. But I didn't deserve to be disregarded so casually. Poor people all over the world often find their most urgent concerns repudiated under a charge of communism. My experience had been that the charges nearly always were false—not in degree but in totality.

Now, in the middle of the week after the South Africa conference, I was being confronted with those same charges made about others. Should I try to ascertain if they were true? Would that be giving more credence to such charges than they deserved? What if they *were* true? Would it make any difference in how the event should be viewed?

I contemplated these questions while re-reading the mass of material and notes accumulating around me in my office. It just added to the general clutter. We had nice, big, though windowless, private offices. With all the space, though, I still didn't have enough. Before heading for another out-of-town assignment, I often found myself dumping my briefcase of materials from the last assignment into a pile on the floor so I would have room for the next set of materials. After a year at the *Reporter*, I had piles all over my floor. It was like walking through a well-used cattle pasture trying to get to my desk—this horizontal filing system worked for me. I knew just where to find each trip.

From the ceiling just inside my door hung a featherless, rubber chicken, suspended by one claw, its eyes staring at me. Perhaps it was to rationalize my behavior in the face of critics. But when I looked at it, I thought of the political figures, corporation executives, small-time business polluters and others who publicly had attacked my reporting in preceding years. The chicken was a sort of silly prod to stick my neck out, go out on a limb, venture onto thin ice because, as I told curious visitors, a chicken or cowardly journalist is likely to end up plucked anyway.

I walked around and talked awhile with my writing colleagues whose offices also opened onto an interior common room where we held our staff meetings. They shared my discomfort about getting into an "is-that-a-communist-hiding-behind-that-bush" exercise. On the other hand, we agreed, if people espousing communism were helping lead a church event that on the surface gave no hint of that and, instead, purported to be something else, that was significant.

I was reluctant to seek help from the executive side of the U.S. government because of the Reagan administration's tendency to slide into red-baiting. I ended up calling the Democratic-controlled U.S. House Permanent Select Committee on Intelligence. Herbert Romerstein, a staff member, said he would help me. He stopped me when I started out by reading the name of Carl Bloice, the coordinator of the church-backed conference on South Africa.

"Carl Bloice," he said, "is a well-known member of the central committee of the Communist Party U.S.A."

"Well-known to whom?" I asked a bit skeptically.

"Bloice has identified himself that way, and public Communist Party literature lists him as a communist leader," Romerstein said.

Labeling a person as a communist isn't always red-baiting or engaging in McCarthyism, the U.S. House official reassured me. "The fact is that some people *are* communists," he went on. "When you report that they are, you're merely reporting a fact."

We very quickly came across another conference planning member, Charlene Mitchell, who he said was listed along with Bloice in Communist Party material. Ms. Mitchell had not identified herself that way in the conference literature. It tied her to the National Alliance Against Racist and Political Repression. Nothing in that name that I couldn't agree with.

Conference literature said Bloice was with the U.S. Peace Council. I ran across that name in a back issue of *Newscope*, the official newsletter of the United Methodist Publishing House. Methodist agencies used to participate in the U.S. Peace Council, it reported, but stopped because its views had been consistently pro-Soviet.

Front Groups, Too

Romerstein explained that a lot of nice-sounding organizations with lofty goals like peace and justice are set up and used by the Soviet Union as front groups. Often most members don't know that, although the leaders of them usually do. Not everything the groups do is necessarily helpful to or distorted by the Soviet Union. But their true roots pop into view on their inconsistencies. Such is the case of some of the obscure "peace" organizations that are against military intervention everywhere—except the Soviet's invasion of Afghanistan, which they support as a neighborly gesture, or Soviet-backed liberation movements.

Many times, Romerstein explained, the front organizations will spawn numerous subsidiary groups with different names and few members to make it more difficult to trace their true connections.

The ruse works, he said, because average Americans just aren't going to know or try to find out what all those groups they're encountering really stand for.

I asked about Lennox S. Hinds, the official moderator of last weekend's conference. He was the one who ran the business meeting so "efficiently" and was listed as a representative to the United Nations from the International Association of Democratic Lawyers.

Romerstein said the Carter administration had investigated the organization and published an unclassified document on it. That report identified Hinds' organization as a Belgium-based group that is "one of the most useful Communist front organizations at the service of the Soviet Communist Party." Hinds also was chairman of the 31-member conference steering committee.

My head was swimming. I had joined the *Reporter* with the idea of taking a couple of years off from the frenzy of daily journalism and devote a little service to the church. But here I was falling into international skullduggery, the like of which I'd never encountered in my years of doing "real" journalism.

I continued trying to identify the steering committee members. A number of them were part of the ANC and SWAPO revolutionary groups. I checked with Senator John Glenn's office where I was told although the ANC is funded and armed by the Soviet Union, that should not be construed as total Soviet control. The ANC was said to contain quite a mixture of ideologies ranging from those seeking some kind of communist regime to those hoping for a democratic replacement of the white tyranny. Some ANC leaders were happy to have the Soviet help because nobody else, including the United States, would provide it. For other ANC leaders the aid was help from an ideological comrade.

By late Thursday afternoon, I had fairly certain identification of more than half the steering committee. Besides the staff member from the United Methodist Women's Division, the rest were identified with the U.S. Peace Council, the U.S. Communist Party, ANC, SWAPO, the International Association of Democratic Lawyers and groups identified by themselves or the U.S. government as affiliates of the lawyers' "Soviet front group." All-in-all, quite a narrow band of folks.

What's The Booty?

Now I was beginning to think that nobody ever had an idea of bringing people together to explore the wide array of South Africa issues. It seemed by this Thursday afternoon that the purpose from the beginning had been to broaden the image of legitimacy of the two revolutionary movements and, perhaps also, to fulfill some goal of raising the status of the Soviet Union and Marxist revolutionary movements around the world.

Despite the very peripheral involvement of a few church-staff people in the planning, that had been enough to entice other church groups into putting their names on the event which brought endorsements from well-known religious figures. A church mailing address made the dress-over complete.

I wondered, *if my scenario is close to correct, what did the apparently Soviet-connected originators get out of the conference?* Then I looked on my desk at the 29 pages of the "Declaration," written before the conference, and "Recommendations for Programs of Actions," written on Saturday.

After the vote, Lennox Hinds had shouted, "You have produced a national program of action." He then quickly moved that the conference secretariat become a permanent committee to act for the "broad-based" conference and to implement the program.

There was no time for nominations from the floor nor were the names of the secretariat read. The audience perfunctorily gave approval. Thus, the narrow ideological group which originated the conference now could claim an endorsement to continue operating. And the endorsement appeared to be from all the religious, labor and community people who quite unwittingly had lent their names to the conference. And the new permanent committee—whose list of sponsors gave it the look of national scope—could claim that its recommendations amounted to something of a consensus of people who are really concerned about South Africa.

Most of those recommendations were somewhat innocuous. Some had punch to them but were general enough to be applied toward a number of solutions. But what the organizers wanted and got for their efforts was the unquestioned declaration that the answer for southern Africa lay in the ANC and SWAPO revolutions. The document called on churches to raise money for the military effort.

I thought about all of this, but it was Thursday evening. The time for thinking was gone. Our copy deadline was Thursday morning to allow time for editing. Fridays were devoted to laying out pages, writing headlines and making up the paper in the back shop. The flats of finished, laid-out type sat for the weekend and could be re-opened for late-breaking stories. One of us each Sunday had duty in the afternoon, often staying through the evening, putting the paper to bed. Printing began early Monday.

But this Thursday evening, I hadn't written a word. I told Sharon I needed to make a few more phone calls. But I'd already used that line too many Thursday nights as it was. She said I had enough grist for my story with what I knew about half the steering committee. Even if none of the rest were part of that vague pro-violence, pro-Soviet network, there was enough involvement to raise questions that probably needed raising, we figured.

Writing: The Agony

I sat down to write and froze at the typewriter keys. *How do I start?* I muttered. After all, this was not a story I had intended to write.

Wads of single sheets of paper with three to a dozen lines of typing on them began to pile up in the corners of my office. Wadding up and throwing the paper was a good release for the frustration borne of being unable to find the proper lead of a story. I just didn't seem to feel right about the direct news approach of, "A United Methodist-sponsored conference last weekend was planned by a committee dominated by people in organizations controlled by, related to, funded by or a part of the Communist Party of the Soviet Union."

The hours passed, and even Spurgeon, who prided himself about how late at night he worked, had gone home. Dan Louis and I had pulled a trick on him earlier this year. Dan and I started at the *Reporter* the same month and both noticed fairly soon how Spurgeon usually would try to stay at least a few minutes longer than the last person to leave. So Dan and I agreed to alternate late nights for a week, pledging not to leave until after Spurgeon did. We had to stay deep into the night, but we succeeded five times in defeating the unwitting and fatigued victim of our plot. Unless he had pressing unfinished business, he was more inclined now to let one of us turn off the lights when we worked late.

This Thursday night I was all alone. Most writers know the feeling. Stuck on a difficult story, you know there's absolutely no way the job can be done without pulling words and thoughts out of your uncooperative head. It's a lonely feeling. My whole floor was strewn with paperwads when I focused on a constant piece of advice from John Lovelace. A 30-year veteran of religious journalism, John had spent the previous five years teaching journalism and carried a professorial manner as a fellow associate editor. He pounded home to us that the most important thing was to remember the average churchgoer while you wrote.

I thought, *what would it be like for a group of average Methodists or Lutherans, for example, to have traveled to New York City because of the church-wide invitation and then seen and heard everything I did? How could I help the readers feel like it was happening to them?*

To set the scene and get the readers in the mood that they were going to walk through the story with me, I decided to start the story with all million *Reporter* readers getting off the subway train with me. After a couple of false starts, I put in a clean sheet of paper and typed three very simple paragraphs:

> NEW YORK—I climbed from the subway tunnel onto sun-drenched Broadway Avenue and into a dimly lit, dingy auditorium at Columbia University. It was Sunday morning.
>
> Several hundred people inside were cheering a harangue against "U.S. imperialism."
>
> Several United Methodist general agencies had joined with a wide variety of groups to sponsor this conference. It was billed as a national mobilizing event "to combat current U.S. policy trends" in relation to Southern Africa.

I had no idea of the ribbing and ridicule I would take through the years for that opening paragraph.

Sounded like a country yokel in the big city for the first time, several said.

Many church leaders took the lead sentence to mean it was my first time to New York and that I simply was overwhelmed by being exposed to urban diversity that didn't look like the Midwest or Dallas.

Mainly, though, it provided a nice joke for people to use in greeting me warmly or icily.

"Hey, Roy, been down in the subway lately?"

"Is that something you learned down in the subway?"

"Well, look who just came up out of the subway!"

"What does he know, he hasn't come up out of the *daaaark* subway tunnel, yet."

Writing: The Ecstasy

Sometime around midnight I wrote the last paragraph on my South Africa conference story. Then it happened. A chill ran through my tired body. The feeling inspired both fear and euphoria at the same time. I'd had that feeling several times before during my years as a reporter. It came when I felt the full emotional impact of the explosiveness of a story I was writing. I didn't feel it on every explosive story, but it seemed to hit me when I knew that the integrity of the story relied largely on my having covered a lot of bases and that no single other person could vouch for its truthfulness.

It was a chill that ran through me when I knew that the minute that story hit the streets, I was on thin ice. At once terrifying and thrilling, the chill was a momentary journalistic ecstasy, the realization that you've provided important information that the public would not know but for your efforts. I was drawn to that thin ice. It wasn't thin because I used information I was unsure of. Rather, it was a matter of helping readers draw as much out of available information as possible, stepping as close to the edge as you could and still be on solid facts.

The euphoria quickly was overcome by the fear, however. I immediately started going through the story once again, checking and rechecking all the facts to make certain I could back them up if called to account. Friday morning I handed the story to Sharon Mielke.

Sharon was a most gracious managing editor despite a tough veneer that seemed to fit her Wisconsin, German farm-girl heritage. Prematurely silverhaired, she had a seen-it-all skepticism from two decades of viewing the inside of the church as a pastor's wife, local church leader, regional church editor and, for six years now, a national church journalist. She always lent encouragement to go for the hard edge of a story. I was taxing her patience on a Friday when she was supposed to be laying out the main news page. I was a day past deadline and was telling her I now needed to turn my attention to researching a sidebar that would include the reaction of the church officials responsible for the South Africa conference.

"Go to it," Sharon encouraged.

I planned to put special emphasis on getting the officials to fill in the explicit Christian aspects of the conference that had not been noticeable to me. Such explicitness was a near-requirement of Spurgeon's for making a story a *Reporter* story. If a story didn't have an explicit religious angle a subscriber could read it somewhere else, Spurgeon reasoned.

I called Mia Adjali of the Women's Division who had staff responsiblity for the conference. I told her all that I had witnessed and all I had discovered during my research this week. Had there been a mistake in sponsoring a conference and essentially turning it over to people with various relationships with the Communist Party, I asked?

"Not at all," Mia said, acknowledging she had been only peripherally involved. "We get involved in these because we think it is important to provide Christian input where we can. We know darn well that in any coalition there's the danger that one ideology will dominate." She said it had been a long time "since we pulled off a major South Africa conference" and that Methodist agency staff people were looking for partners "to try to get United Methodist interest alive again in South Africa."

"Wouldn't a primarily Christian conference have done a better job?" I asked.

"Oh, we've tried many methods. Most of the time we try to find a different process to get more people involved. Often, it's too expensive for us to do on our own," Mia explained.

"But you didn't get many Christians into this one."

"We didn't seek a lot of grassroots people for this one," she said. "We just asked national leadership."

"What is gained by providing a forum for the kind of rhetoric I heard?"

"Considering the potential for statements far more radical, there was less rhetoric than could have been expected. I think our influence was felt. Our main concern is our own government. Sometimes we get pretty rough with our own. How often does the U.S. media quote ANC or SWAPO at length? We like to give them an opportunity. We bend over double to make sure that those voices get the limelight."

I asked, "If a United Methodist were looking for some unique sign of Christians having been involved in the conference or in the recommendations, what would you show them?"

"Often we don't know what we bring into these coalitions that is uniquely religious. We're struggling with that. We need to find where faith has something special to offer. But we have difficulty expressing that and putting it on paper."

I questioned Mia's subordinant, Melba Smith. Why was Melba the only religious representative on the 31-member steering committee and why were no United Methodists part of the Sunday program?

"We weren't trying to have it overloaded with United Methodists," was Melba's reply. She said the seeming imbalance on the last day was planned. The idea was to have several religious people dominate the opening sessions on Friday, labor people on Saturday and then the "international groups" to have control on Sunday (the day when decisions were made).

Well, I thought, this isn't real convincing to me, but who knows? I'll just write it straight, and maybe it will help our readers feel good about what their church's money, time and name were able to achieve in consort with the very interesting Soviet-connected political groups.

Another Late Night Call

I drove home Friday evening, satisfied with a major piece of work completed, and for the first time was able to devote my attention to Shirley's parents who had come earlier in the week from Missouri.

Around midnight in the midst of one of my lengthy family slide shows, I was startled and Shirley's father was awakened on the couch by the ringing of the phone. I flipped the projector switch to the fan position and went to the kitchen.

"Roy, this is Spurgeon."

My heart sank. I was tired. I'd planned to go to bed soon. I wanted to be done with the week's project. A Friday night call from Spurgeon could only be trouble. He was notorious for reading a major, past-deadline story late on Friday afternoon and coming into our writers' offices and plopping down a manuscript awash in his turquoise ink. "This needs a lot of work," he might say. Or worse, "I cannot allow this to run in our paper." Usually, the story already was laid down on the flat in the back shop. If the story was killed, at least for the week, you had to scramble to find something else to anchor the paper. You might have to work through the night or all day Saturday to make up for the loss. The thought of his ripping up a whole laid-out page on Friday evening was a true nightmare. When I had left the office around 8 p.m. my two stories filled the bottom half of the main page. Spurgeon hadn't looked at a thing because he was tied down Thursday and Friday with the executive committee of our board of directors. That meant he was now highly sensitive to the effect of stories on "the higher powers."

All of that passed through my mind at the sound of Spurgeon's voice. There was time for it to pass through, for he had a slow way of talking.

"I just read your stories," he said. "They're explosive."

But will I be able to go to bed tonight, I thought. I just grunted in response.

"We can't run them the way they are."

There, he said it. My weekend once again would be a goner. But Spurgeon had a manner of often stating things in the worst possible way. Actually, my main story on the conference was fine. So was the sidebar, except that Spurgeon noted I didn't have response from the bishops who were listed as sponsors of the South Africa event. "We've got to have them," he said.

"I tried to get their response, but two of them are out of the country."

"Where?"

"England, I think, at some conference."

Spurgeon was matter of fact, "You'll just have to call them."

"I don't have a number and have no idea where they are, Spurgeon."

"Somebody must know."

I said Ned Dewire might know. Ned was the chief executive of the General Council of Ministries which coordinated all the national program agencies and basically kept track of many of the bishops' events.

"I'll check tomorrow," I said.

"No, we might miss them," Spurgeon said. "You'd better get hold of them tonight." He wished me good luck and told me to bring a copy of my revised story by his house on Saturday. "And by the way," he added, "good job."

It could have been much worse, I thought. And, to tell the truth, Spurgeon's intensity in pursuing a story and in demanding thoroughness and excellence was something I loved about the job at the same time I lamented it.

Shirley's folks had given up on seeing the slide-show finale and were coming through the darkened kitchen.

"Who's calling you this late at night?" her father asked.

I explained briefly and said I had to stay up to do some telephone interviews.

"At this hour!" Shirley's mother exclaimed.

I'm sure that's what Ned Dewire thought, too. It was nearly 1 a.m. when I awakened him at his home in Dayton, Ohio. Actually, he didn't seem all that surprised to hear my voice. The *Reporter* staff had turned to him for urgent information before.

Yes, he knew where my target bishops were. Symbolically, for the purpose for which I was seeking them, they were attending a conference at Wesley Chapel in London on Methodist heritage in relation to politics. George McGovern and Margaret Thatcher were to speak, he said.

Ned was interested in hearing all the details of my story. "That's too bad," he said when I finished. "Every once in awhile the New York staff seems to lose control of the reins and lets one or two staffers do something that totally ignores who their constituents are."

Good Morning, London

Ned advised that I wait until 2 a.m. to call the Wesley Chapel manse. I did.

"They're at the Mount Royal Hotel," the woman at the manse told me when I called.

At the hotel, I first asked for my friend Bishop Hodapp. I'd been calling him regularly all year for comments as president of the Board of Church and Society about a long list of public issues. Last spring we had brought him in to our headquarters as the newsmaker for our annual conference for *Reporter* edition editors. I'd spent time with him at a World Council of Churches' sponsored meeting in Atlanta. And just the month before I'd ridden through southern and central Illinois with him as he led back-to-the-Bible conferences. Like most bishops he was not an ostentatious man, far different from the blow-dried TV evangelists. A big, informal-looking fellow with a round balding head and jovial hearty-har laugh, he reminded me of some heart-of-gold Ozark farmers I'd known in my childhood. I admired his unflagging commitment to justice.

Bishop Hodapp had just gotten up and begun shaving when the phone rang. He was a little surprised to have me as the first person he talked to in London that day. But then, the *Reporter* staff had turned to him for urgent information before. I said I was calling because his name was on all the literature as a sponsor of the conference last weekend. I tried to tell him the details as dispassionately as possible.

Bishop Hodapp said he had had no contact with the planning of the event. He consented to have his name listed because agency staff presented the conference as one "to openly discuss the developing independent nations of Africa. Since these kinds of concerns have been continually expressed as concerns of our General Conferences, I felt it was in order to join as a sponsor to call the conference together."

He expressed surprise at the makeup of the conference planning committee and the last day's session. "Your report indicates the conference was not what I anticipated." And not knowing for certain what happened at the event, he could only state in general that he repudiated United Methodist participation in any meeting or event that is manipulated by persons of one particular ideology. He went on to say that if the United Methodist name and money are offered to an event, then Methodist leaders should be in positions of influence both in planning and at the actual event.

I then called Bishop A. James Armstrong of Indiana, once called by a national magazine America's most activist bishop. I told him I was calling him because his name was on a list of 100 called the "preparatory committee."

Armstrong said he didn't know his name had been used and that he knew nothing about the conference. That was the same thing I'd heard from another person on that list, Lois Miller, chief executive of the world missionary unit of the Board of Global Ministries.

The bishop didn't like the sound of the way resolutions had been passed. "Any conference that is so closed that participants do not have the freedom to amend is not in the tradition of the United Methodist Church and is not worthy of UMC participation."

All told, I spent 51 minutes on the phone to London at a bargain rate of $32.80. What a breeze this job was. I was sleeping like a baby by 3:30 a.m.

Rewriting A Headline

That Sunday it was my turn for putting the paper to bed, not a happy circumstance for helping to allay my in-laws' growing concerns about whether I *ever* had time for my family. I had spent part of Saturday rewriting and running the copy over to Spurgeon's house. I'd worked through the previous weekend in New York and an earlier weekend in Dayton. During that 34-day period, I had a grand total of three days off, not an uncommon ratio for *Reporter* editors and writers trying to keep our readers apprised of the church's very busy fall activities.

While I was performing my Sunday afternoon duty of working with a paste-up artist to get all the corrections down, Spurgeon walked in with my revised manuscript. The stories were fine, he told me, but when he looked over the flat of the main page, he didn't like the six-column headline over them.

I'd helped write the headline Friday with Sharon, who had made the decision to avoid the appearance of exploiting a volatile story. She ran it across the bottom of the page and put brighter stories on top. In a large box was a jubilant picture and review of Tom Key's then-new Cotton Patch Gospel musical playing just off Broadway. After sort of backing into the controversy in the story we decided to put the whammy on the reader with a direct headline, something like, "UMs Gave the Name and Money, Pro-Soviets Ran the Show." We often changed headlines on Sundays. I had no problem with Spurgeon wanting to tone this one down a little.

Spurgeon and I worked and worked on something that would fit. He really liked, "UM Endorsed Event Seemed Controlled By Pro-Soviets." It had the qualified, tentative tone that Spurgeon liked because it didn't claim any absolutes. But it was too long to run in headline type that was 48 picas high. And the *Reporter* did not have 42-point headline type. A 36-point head would be far too small for a six-column story and Spurgeon's preferred wording would come way short in that size.

He was so committed to that wording that he had the head set in 48-point, took it to our camera shop and had the photographer take a picture of it and print it at 87 percent which gave us about a 42-point headline that fit.

On the flat, tucked in what we called the right armpit of the main story was the reaction story of church officials with the headline, "Officials Explain, Question Participation."

In the stories, I had abstained from offering any opinions of what really led to such a conference. I tried to select enough facts to give readers an accurate feel of the event.

Early the next morning the presses started rolling.

4

Rolling With the Presses

When I got to work early Monday, the pressmen were attaching the metal imprinted plates of the first of that week's editions. My South Africa conference story was on the main news plate.

The press room was quiet. Several hundred of my words were poised to becoming THE NEWS for hundreds of thousands of people. But right now the story remained known only to the few hundred people who had attended the New York conference and to my colleagues. All would change once the press button was pushed by Johnny Brown, Danny Brown or Johnie Stailey, who always called me "Slant" after we ran a letter accusing me of slanting the news.

My thoughts abruptly were interrupted. The howl of the presses filled the room.

Local church and annual conference editions for California— the ones needing the most truck time to reach the homes of church members by Friday—rolled off the presses. The machinery automatically cut and stacked them to the side. Workers placed them on a gurney and pushed them out of the press room into the mail room where they were stamped with mailing labels and placed into bags that were thrown onto other gurneys, rolled up a metal ramp into the mail truck and whisked off to the post office about a mile away. Californians now were destined to know the story, too.

Every 15 minutes or so, the workers stopped the presses to put new plates on for a different local church edition or annual conference edition. There were more than 400 additions in all. But in each edition and on the main news page of every paper was my story. Journalists seeking humility shouldn't watch the presses roll.

All day and all night the presses ran and the mail trucks rolled, spreading the news to nearly every county of the land. Every half-hour or so there was a deadline for meeting a truck at the post office before it pulled away from the dock for a new American destination.

Off they rolled to disparate shores of Maryland and Florida. There they went to Minnesota woods and the Utah desert. Later, they headed to Ohio mill towns and Tennessee hills.

The presses just kept rolling 24 hours a day right on into Wednesday when the trucks headed for Oklahoma and all across the endless expanses of Texas until the last hometown Dallas editions were impregnated with ink in the shape of all the words that made up mine and the other writers' stories.

Wednesday evening, the frenetic, seemingly ceaseless operation stopped cold. Abrupt silence signalled that now, everybody could hear the story. I thought about the courage needed by the top decision-maker to go ahead and say, "Roll the presses; put 'em on the truck; get the news out," when it is quite certain that he and his institution will suffer repercussions.

On Friday, the papers hit church members' houses across America. An uproar followed. Most of it was anger at church agencies for "tarnishing" the church's name in that way. The Methodists' Board of Global Ministries was something of a punching bag, taking the frustration aimed at all New York denominational agencies.

The Readers Speak

Our office was inundated with mail. A lot of it jolted us with its paradoxical ring.

A Massachusetts man wrote:

> Congratulations to the *Reporter* and to Roy Howard Beck for printing that some of the money our church members have given in their apportionments was used to support a meeting which appeared to be controlled by organizations which are at the service of the Soviet Communist Party.

"I was deeply impressed by your article," said a Montana man. "What a wonderful surprise I had in reading your report," a Tennessee physician wrote.

It was strange to have so many people act so happy about my story, even though their letters indicated they were furious with the church agencies and officials.

The joy came from the fact that they had been suspicious of such goings-on or had heard rumors for years and believed the church and its journalistic institutions had been part of a conspiracy to withhold the information from the members. They were joyous because they felt so uplifted by being trusted to know the details and judge for themselves.

Long-time conservative critics of the *Reporter*—some of whom had riled me so much during my first year—fell all over themselves to praise us.

One prolific letter-writer in New Mexico several times earlier had questioned my integrity and professionalism and tarred me as representing only the liberal point of view. Now, he wrote: "You are standing tall, Roy. May your checks be ever larger. I may not survive the cheering each week when I see your latest."

I wrote back, "Every reporter has to earn his credibility with readers. I hope that I finally have done that with you."

To another conservative, I responded:

Thank you for those warm words of support and affirmation. Please know that the editorial integrity and sincerity that went into this story also go into the stories in our paper with which you don't agree. That is not to say, of course, that we don't value criticism, especially when it points out factual errors.

I was, at the same time, trying to remind liberals who were busy attacking us that we were the same people they loved for our exposures of Religious Right activities throughout the previous year.

Some were buying into that. A liberal, social-activist district superintendent from Illinois called to say that my story was the kind of self-cleansing always needed to keep a movement strong. The agency officials, he said, had squandered an opportunity to promote a solid liberal cause by linking themselves with groups that on other issues—such as Afghanistan and the Baltic nations—stood with the oppressors, not the oppressed.

From the broad middle of the church came additional passionate letters. Representative of them was a Florida minister. He applauded the church agencies for stepping out on issues like the South Africa situation, but chastised them for failure to "exercise prudent responsibility":

> The agencies have allowed the good name of our church to be used, but failed to provide for responsible stewardship of that usage. . . .It is important for the church to be on the cutting edge in world needs—independent of political ideologies—in order to be a creative ministry.
>
> But "cutting-edge ministry" demands greater responsibility in involvement and follow-through than has been exhibited in this conference.

The conservatives, though, were the most colorful. It was clear that many would be reading our stories with much more openness in the future. Because of that, the church's national programs probably would get a fairer assessment from those people than before we printed my sizzler.

A Texas physician displayed this with his letter.

> As a follow-up to past letters regarding my allegation to you that the *Reporter* has been a leftist newsletter, I feel now I must accept your explanation that the paper merely reports religious-related news events as they transpire, regardless of their socio-political implications.
>
> The *Reporter*, and particularly in the recent article by Roy Beck, has demonstrated courage and honesty beyond that expected. May the Lord be with you and keep you during the predictable siege of contrived criticism. May you be shielded and protected from intimidation and church pressure politics.
>
> In honor of your recent great hour of truth in journalism, I will no longer refer to your publication as the "Weekly Worker." Please accept my apology for past insults of which you have not even been informed.

The reaction from our readers in the national agencies, however, tended to be anger at me and the *Reporter*. We were accused of stirring up right-wing anxiety and anti-communism, of engaging in guilt-by-association tactics and McCarthyism. Our critics just couldn't understand how we could run a story that we knew would bring scorn on our church's agencies and on a justice issue that we said we largely supported.

Leaders Say, Be Proud of Conference

Early in the week, while the presses still were running on the paper carrying my story, Sharon Mielke flew up to St. Paul, Minnesota, where the Methodist mission board was having its big fall meeting. It was rather awkward timing, since the board and its Women's Division were two of the key players in the South Africa conference support.

We thought it wouldn't be fair to let the 150 or so directors meet all week and then encounter our conference story when they returned to their homes. So Sharon took about 100 copies of the week's *Reporter*. She set the papers on a table near the mail folders where all directors checked several times a day for handouts and mail. The murmuring began quickly. You couldn't miss the "pro-Soviet" headline.

At the end of the first day, Sharon went back to the mail folders and found somebody had pushed the pile of *Reporters* into the waste basket. She put them out again.

Thursday I got a rather urgent call from Sharon. She had just stepped out of a meeting of the Women's Division. The papers had stirred a request for official response. So Mia Adjali made a 15-minute presentation on the board staff's role in the South Africa conference.

"Your story doesn't have a chance" against the credibility of a presentation by a very pregnant woman, in the autumn of her childbearing years, wearing a "cute little maternity dress," Sharon said.

Mia, sticking with the opinions I had reported for her in my sidebar, told directors they should be proud of their role in the conference. The Women's Division directors were convinced. They later voted unanimously for their president to consider preparing a rebuttal to my story.

"However," Sharon said, "nobody even attempted to refute any fact of your story."

Critics of my report mainly sought to minimize the importance of it by saying the recommendations passed on the final day had no meaning and that the first two days of the conference were what mattered.

Sharon told me the women were especially concerned about my having gotten a copy of the conference secretariat list. That wasn't supposed to be made public. Considering the membership, we at the *Reporter* thought we had a pretty good idea why.

Mia told the board my story suggested that few United Methodists attended the conference that had the Methodist name on it. True, she said, she wasn't there, but of the 1,200 to 1,500 people who were, she knew of at least 10 and probably more United Methodists attending during the first two days, but not on the last day. I didn't find her numbers very impressive.

She acknowledged that there were relatively few religious leaders on the platform during the conference and then only in ceremonial roles. Since I had interviewed them, the Women's Division officials had discovered that two other religious representatives were on the 31-member steering committee, a layman from New York's Riverside Church and a member of the activist group, Clergy and Laity Concerned.

Much was made by several people in St. Paul of the fact that the first day of the New York conference had begun with a prayer by Riverside Church's Rev. William Sloan Coffin. That was supposed to show that the religious folks were having influence on the non-religious leftists who predominated in the audience. But that prayer actually was a source of even more controversy after reports from the first day were published.

Coffin had appeared to be a bit embarrassed to be praying, when the seats of honor were filled with the likes of representatives of the Soviet Union, East Germany and the chairman of the Communist Party U.S.A. Before beginning his prayer, he apologized to those in the audience who might be offended by his reference to a supreme being.

Sharon dutifully reported the Women's Division meeting in a story running under the headline, "Be proud of conference / despite pro-Soviet allegations, event success, women's unit told." It was becoming clear to all of us at the *Reporter* that nothing about the conference was going to be questioned or be a cause of rethinking inside the national denominational bureaucracies.

I hadn't even thought of bureaucracy as a word to be used in connection with the church when I joined the *Reporter* a year earlier. I had a very idealistic image of the national church agencies and an innocent loyalty to them. But I had been losing my unrealistic image of the agencies during the preceding summer as I sought information from New York mainline Protestant headquarters concerning a controversy involving support for a Native American woman in Oklahoma who had been convicted of murdering a policeman.

Nobody in any office would take or return my phone calls. I kept trying. Finally, I was asked to submit questions in advance of any interview. This went on for months, and I was fed up. I fired off a letter to church executives telling them that their bureaucracy was just as unresponsive to public news interests as the Procter & Gamble Co. in Cincinnati, notorious for its sealed lips. In fact, I said, I'd have to lump the New York church bureaucracy as being pretty similar to, if not worse than, the bureaucracy of all the governments and businesses I'd covered in the past.

I got their attention with that and some helpful response. "That's hitting pretty low," one executive laughed, "to compare us to a multinational corporation."

Backlash Includes Media Peers

Soon after the jab at us from the St. Paul meeting, the United Methodist Publishing House's newsletter delivered a new blow. Not only did it carry Mia Adjali's objections to my stories but a report that Bishop Hodapp was changing his response. He had called *Newscope* to say that when he returned from London he contacted several people who had been at the conference the first two days. "Not one has been in any way negative about the conference or its actions," he said.

Mia was quoted as discounting my report because I had attended only the last session. That was untrue. I had attended the second and third days of the conference.

Then the denominational news service put out a report that Bishop Hodapp and Bishop Jesse DeWitt, president of the Methodists' Board of Global Ministries, had protested to the news service about my stories. The two bishops called my stories incomplete. They said they did not question the accuracy of anything that I had written, but that I had not seen everything. Bishop DeWitt said the actions of the last day did not have "the significance given them in the Beck reporting. His account seemed to be out of proportion to the meeting itself."

Charles Brewster, managing editor of the denomination's *New World Outlook* missions magazine, shot off a letter to the editor to us accusing me of breaking "the first law of interpretive or investigative journalism."

> That law is: if you are going to attack a meeting make
> sure you are there for the whole meeting. . . .I shall not go
> into all the presuppositions and guilt by association evident
> in Mr. Beck's reporting of the one day he did attend the
> conference. . .I'm afraid this report is a lowpoint for the
> *Reporter* and I am indeed sorry.

Not Reporting But Paul Harvey

By the first of November, the *Reporter's* support base among some
of the church hierarchy was being eroded. Officials in some of the annual conferences were questioning if their conferences should be attached to a newspaper that would report what I had.

"I protest the timing of your article," came the cry from a California local church leader. "Did you deliberately plan to run this expose
just before Stewardship Sunday? Some laypeople who do not understand the economic, social and political implications of liberation
struggles may be tempted to withhold or reduce their pledges to the
local church." Then in a comment laden with interesting judgments
that seemed to undercut the very support he was trying to give to the
agency, the writer concluded, "Our leaders in New York need support,
not criticism from Dallas. In future years, please wait until after
Stewardship Sunday to run articles about the activities of our General
Board of Global Ministries."

A Western New York district superintendent wrote about the "contribution of Roy Beck." He put the word "contribution" in quotes. "It
was not reporting as I understand reporting. The article which he wrote
was more of a Paul Harvey type of thing."

Paul Harvey? With the release of one story, I'd gone from a darling of the church left and scourge of the Religious Right to Ronald
Reagan's radio altar ego! I was feeling a real identity crisis. I didn't
like being labeled a right-winger or McCarthyite or Paul Harvey.

Never before had I done anything that was so despised by liberals.
These were the kinds of responses I'd become accustomed to getting
from the right. I'd always wanted to prove to conservatives that my
sense of journalism let the chips fall wherever they might, regardless
of which ideological group's yard got littered. But I guess I'd never
had that much of an opportunity.

The more I thought about it, the more I realized that every other institution I'd ever reported on had been basically a conservative one. And conservatism had prevailed in the political climate in each of the communities. Therefore, holding institutions accountable almost always tended to please liberals and anger conservatives.

Now for the first time in my life, I was covering an institution dogmatically liberal in its leadership. And I was finding that liberal power figures squeak the same way that conservative power figures do when their deeds are held up for public observation.

None of this was new to my mind. But it was different experiencing it.

Reassessing In The Grotto

I was feeling vulnerable and isolated, especially the day Spurgeon and Bishop Hodapp had a lengthy phone call in which the bishop continued his strong complaint about my story. Afterward, Spurgeon grilled me about a number of points and asked for all the material I'd gathered concerning the conference. He then shut himself in his office.

I felt like the jury was out—a one-man jury that immediately after deciding the verdict would turn into a judge to mete out my sentence.

Across the hall in my office, I was feeling extremely frustrated. *I willingly would acknowledge a mistake if anybody would point out errors*, I thought. But the only criticism was that I reported the final day's activities and the conference-control information without telling what happened on the first two days of the meeting. That was like saying a reporter should write stories like the minutes of a meeting.

Nobody in officialdom was dealing with the substance of my report. The only response was on peripheral items and in attacks on my own integrity. All of the *Reporter* staff's discussions prior to the printing of my story may have seemed melodramatic and overdone at the time, but the possible repercussions were coming true in spades.

Trying to keep busy in my office, I remembered many other times at other papers when this kind of thing had occurred. A threatening gesture from a governor, a corporate bigwig, a police chief and other power figures who had challenged the integrity of a story or series I'd written. Always before, editors stood behind my stories because they believed them and in me. Maybe I'd just been lucky before. I waited— with my suspended plucked chicken.

Spurgeon eventually emerged from his grotto with the materials and the good news that he could not fault my report. He gave me an assessment that he later that night would dictate in a letter to Bishop Hodapp. He said the more he heard and read, the more convinced he was that "if a cross-section of United Methodists had shown up at the meeting, 90 percent or more would have perceived matters as you did, except most people would not have been nearly so thorough and even-handed in the follow-up checking."

Spurgeon told the bishop that if my report could be discredited in substance or as a distortion of reality that he would accept responsibility and, if necessary, resign his editorship because of it.

Let's not go overboard, I thought.

Until somebody offered substantive criticism, Spurgeon said, "I'm not willing to stand idly by and witness efforts to discredit our report in general."

An Admission Of Error

Spurgeon invited Bishop Hodapp to write an opinion/editorial piece for the *Reporter's* editorial page if he still felt our report needed more challenging. The bishop did. It filled the top right quarter of the page on November 13 under the headline, "UMR report short-changed church; faithfulness required participation." He repeated his earlier stated criticisms.

Tucked in the middle of the article, however, was a statement that agency staff had erred in lending the church's name to the conference. Such identification shouldn't have been lent ahead of time to something the church didn't have control over, he said, because it gave the appearance of church approval of the contents of all conference reports and actions.

"I have expressed this concern to agency staff members and have been assured that this will be corrected in the future," he wrote. It didn't take much space in the article. But that action on his part, combined with the publicity from my story, significantly changed some staff operating procedures that had been somewhat common, though un-reported, in years past.

Spurgeon's equally long editorial ran in the upper left quarter of the page and saluted Bishop Hodapp for doing far more than any other leader—in any denomination—to respond to serious concerns raised by my report. Spurgeon criticized all other leaders of the New York and Washington agencies for not giving straight answers on nine key issues.

Among the issues was the question of the use of a "sponsors" list when sponsors have no say in the planning and conduct of the meeting. The editorial also asked, "If, as the *Reporter's* critics were contending, the third day's session had no meaning, why did its leadership bother to go through the gesture of receiving motions and taking votes. It continued:

> Even though many religious leaders consider the revolutionary groups to be the most viable political vehicles for bringing about majority rule in Southern Africa, how can one justify billing as broad-based a conference which excluded by design any expression of alternative view points?
>
> How does one justify the unwillingness or inability of officials for the church agency most directly involved to identify any uniquely Christian witness included in this conference?
>
> How does one justify the efforts of agency officials to avoid dealing with these substantive issues by means of diversionary attacks on the individual or publication raising them?

Those questions never received answers from church officialdom.

Not An Isolated Incident

A rich flow of mail from all types of readers always kept us apprised of not only feelings but also new information. Several letters in this round alerted us to other activities of some agency staff that suggested what I witnessed at the conference in New York was not an isolated incident.

A woman from Indiana wrote:

> Next weekend, the Board of Church and Society here is sponsoring a peace with justice weekend. The final speaker will be Lubomir Mirejovsky, general secretary of the Christian Peace Conference of Prague, Czechoslovakia, an internationally known communist front.

Her labeling was the same as I had learned in my conversation
with the U.S. House official while preparing my story. The group was
another of the so-called peace groups with curious actions such as
resolutions applauding the Soviet Union for invading Afghanistan.

An Illinois member of the church women's organization wrote:

> It seems that we would have learned from the mess in
> Zimbabwe/Rhodesia, but the wealth of Methodists will
> constantly be tapped for propagation of ideologies opposed
> to Christ if the trusting majority don't speak up.

From an Indiana pastor came this:

> Five months ago our congregation's United Methodist
> Women decided they had had enough with the Women's
> Division of the Board of Global Ministries and sent the at-
> tached information to all churches in our Conference. After
> hearing of our action, a missionary on furlough from Africa
> said, "Great for you, we missionaries are tired of being shot
> at by Cuban guerrillas funded by the United Methodist
> Women."

Donald Morris, a *Houston Post* news analyst, wrote a column on
my "out-of-the-subway" experience. We had a lengthy conversation
in which he revealed that for many years he worked for the CIA and
monitored one meeting after another around the world that he said was
set up like the South Africa one.

The purpose of such conferences, he said, was to allow the conference leaders like Bloice of the Communist Party and Hinds of the
Soviet front group to be able to claim church support for all kinds of
things and still be able to stand up to superficial scrutiny. "Then," he
said, "they will say, 'This isn't a commie program; why, it's the official stand of the United Methodist Church.' "

He continued, "Such shows as the South Africa conference are
structured to pull in liberal groups. Your church, like any other, is
staffed with scores of people with a deep concern about human rights
and oppression, troubled and earnestly hoping to support worthy
causes. The conference is the catnip."

Morris was a fascinating fellow. He said some things that should have moderated some of my new-found conservative admirers in their rush to use my experience to prove a clear-cut choice between communism and the "right way." Despite his absolute belief that the church had been snookered into one of the most common Soviet sting operations around, he said he had considerable sympathy for South Africa's African National Congress the conference had endorsed.

"The ANC, despite Soviet backing, is a valid organization," he observed. "SWAPO isn't. It is a complete Soviet creation."

A district superintendent from New Mexico wrote to recount his experience four years earlier that Sharon Mielke had raised a stink by reporting:

> A group at a Global Ministries' girls' school in Albuquerque told me they were pro-Chinese Communists working for the violent overthrow of our government. The *Reporter* helped us get the truth out. It took me about 20 hours a week for four months to get action, but it can happen. Persons with our Board of Global Ministries called me a racist, and my life was threatened, but what the *Reporter* did helped me bring more accountability through the 1980 General Conference.

A Michigan writer said the Women's Division of the Board of Global Ministries obviously needed to be reminded of the law of the denomination established in 1980 that deplores "all political and economic ideologies that lead to repression and totalitarianism." He went on: "Who are these women? How deep is their commitment to Marxism? Obviously they have an extraordinary tolerance for it."

The depth of feelings and rancor I had tapped with my story was almost overwhelming to me. I had to face up to the fact that were I not the one writing these stories, I would be more inclined to react like the church leaders who basically were trying to ignore this red-baiting-sounding exercise.

But I thought, *With so many people feeling they had examples of agency officials improperly using the church for leftist ideological purposes, maybe there really was a problem as real as with the way the Religious Right was misusing the Christian identity to baptize political agendas.*

Yet, I was more than a little concerned that I'd started a runaway reaction. Many people seemed to be reading more into my story than I thought I'd put into it. So I tried to include in each response some words appealing for moderation in assessing the situation.

To people who spoke of withholding money from the church's general program fund, I said, "I do not believe that some of the questionable antics of staff involve enough money to negate the great good that our denominational giving does." Use the process if you think changes are needed, I urged. Every congregation elects a lay representative to accompany the pastor to annual conference. Each annual conference sends a member to each of the national boards. Work with your representatives, I told each disgruntled writer.

All the outpouring of support from lay readers and even from many annual conference officials pleased Spurgeon. But he was concerned that I might be shut off from the top officials of the church, whom I would need for news sources on all kinds of subjects in the future. He assigned me to attend the fall meeting of the Council of Bishops." I want them to see that you don't have horns," he told me.

Bishops Over Cookies

At Pittsburgh I didn't receive the warmest reception of my journalistic career. Nearly all of the hundred active and retired bishops at the hotel in the Golden Triangle were seeing me for the first time.

In the big reception area outside the meeting room, bishops on break hovered around the tables piled with polite, homemade, calorie-laden cookies provided by local congregations. Methodist moderation was nowhere to be seen around the goodies. Most of the current presiding bishops milled around, while many of the retired white heads sat around other tables entertaining each other with old war stories from their days of "bishing."

With my reporter's note pad and my age that was about 25 years under the average in the room, I felt conspicuous and like everybody surely had noticed my name on the tag I was wearing. But nobody approached me. I felt remarkably shy, and I was fighting an awful head cold and sore throat. I gingerly worked the crowd, introducing myself at a slow pace.

A few bishops had gotten a letter I'd sent out a few days earlier to combat rumors circulating about me. Most rumors attempted to explain how I could have done such a thing as write the South Africa conference story. They portrayed me as a naive midwesterner who apparently had never been to New York City before and simply was overwhelmed by the cosmopolitan atmosphere and the exposure to a few radicals. One conspiratorial rumor was that I was a "plant" of conservative church caucuses and had slipped undercover into the *Reporter's* staff. Criticism focused on discrediting me.

I had addressed the letter to Bishop Hodapp, with copies to a number of people. The whole exercise now was embarrassingly self-centered. But I felt so defensive. Mixing with the bishops, I shared some of the same information of the letter, such as names of eyewitnesses who could document that I attended the conference more than the one day, since that seemed to be of great importance to some.

As a Missouri-Ozarks native, I already had experienced too many years of put-downs because of my hills accent and background. Emotionally, I took the naivete charge against me as being something of an ethnic slur.

New York City was not new to me, I told the bishops. Shirley and I had bummed around the country for three months after college graduation and camped out in a basement of a Brooklyn church for a while, riding the subways and walking the streets in the wee hours of the morning. Then, after being drafted, I had been stationed for awhile in New York City, getting a fairly liberal pedestrian view of the city nearly every night. Shirley and I had visited New York other times since, including a week I spent pounding 57th Street trying to interest a publisher in my musical compositions.

As to being frightened or shocked to see real live Communists on the stage at the South Africa conference, I told the bishops that I thought I was writing out of a little more experience than that. I'd spent a week reporting out of Cuba just last spring. Four days before I walked into the conference in that Columbia University auditorium this fall, I had spent an evening taxiing around the city and dining with two Communist Party officials I had met in Cuba and who at that time were working at the United Nations.

Mainly, I tried to help the bishops feel how important the church and its mission were to me. I think I met Spurgeon's primary aim, most didn't think I had horns. Other than that, I'm not sure of their initial appraisal.

Cause for wondering came at the end of one of the business sessions. Perhaps two dozen bishops stood to make emotional speeches about President Reagan's recent speech in favor of nuclear armament reduction. The council approved a statement that Reagan's speech was a "sign of God's grace." I went to the podium at the end of the session to ask some questions. A bishop who was an officer of the council treated me roughly, rhetorically questioning in front of the press corps whether I could be trusted to handle any information fairly.

Several bishops, however, one-by-one, let me know privately that they thought the *Reporter* was doing an important thing in exposing the workings of a few staff who were in need of reins.

I first encountered Bishop Hodapp while the bishops were divided into several rooms for committee meetings. I rounded a corner and saw him coming up the hall toward me. He immediately flashed a big smile and a hearty laugh, "Well, Roy, how are you doing?" He stuck out his hand as he approached me. I almost thought I detected a slight edge of embarrassment or uncertainty from him, as this was our first encounter since he had begun publicly upbraiding me. He didn't know me well enough to predict whether I'd be angry. He was safe. One-on-one anger was not my style. I'd do about anything to avoid personal confrontation.

His warm greeting really reduced the tension in me. I clasped his hand as firmly as he did mine.

He told me he'd gotten my letter and that I need not have felt I had to prove my integrity with him. He had no doubt of that, just of my judgment. I indicated I was doubting some of his judgment, too.

He said that he'd heard many of the rumors that I'd listed in the letter and that he may have been the source of one of them because of a misunderstanding of something I'd once told him, and he apologized for having passed on inaccurate information.

Cuba Over Lunch

I ran into Bob McLean at lunchtime. I figured the denomination's top peace officer might have some great conspiracy theories worked up about me. But he also was friendly. He'd received a copy of my letter to Bishop Hodapp.

"You know," Bob said, "I saw your story last week, and you *are* a good reporter." He was referring to coverage I'd done of 25 Soviet citizens touring America and pleading for peace as a project of USA-USSR Citizens' Dialogue Inc., for which Bob served as treasurer. Maybe I wasn't a mindless anti-communist after all, given the sympathetic treatment I'd given the visitors in my story.

I walked across the street with Bob and some other New York agency staff people to a busy diner. It didn't take long for the conversation to get around to the value of Marxist systems. Leading the way was Nora Boots, head of the Board of Global Ministries' mission efforts in Latin America. A Bolivian native, she grew up with bitter experiences from missionaries and U.S. policies she felt were misguided. She now was in a position to place her own imprint on missions.

Short and full-figured, Nora had a voice that could vary from the sound of a lilting musical instrument to that of a spewing volcano. Her English always was understandable even as it always carried rich accents and trills of her Latin roots. As I took my first bite of a BLT sandwich, Nora took a bite into my profession.

"There's nothing particularly free about the press in the United States," she said. "The press is much freer in Cuba." Nora had a way of offering ideas for people to choke on.

People try to put down Cuba by calling it Communist, she said, but Cuba's is one of the few governments in the Americas truly trying to help the poor. On the other hand, she continued, most newspapers in America are in the hands of a few dozen media corporations which run them to make a profit. In Cuba, the press does not have to be beholden to fat cat corporate advertisers but is run for the benefit of the people, Nora continued.

By the time I got fully involved in this conversation, the others at the table had taken to the sidelines and merely observed. "I agree that the continued media concentration in this country is troubling," I said. "And the advertiser-supported system of newspapers is not perfect. When I worked at daily newspapers I had quite a few disagreements over what I thought were influences being allowed over our operations by certain elite groups, whether advertisers or the people who played golf with the publisher. But it is the multiplicity of publications that allows all views to be heard and readers to judge for themselves."

Not all views are heard, Nora said. The U.S. news media are so conservative people rarely hear the views of liberation movements presented in fairness, she said, in a labeling that defied the most common public epithet that the news media are too liberal.

"Well, I visited the *Granma* newspaper in Havana last spring," I replied, "and there just is no way that publication, controlled entirely by the Cuban Communist Party, can rival the free flow of information in this country's publications."

The mission executive and I had to call it a draw. We just didn't seem to have enough common ground to reach for consensus on the topic.

A Secret Strategy Meeting

I couldn't figure out why so many agency people were showing up. I was told few usually attended the Council of Bishops. After an afternoon bishops' session, I noticed that all the agency people had disappeared.

I looked around the cookie tables and felt that several of the bishops seemed to be missing, too. I asked around and found that most of the bishops didn't seem to know what was going on. But one told me he understood that the bishops' executive committee was meeting in a secret session with agency officials.

A secret session at once piqued my attention. The church had a sunshine law requiring that all denominational business be conducted in public unless it involved property transactions or personnel matters. Even when an agency did close a session to the public, it was to be a publicized closed session with a report of some kind at the end. Secret meetings, thus, were cause for keen interest.

Late that evening, I tracked down one of the bishops who had been in the meeting. We had to meet clandestinely out of view of the others so he wouldn't be discovered, said Bishop Finis Crutchfield of Houston, who had a penchant for being mysterious. He explained that the secret meeting was to discuss strategies for counteracting the Institute on Religion and Democracy (IRD).

The IRD was a half-year-old group begun by some big-church pastors and academics in the mainline Protestant churches. They contended that the churches' agencies had become "apologists for oppression," justifying the loss of individual human freedoms under leftist regimes. It really had people shook up, the bishop told me.

I knew that. Just the previous week I had reported that a meeting of the NCC had included the unveiling of a previously secret, $6,000 study of the IRD by United Church of Christ and United Methodist national agencies. For three months private investigators had undertaken to find out who was really behind the IRD.

Like so much of the conspiracy-tinged work around the church, it just seemed overdone to me. Why do it in secret? I had covered the founding meeting of the IRD and had gathered much of the information openly that the secret study had gotten. The church leaders in IRD charged that it was more than overdone and had involved "subterfuge and Watergate-style" tactics.

Mainly, the study found the IRD was heavily funded by ultra-conservative foundations and was full of people tied to organized labor who were conservative on foreign policy and fairly liberal on domestic causes. It was pledged to root out "anti-democratic" sentiments in mainline Protestant agencies. One of its chief arguments was that in many oppressive societies ruled by dictators there are groups and movements trying to bring about change. The IRD claimed U.S. church groups often threw their weight behind the more radical, authoritarian-Marxist groups when more democratic reform groups existed.

Bishop Crutchfield told me he thought the full Council of Bishops would resist proposals to further try to formally discredit the IRD. The next day, the council proved him correct.

I ran into Rich Peck, editor of *Newscope*, during the meetings, and we took a hike for lunch. Tall and lean from his regimen of jogging, Rich threw an arm around me as we strode along in the brisk air and said, "There, you need a hug, Roy, with everybody coming down on you."

I had enjoyed getting to know Rich while we covered the Board of Church and Society meeting the days running up to the South Africa conference, and I had sent him a letter complaining about a couple of things in his story about Bishop Hodapp's and Mia Adjali's displeasure with me. He acknowledged on the Pittsburgh street that the Women's Division had misled him about the points I had contested.

"Sharon [Mielke] asked me what I thought about your story," Rich said. "I told her I thought your only error was in not carrying a news report on the conference along with your story."

"What I did *was* a news story."

"I mean a basic kind of story that told what happened over all three days. I think that omission made your piece more questionable."

We walked a while longer. "I also wondered how much you manipulated Bishop Hodapp into supporting your thesis when you called him in London," he said.

"I certainly wasn't trying to manipulate him," I said. "I just told him everything I knew." I thought a bit, and added, "But it's true that my assignment was to try to get something out of him, if he was willing. That would reassure our readers that somebody at the top disapproved of the way the conference turned out. Maybe we did unintentionally guide him past where he really wanted to go."

"At times," Rich said, "there's great tension between loving the church and telling the truth. I go by the standard that when our truth-telling in our publications might hurt the church, it seems to me we have to bend over backwards to make our reports as fair as possible."

Rich's advice seemed reasonable, but to me it had the sound of bending over backwards to protect the church from the truth. It wasn't until many months later, after a lot of rehashing everything in my mind, that I came to believe Rich was right on his earlier point. If we had also run a very straight, typical church-event news story—perhaps using the *United Methodist News Service* report on the first day of the conference—then my "out-of-the-subway" story would have combined to make a broader and fairer presentation. I never did believe, though, that any change in packaging, other than suppressing the information I discovered, would have made the conference seem acceptable in any way to the vast majority of church members.

I flew back to Dallas just in time for the annual meeting of the *Reporter's* Board of Directors.

The membership of our board was determined as follows: Each annual conference that published an edition with the *Reporter* was allowed to send a director as a member. The Texas conferences, as the founders, chose two directors each. The board was a good one, made up of people who believed substantially in United Methodist principles of openness, reason, pluralism and accountablility.

On The Board Of Directors' Grill

The first evening traditionally was given over to an open forum for all directors to ask any question and make any judgment about the content of the paper during the previous year.

During dinner, catered to our sloping back-of-the-building conference room, I got an early warning of what was to come. A couple of the directors sat down across from me, and one said, "Tell us about what was going through your mind when you wrote that story."

"That story" was the agenda for the evening. Fortunately, enough directors loved it that they ended up debating each other for much of the time. Clearly, though, several of them had received great pressure from their home conferences to express grave displeasure with my reporting and the paper's editorializing about the South Africa conference.

The *Reporter's* editorial independence from the top brass of the church was aided by two factors. One was that a 50-member board is too large to control many of any day-to-day details, and on whatever subject some directors might want to suppress information, there nearly always were others who would fight to publish it.

The second protection was that the board a few years earlier had approved a lengthy statement of editorial policy that was an excellent journalism treatise. The board could officially act on editorial matters only if it determined the staff had violated the editorial policy.

After this board meeting, I had one more opportunity for playing such a "celebrity" role. The United Methodist Joint Panel On International Affairs met December 8 in the Church Center at the UN that had served as the headquarters of the South Africa conference planning. We at the *Reporter* had not even known of the panel's existence until a few months earlier.

It was composed of approximately 30 representatives from the staff and directors of the social action and missions agencies. But most of the other directors on those boards didn't know the panel existed, and the general membership certainly was unaware.

Sharon Mielke had stumbled into one of its meetings earlier in the year while looking for another group, and had sat in it long enough to hear the group talking enthusiastically about an upcoming fall event to mobilize United Methodists on the South Africa issues.

I was not expecting a great deal of affirmation of my work from this group, but after what I ran into up at Columbia University, Sharon determined we'd better start covering this little-known body. We soon learned that it was rather like a kitchen cabinet. The members met for two days three or four times a year to hear an amazing array of experts on international issues. They then formulated positions that ended up being the basis for what both boards usually adopted as their own.

In The New York Barbecue Pit

I was wearing a hat, scarf and heavy topcoat when I arrived a few minutes after the meeting started. I'd recently bought the hat, my first as an adult, thinking it might be time to add a dash of maturity to my persona. I'd tried at times to grow a beard or moustache to give my medium frame and too-young face the appearance of their chronological age. But the whiskers wouldn't grow right.

I tried to slip into the back of the room, but the chairman noticed me.

"Let the record show," said the Rev. Randolph Nugent, chief executive of Global Ministries and chairman of the panel, "that we have another member of the press with us, Roy Howard Beck from the *United Methodist Reporter*. And let the record show he arrived late." The quip brought heavy laughter around the room. Obviously, my name by now was well connected to the concept of missing the first of a meeting.

At the first break I went around introducing myself to the several people I'd not met before.

"Oh," one woman said, looking up and down my 5-foot-8 presence, "I thought you would be taller."

"I thought you were older," several others observed, as I wondered if I should wear my new hat during the meeting.

The whole evening session was devoted to discussing the "fall-out" from the South Africa conference and the *Reporter* coverage. The tables were set up in a big square. Betty Thompson, Global Ministries' communications executive, congenially had invited me to eat supper and visit with her. So I'd seated myself on the inside of that square across from her. I had lingered too long in conversation and found myself trapped in the middle of the panel when the meeting began.

It felt more like a barbecue pit, and I was the meat. Most of the discussion lambasted my coverage. But nobody referred to me by name. They were tactful, referring to me in the third person and avoiding making it a feud of personalities. Still, everybody knew exactly who the culprit was.

I kept my head down and kept taking notes. After an-hour-and-a-half of it, though, Melba Smith couldn't keep up the strange protocol any longer. She looked at me and said, "I just want to know. Why did you write that, Roy?"

To be asked a question as a reporter covering a meeting is to be asked to become something totally different from what you are. For a second I sat in mute bewilderment. Peggy Billings came to my rescue. The head of the Women's Division social action unit said, "I don't think it's appropriate to ask Roy to comment. He's here as a reporter. The purpose of our discussion isn't to quiz him."

Whew!

Panel members expressed no reservations about the church's involvement with the South Africa conference. They emphasized the importance of the church not being afraid to talk with groups such as Communists who might hold greatly different philosophies.

The raising of questions about the ideology of the group that controlled the conference pulled people off onto "peripheral issues" and away from the important issue of fighting apartheid, several said.

"How many letters did we get complaining about the conference?" somebody asked.

"Only about 50," another answered.

Several comments around the room indicated that they felt 50 was a small number that suggested few United Methodists were upset and that the panel need not spend much energy responding to criticism of the conference.

I reported all of that in my next week's story, prompting another round of letters protesting that 50 letters "were a very large number indeed on a relative scale." Several wanted to know addresses so they could "make it 51."

The panel recessed late in the evening. I left quietly, some might say with my tail between my legs. I put on my hat, scarf and coat and walked in the New York winter's night through Ralph Bunche park across from the UN and over to the Tudor, my usual Manhattan home away from home. For the bargain rate of $50, I got a room so small that the door to the bathroom could not shut because part of the bed was in the way.

I was distressed. If I had met these people under different circumstances—before I wrote the "out-of-the-subway" story or with my having followed through on my intention not to write it—I think we would have felt ourselves to have been kindred spirits. I shared the panel members' interest in international affairs and admired their perseverance in finding ways to express a Christian witness in the midst of overwhelming issues and events.

But I couldn't understand their response on this conference issue. It wasn't that I expected or even thought desirable that most of the panel think I had done the right thing and turn against its decision to endorse the conference. But not one person spoke up to say there was any legitimacy whatsoever in the questions that had been raised about the conference.

I just couldn't understand how there could be such unanimity of confidence about something so controversial with large segments of the denomination.

No, I remembered, *there had been one sign of a break in unanimity.* When others were saying the criticism of the conference was based on white, middle-class fear, Bishop Wayne Clymer of Iowa had said, "Let's not be overly hard on our members. I don't think they're against fighting apartheid. But the rhetoric at the conference gave the impression that if you're against apartheid, you're for communism, anti-American and pro-Soviet."

A Bishop Swims Against The Tide

The next morning the panel spent another hour-and-a-half talking about ways to counteract the Institute on Religion and Democracy and about the $6,000 study of the IRD the panel had initiated.

Toward the end, Bishop Clymer asked for the floor. Nearing retirement, the bishop retained the intellectual facility of his academic background and the dulcet voice of a preacher. He was chairman of the United Methodist Committee on Relief, a massive international development and emergency aid organization.

The bishop took the floor and spoke in quiet, measured words, but he had everyone's attention. Then he did something you don't see much of in these kinds of meetings; he spoke against the prevailing tide of opinion at the meeting. He began by saying he'd gone back to his hotel room last night troubled. The morning's conversation had bothered him more. Now he felt he had to speak.

"We United Methodist leaders of agencies are more comfortable dealing with international problems caused by right-wing elements than those caused by the left. Thus, groups such as the Institute on Religion and Democracy have risen to challenge us to greater concern for the losses of freedom under leftist regimes."

The morning's discussion had treated the IRD like an enemy, he continued. "There are many institutes, but this one is more like family." He pointed out that more than a dozen of IRD's 31-member board of directors were United Methodists. "These are our people. We find it easy to engage in conversations and coalitions with communists and various leftist groups, but I haven't seen us work with more conservative groups, even when they are other United Methodists. Conservative groups tend to emphasize freedom while the panel has emphasized justice. We never call for peace with freedom; we say peace with justice. But for Americans the normative category has been freedom. Our country's motto 'liberty and justice for all' is very difficult in this world. One seems to play against the other. That has created a communication problem for the panel."

The bishop felt there was a tendency to undersell the commitment of the laity in the churches, to assume they couldn't be mobilized behind a Christian social concern and therefore to not be careful about how the concern is presented.

"The panel often is critical of the United States when it fails to live up to its own high ideals of liberty and justice. But I never recall in five years around this table a strong affirmation of something the United States has done."

Bishop Clymer called for the panel, instead of plotting against the IRD, to set up a dialogue with its leaders.

Nora Boots strongly objected, "The Institute is part of the diversionary tactics to keep us from the real issues. For the first time the church in Latin America represents the salvation, not the oppression, of people. By spending time with the Institute, the agencies will be playing into its hands by being sucked into defending ourselves."

Peggy Billings warned against dealing with the non-profit, political IRD as a co-equal of church agencies.

John Stumbo, a bearded, gruff, bow-tied lawyer from Kansas, could see that all the protest sounded strange from people willing to let communists and members of Soviet front groups run their South Africa mobilization event. "It sounds like we have a lot of paranoia about another group we don't like. This bothers me. I think we're trying to withhold diplomatic recognition. I think if this were a liberal theology group, we'd spend a lot of time with them."

As the discussion developed, I marveled at what a difference it makes to have one person speak with conviction to a point of view different from the prevailing one in a group. It frees others to speak. Real searching now was occurring, and that is good no matter which side of a debate one might be on. *Perhaps my reporting had precipitated some discussion after all,* I thought. That was a common experience for city hall and legislative reporters, but seemed rare in the religion field.

The panel agreed to set up a dialogue. But it never really took place, it just kind of slipped between the cracks. What also may have slipped away was a chance for the agencies to calm the IRD people through explanation or change. An unmollified IRD would a year later help create international havoc for the agencies.

An Autumn Change Of Colors

As for me, the autumn had been one of intense challenge to long-held perceptions. I had been jolted off my trajectory more than I even then knew. I would evermore look upon the church as an institution just like all others that must be subjected to the light of public scrutiny if it is to have a chance at remaining true to its own principles.

I was bothered by that. It made me feel somehow disloyal. But as the weeks and months passed, I was, for good or ill, deeply confirmed in the path I had trod thus far.

Jim Wall, the editor of the prestigious liberal-thought journal, the *Christian Century*, responded to my request for his reaction. I had spent Holy Week the previous spring with him in Cuba.

He wrote:

> No, I don't think you over-reacted with your story. As journalists we have to give both sides in this kind of argument access to our pages, and when the Board of Global Ministries does something as blatant as it did in the South Africa session they deserved to be exposed. I agree completely with the approach that we report ideological excesses from every side.

When church journalists and publicists gathered at a National Council of Churches event in Cleveland, some began to roast this new Roy Beck reporter who had recently popped up in the religion reporting scene. Martin Bailey, veteran United Church of Christ journalist, who also was on the Cuba trip, stood up for my professionalism and commitment to the church. When I heard of that and thanked him, Martin cautioned me not to be overly prideful in my journalist training.

> I'm convinced there's no such thing as objective reporting. We bring our loyalties and our experience to all we write. We're better understood when we admit all that.

In the spring, a group of Minnesota journalism professionals honored my "out-of-the-subway" reporting. Holding its annual meeting there was the Associated Church Press of 120 mainline Protestant and Catholic publications. The judges named my story the religious newspaper news story of the year.

Spurgeon's editorial that asked why church leaders weren't answering the important questions didn't get an award, but the judges said the editors "should take a bow for an excellent job of outlining for readers what controversy means and the newspaper's role in controversy."

The announcement of my award at the meeting was memorable for those there because of the audible outburst of protest that came from a Presbyterian journalist. At the close of the meeting, he heatedly and loudly accosted Sharon about the disgrace of the award. Affirmation by professional peers always is sweet succor for the honoree and a bitter pill for the critic.

But, more than anything, I sought a personal peace that I was not engaged in damaging the church I loved. I thought I would rather go back to my public newspaper career than do that. I began to feel an assurance and security about continuing to work inside the church shortly after Bishop Clymer's stand at the Joint Panel meeting in December. A bishop whom I had not talked to at all about the whole episode surprised me with a pastoral letter.

> Dear Roy,
>
> You have tackled a biggie. I have been reading your reports. I appreciated the quotes from Wayne Clymer. There has long been a feeling that the Board of Global Ministries has become too leftist. This may not be true. The kind of reporting you are doing will make possible dialogue and truth. You are probably discovering that the church is no more open to self-revelation and truth than multi-nationals. We can be exceedingly defensive.
>
> Now let me add a word of caution. You have challenged the most powerful bureaucracy in the denomination. Because of the amorphous organizational style of the board, the professional staff has experienced very little accountability. . . .
>
> . . .The Board of Global Ministries has ignored develop-

ing a strategy for reaching the world's unchurched or non-Christian population. The focus is on bread, and appropriately so in many countries, but the intent must be broader than that. At least some of us think so.

I guess, Roy, I'm suggesting that I hope you will keep reporting. I'm part of the establishment. I hope you will find positive things to say. But it is high time someone includes BGM in the accountability process of which we are supportive verbally but ignore in practice.

I hope for you and your family a blessed Christmas.

5

Mississippi Maze

It was the trees. That's what was giving me the vague sense of uneasiness. Dense stands of Mississippi evergreens crowded the road, creating a foreboding conifer canyon. I was driving alone. Was I thinking of Westerns and people getting trapped in canyon ambushes? Had I gotten so used to Texas plains that I felt uncomfortable driving into an area where you couldn't see somebody coming for miles around?

My assignment this May of 1982 was to find out what was really going on in Holmes County, one of the 10 poorest counties in the nation. It had been described to me as a backwoods, edge-of-the-Mississippi-Delta remnant of the unreconstructed, unrepentant Old South. There, I was told, blacks still were kept in their place while the minority white community controlled nearly everything—South African apartheid right here in these United States.

The civil rights cause celebre of 1982, if not the decade, was said to be in Holmes County where the white power structure had succeeded in hounding a town's first black mayor from office last year. Then a month ago, the white powers were said to have framed him on a charge of paying a gunman to murder his chief political opponent. They obviously had a legal lynching in mind.

The sun began to set behind the pines. Shadows lengthened. The trees seemed to close in more tightly on my road. I continued driving my rental car and thinking, *It's not Westerns but "Southerns" that are giving me the heebie-jeebies. This is Mississippi—my first trip to Mississippi, and all those old movies about the Deep South are playing with my emotions.* The old song was running through my head as I turned on my headlights, *Bye, bye, Miss American Pie/ Drove my Chevy to the levy but the levy was dry.* Civil rights workers and freedom riders were harassed and beaten in Deep-South places like

this. *Good ole boys drinking whiskey and rye.* Some civil rights
workers had been murdered and buried in an earthen levy not far from
where I was driving. I saw the movie. They got trapped on a road, suf-
focated by trees like these.

Over on the western side of the county, down in the Delta where
white folks had continued the plantation-like subjugation longer than
in most other places, 28-year-old Eddie James Carthan had burst onto
the scene in 1977. He already was president of the school board in
Tchula, a town pronounced CHEW-luh. But in 1977 he became
Tchula's first black mayor in an election that filled four of the five city
alderman seats with blacks as well.

Like a Third World nation throwing off the shackles of a colonial
oppressor, the 80 percent black population finally had achieved self-
determination. That was the story I was getting from current literature
I'd been reading all week. I was driving to Holmes County for a first-
hand look.

A white minister had called me to say there was no white conspiracy at all. He had some fairly persuasive arguments to make, if his
facts were right, and my South Africa conference experience with New
York church activists the previous fall left me capable of doubting the
activists.

But if Sheila Collins' facts were right, Holmes County was a racist
mess. A scary one at that.

I kept an uneasy eye on the rear-view mirror and the headlights
approaching from behind. A car menacingly pulled up parallel for what
seemed an excessive period, but then sped on around and disappeared
into the trees ahead.

I continued in my mind to review the facts of the story I was checking out. Sheila Collins was the church worker out of New York who
brought Eddie Carthan's case to the attention of the national Protestant community. Now Carthan's cause was being supported in one way
or another at the national level of the Lutheran Church of America,
Episcopalians, Presbyterians, Orthodox, American Baptists, United
Methodists and many others.

I had Sheila's definitive account in the file folder on the car seat.
"Revenge of the Good Ole Boys" from *In These Times* magazine explained that "it's one thing for a black to win an election in a small
southern town. It's another to use the power of the office."

Sheila wrote that "to hear Carthan speak about freedom, justice and the responsibilities of citizenship in the simple, eloquent manner characteristic of many rural southern blacks, was to feel once again the spirit King evoked during the heyday of the civil rights movement." Out of impoverished sharecropper roots, Carthan had risen to lead his people out of their long suffering and to take advantage of federal programs to help the town of fewer than 2,000, she said.

The Carthan supporters put together a long list of his accomplishments after becoming mayor in 1977. Among them were:

A federal community development block-grant to rehabilitate substandard housing.

A 50 percent matching grant from a foundation to build a new library.

A health clinic for the poor.

A federal Comprehensive Employment and Training Act grant to help unemployed residents.

A day care center.

In short, the young black man had tapped into federal, state and private anti-poverty programs that the white power structure had ignored in its efforts to keep blacks dependent on whites. The whites felt threatened by all that. So Holmes County's white merchant aristocrats were said to have intimidated and bought off enough blacks to stack the city council against the mayor so that he lost basic control. Then some feds were persuaded to join in, and the FBI began harassing Carthan.

Telegrams In The Heat Of The Night
During 1980, the Tchula political bickering took a bizarre turn. The opposition aldermen locked the mayor and everybody else out of city hall for two months because the mayor wouldn't do something they wanted.

What happened next would turn the obscure, small-town feud into a national cause. The police chief resigned. The mayor chose a black replacement. But the majority of the aldermen chose a white man who actually took over at the headquarters. When Carthan and six associates confronted the aldermen's white chief and ordered him to leave the headquarters, the state court system concocted a bogus charge. The so-called Tchula 7 were convicted of assaulting a police officer, and Carthan was sentenced to three years in the state pen.

The Delta dawn of black self-determination was over just like that, and all federal programs to Tchula by that time had been cut off, Sheila reported. Apartheid had reasserted itself.

The National Campaign to Free Mayor Eddie Carthan and the Tchula 7 said the case was representative of a white conspiracy throughout the South to drive blacks from office, under sanction of the new Reagan administration's anti-civil rights policies. Endorsements of the campaign by national civil rights groups and activists were snowballing. Holmes County was where church and other civil rights groups would take their stand against further encroachments by the Reagan administration.

Sheila was the point woman for the churches. She'd been in and out of Holmes County since 1980, when she linked the United League of Holmes County with the United Methodist grassroots activist network sponsored by the denomination's Board of Global Ministries. Thousands of dollars of church money had gone into the support. She'd been instrumental in a National Council of Churches' team doing an on-site investigation in April.

Now a month later in May, Holmes County whites—especially white United Methodists—were furious about all of this. They were among the people I was on my way to see. And they knew I was coming. Although the *National Christian Reporter* and *United Methodist Reporter* were independent, many people saw the papers as part of the church hierarchy and, therefore, responsible for actions they detested.

It was dark as I continued to drive toward the scene. The forests were black walls encasing my headlight beams that pointed the way to Holmes County. In April those black walls almost swallowed up former Mayor Carthan when the county sheriff suddenly hauled him into the county jail and told him he was charged with murder.

A St. Louis gunman had committed the murder during a robbery at a convenience store the previous June. In a highly suspicious maneuver, Mississipi officials allowed the St. Louis gunman to plead guilty to a lesser charge in exchange for his testimony that Carthan had hired him to pull the trigger. Now, the Mississippi criminal justice system was aiming to put the aggressive young political leader in the gas chamber.

As soon as they got word on the April night that Carthan was behind bars, Global Ministries officials fired off after-midnight telegrams to the rural Southern sheriff. They protested the "frame up" and the "major violation of American judicial system." The church officials were veterans of civil rights actions. They knew what could happen in those backwoods jails. They knew how blacks and other activists in the past had just happened to end up beaten or killed because of supposed escape attempts or alleged attacks on jailers.

"The entire country is watching process of justice in Holmes County," read Sheila Collins' telegram. Like an Amnesty International communique to a brutal, right-wing dictator concerning political prisoners, the telegram's language was designed to preempt any violence by taking away any thought that nobody would notice. The warning apparently worked. Carthan soon was released unharmed on bail.

I planned to talk to the sheriff tomorrow.

Brakes Fail

Right now my headlights were illuminating a sign that indicated I should turn off just ahead. I let up on the gas and coasted at a fairly high speed onto a curved road to the right, where the trees had backed away to make an opening.

I stepped on the brake pedal just before the curve sharpened. My eyes sent an instant panic signal to my brain. Nothing was happening. In a split second, my right foot pushed harder on the brake. My view through the windshield no longer was of the road. My headlights shown on something else. It was the trees. *The power brakes aren't working!* my brain screamed as the car left the road. Reflexively, I lifted my right foot up and slammed it back down with all my might. My arms were fully extended, pulling on the steering wheel to force the complete weight of my now-rigid body the other direction into the mushy brake pedal. The car came to a stop before hitting anything.

At first I was dazed. Then the underlying sense of conspiracy that had been toying with my emotions the last hour took over. I swung around in my seat to see if anybody was around. Nothing but night and whatever secrets it chose to hold.

Did somebody do this to me? I thought. *No. How could that happen? But then. . . .*

I mentally retraced my steps that day. My plane had landed in Jackson that afternoon. I rented a car there. True, before I got the car I'd listed my journalism profession on the rental form and talked to the clerks about getting to Holmes County. I asked them what they knew about the Eddie Carthan situation. They knew of the case. It had been getting a lot of press lately, especially the role of outsiders.

I thought about what I'd heard about southern hostility to outside agitators during the '50s and '60s civil rights era. *Could they. . . ? Surely not*, I thought, choosing to exonerate the rental car people.

I had driven directly from the airport to the state capitol. It was being renovated. Weeds grew around it, and in the blocks surrounding it were aging, dilapidated structures. Not an impressive sight. It reinforced the image created by the state's poverty statistics.

The United Methodist building was across from the capitol. I parked nearby and went inside. About two dozen pastors and lay people from Holmes County and annual conference offices were headed into a conference room to vent their anger at the Rev. Rene Bideaux.

Most of the Holmes County Methodists had not known a thing until a week ago about the Board of Global Ministries' involvement with the Carthan movement and with the United League in their own county. A Jackson newspaper article about that involvement had blown the cover and ignited an outcry. To try to calm a spreading grassroots rebellion, Rene had flown from New York City to Jackson to the hastily called meeting. He was the new head of the national missions arm of Global Ministries, the division in which Sheila worked.

"Rene says you can't go in there," Roy Lawrence, the Mississippi Methodist editor, told me when I approached the meeting room. I asked him to call Rene out so I could try to change his mind.

Rene was flustered. "Look, I know this kind of thing sells papers, but I'm trying to build a program. One man here has raised all this fuss, and I need to settle this without reporters." He whisked back into the room.

Soon I heard shouting. After awhile my hallway seat was in the middle of a parade of people shaking their heads and mumbling on the way to restrooms.

"Not getting anywhere," one offered as he passed. A few minutes later, a sizeable group—all whites—walked out in disgust.

"That's the sorriest thing I've ever seen," a layman said.

"We've tried hard and made a lot of progress in the last 15 years in race relations," another said. "Then they come in here and destroy everything."

"You can kiss the Methodist Church in Holmes County good-bye," a minister said. "We came down here to get something."

I asked, "Is it over?"

"Nah, Rene's still in there talking, but he's not going to give us what we want."

I pressed, "I thought he was going to apologize for not having consulted first with local church leaders before getting involved in the Carthan case."

"Yeah, he did that. And he apologized for the telegrams to our sheriff. But he won't promise to get Sheila Collins and the others out of our county."

Another explained, "He says he can't do that and keep the agency true to its mission of justice and concern for the poor. But these outsiders don't know what's going on. Carthan's problems are of his own making. They have nothing to do with racist conspiracies."

From the meeting room, Rene was calling for the Mississippians to return to the discussion. Most reluctantly did, though one young Holmes County banker refused, turning to me and saying, "The Northern liberals just can't figure out that things aren't the same here anymore. If those juries and elections were rigged, the federal government would've gotten us. We don't need the Board of Global Ministries to come investigate us." He had tears in his eyes.

Now as I sat on the side of a road in the north Mississippi darkness several hours later I wondered, *Might anybody have tampered with this outside reporter's car while I remained inside the headquarters to talk with Rene and another Global Ministries official?* I couldn't imagine that any of the local church people would have a reason or the will to do such a thing. But who else would know I was even there? To consider that somebody deliberately would send me into north Mississippi without brakes was just too paranoid.

It was the trees again, I thought, *stirring an overactive imagination based on civil rights folklore.* I felt claustrophobic for they seemed to close in on me as I began driving again.

Keeping the speed below 15 mph, I could make the mushy brakes work for me fairly well. The few communities in these parts already were bedded down for the night. Most were without a motel. My custom had been to travel without reservations—more flexibility.

The little town of Durant had an old-style motel connected to a late-night diner. I limped into the drive beside the office window.

"Anywhere around here I can get some brakes fixed?" I asked.

"There's a Ford place just over there. Be open tomorrow," the white, woman manager said.

I filled out the motel form, including the blanks for company and occupation, and went into the diner there at the office.

No Biscuits Or Southern Hospitality

After quite awhile a waitress came by, and I tried to order.

"Too late," she said.

"Too late? What about all of them?" I motioned to a large number of people who had plates of freshly cooked food.

"We turned the grill off," she said shortly.

"Well, how about a tuna fish sandwich," I called futilely to her back.

I phoned home to Shirley and tried to take the emotion out of my failed-brakes tale. She was very concerned. She'd seen all those "Southerns" movies, too. "Don't take any chances," she urged.

The motel room looked like something the Bates family furnished in "Psycho." Quite spartan. As I pulled a worn bedspread up over me, my mind fretted about the motel registration form. I got out of bed and walked over to check the lock on the door and went to sleep with visions of Jack Nicholson and "Easy Rider" dancing in my head.

The next morning I tried the diner again. The menu was classic. "Biscuits and gravy, sausage, grits and fried eggs," I ordered.

"No biscuits today," the waitress said. It was a different one but with the same curt manner as my friend last night.

"No biscuits! Is this Mississippi?"

"She burned 'em!" the white waitress snapped, jerking her head toward the kitchen. "She ain't done nothin' right today."

I recorded the exchange in my notepad and noted, "Cook is black."

Southern hospitality was no better at the Ford garage. As I eased my car into the driveway, I determined I would not divulge my identity. But these people had a way of making you feel you were hiding a background as a psychotic slasher unless you identified yourself fully. Even after I explained that my editor wanted me to finish the job by tomorrow, they told me they couldn't look at my car at all today. "Check with the guy on up the road," they said.

I parked the car in the dusty driveway of the mechanic's garage. "I just got this at a rental place at the airport yesterday," I said. "I don't know what's wrong with it, but I have no brakes."

"From out of state, huh?" the white mechanic said.

"Dallas."

"Where ya headed?"

"I'm going over to Lexington and Tchula a little later," I said.

"What's to see up here?" he said, looking at a white partner.

I hesitated and then figured I might as well start getting some local flavor, "Oh, I'm a reporter for a church publication. I was checking into this situation with Eddie Carthan and the Tchula 7."

"Never heard of the Tchula 7."

"You know, the black mayor that got run out of office over there?" I prodded.

The mechanic acted repulsed, "I don't pay no attention to niggers."

He immediately defied his words and turned his attention to a customer coming toward the door. A middle-aged black working man inquired about something for an antiquated truck that looked like it might be used in the logging business. I didn't relish hearing the racism that might pass between them. But the white mechanic dealt with the black trucker in a business-like, yet congenial, familiar way.

When the mechanic returned, he had some advice, "Tchula has some crazy niggers over there. You'd better take a gun."

"You a church-going man?" I asked.

"Yeah, I go to the Church of Nazarene and I don't pay no attention to niggers, including that sheriff we got."

I was taken aback. "What was that? Are you saying the Holmes County sheriff is black?"

"Yeah, our nigger sheriff is a real slouch. Looks just like Fred Sanford." The mechanic grinned, looking over at some other people who all laughed and nodded agreement. I had pictured someone more like Rod Steiger.

"Somebody's Been Fooling Around With It"

Another mechanic called over to me from my car out in the driveway, "You been fooling around with the brake fluid?"

"No. I've not even opened the hood," I answered.

"Well, you don't have any fluid at all. You don't have a brake fluid cap, either. Somebody's been fooling around with it."

"What do you mean?"

"Come over here and look at this," the mechanic said.

When I looked under the hood, he pointed, "See all the marks? Somebody's had a screwdriver or something in here messing things up. Looks like you've got a little bit of a leak, but you're dry because there wasn't a cap on it. When you taking this car back?"

"Probably Saturday."

"I'll fill up the fluid and get you a cap. That oughta hold you fine until then."

In the daylight it was easier to just put off thinking about what any of that meant, but I pulled to the shoulder when I got out of sight of the garage and made notes of the preceding conversation. Background color on the racial mood, I figured.

The winding, tree-lined road across to Lexington, the Holmes County seat, left me feeling as though I was going into an inner sanctum. The town square seemed out of *To Kill A Mockingbird*. The courthouse in the middle had that old redneck aura plenty capable of housing white judicial conspiracies. I drove over to the First United Methodist Church—similar vintage as the court house—just off the square and went in to see the pastor.

The Rev. Dudley Brown was the ringleader of the confrontation in Jackson the day before. He was the one who called me during the *Reporter* staff's Monday morning meeting. He said he'd been referred to me because of my writing on the South Africa conference the previous fall. Some people told him I might be a reporter who would tell the truth about what was happening in Holmes County.

"I can only listen and try to find out what the truth is," I told him.

Now that I was face to face with Pastor Brown, I was armed with a lot more information I'd gained from the national mission staff since I talked with him by phone.

Dudley took little time to tell me I'd been reading a bunch of lies that were stirring up racial hatred in Holmes County.

"But I'm told racial hatred already is here," I said, thinking about my time at the garage.

With moustache, big dark-rimmed glasses and hair cut with almost-boyish-looking bangs, Dudley had the general appearance of calm, but I quickly had the feeling that a volcano was smoldering underneath the surface. He was full of righteous indignation.

"You don't bring justice in a court case by educating the public," he said. "You hire a good attorney. You don't try to prejudice the potential jurors."

"So you're trying to stop national church workers from prejudicing jurors?"

"I'm trying to save this church," Dudley told me. "My people feel personally attacked by this Sheila Collins stuff that is showing up all over the place. They want to stop paying any money that goes outside of Mississippi to mission projects out there. Some are being enticed by some independent Methodist congregations that pulled out of the denomination during the civil rights battles of the '60s."

"What makes them so mad?" I asked.

"When they read the Jackson paper last week and saw what Sheila Collins, their national church representative, was saying about them, well, they resented that stuff about a white conspiracy. I guess that means the people of this church are part of the conspiracy. They're an important part of the whites that have any power in this county."

"But," I asked, "if an injustice were occurring, you'd have to acknowledge that the church should be involved, wouldn't you?"

"Of course," Dudley said. "But there are right ways and wrong ways to do things. Those folks in New York don't even know what's going on here. They talked with a few black radicals here and made up their minds. They didn't talk with any of our white people or with any of our black officials."

"Yeah, I hear your sheriff is black. Is he a token?"

"We've got black political leaders all over the place," Dudley sort of cackled. It was a mannerism that rose when he described things he thought were ironic. "We've got more than 30 elected officials in this county who are black. What kind of white conspiracy allowed that to happen?"

Thirty black officials. That sounded like a lot to me.

"We're pretty upset at those insulting telegrams the Global Ministries people sent to Sheriff Howard Huggins, too," Dudley continued. "They're protesting treatment of black leaders and at the same time they insult our black sheriff. We want them to apologize to him. Our state legislator for years is a black man, Robert Clark. Long-time civil rights leader. He's running for U.S. congressman this year."

"None of that is in the Free Eddie Carthan literature," I said.

"Of course not. That stuff is full of lies," Dudley said. "They're trying to stir up race hatred here, not to foster racial understanding."

"This state representative . . ."

"Clark."

"Yeah, Clark. Where does he stand on Mayor Carthan?" I asked.

"He's staying out of it. Look, the blacks in this county don't need help from New York in deciding who they want to elect. They make up 75 percent of the county. They can control the elections by themselves."

"What about the justice system? The national church leaders are saying the white power structure controls it."

"Here, let me check something." Dudley thumbed through a sheaf of newspaper clippings and photocopy papers. "Here it is. The jury last fall that convicted Carthan on the assault charge had nine blacks on it. Nine out of 12. And the grand jury that just indicted him for murder had 17 blacks out of 19. This is ridiculous to make a national issue out of whites supposedly ganging up on blacks."

I told Dudley that it bothered me that his story differed so radically from the national church leaders'.

"Of course it differs," he said. "They didn't try to find out the truth. They broke church law to make sure they didn't find out the truth."

"Just Some White Nuns And Black Radicals"

Dudley pulled out a *Book of Discipline.* United Methodists continue to be very methodical and have more than 600 pages of rules, or laws, for running the national, regional and local church. These are bound like a hymnal, about the same size.

Church law required that before the national agencies put money into a program in an area they had to "consult" with the area bishop and head of the annual conference's Council On Ministries. The regional people couldn't veto a project, but presumably they could ensure that all local information and ramifications were known and would be taken into consideration by the national agencies.

Such consultation had not occurred, Dudley said. And to keep with the spirit of searching for truth, why didn't the agency people talk to him, the members of his church, the pastors and members of the church in Tchula and elected officials of the county, white and black, he asked.

"How do you think our people feel to find out that people their offerings are supporting have been coming right here under their noses for two years without telling them?" he said. "Now they find out that their mission board has been supporting this radical United League that none of the local United Methodists has any respect for and not told them it was happening."

Rene's apology the day before for not consulting was appreciated, Dudley said; but "our people want to know that Global Ministries has cut all ties to the United League."

"But why shouldn't the mission board support a group advocating civil rights and representing black political leaders?" I asked.

"The United League doesn't represent much of anybody but three white nuns and a few radical blacks," Dudley said. "The black elected officials don't agree with it."

"White nuns?"

"You haven't heard about our nuns?" Dudley was cackling again. "They moved down here from Minnesota about 10 years ago to save the blacks. They're into everything."

"How many black members do you have in this church?" I asked, changing the subject.

"None. There are black United Methodist churches in the county."

Dudley was frank. Holmes County was slower than a lot of other Mississippi counties to adapt to the end of legal segregation. He had no illusions that his congregation had worked through all problems of racism. "I'm trying to lead them and help them. But I can't do it with this other stuff going on that the members know is based on lies."

He showed me recent newsletters in which he had pleaded with members not to act too hastily by doing things like cutting off mission funds. Then he had to leave but told me to make myself at home with the phone.

I had a lot more to learn, but I was deeply troubled by all the facts that either were left out by the Free Eddie Carthan people or were contradicted by this pastor.

Human rights campaigns don't need distortions to make them work, I thought. *This pastor was engaging. Was he distorting things? Was he using reason as a cover for racism?*

"Blacks Hindered By Plantation Mentality"

I made several calls to Mississippi United Methodists and then called New York to talk to Sheila. She wasn't there. John Jordan came on the phone. He was a middle-level executive above Sheila and involved with the Carthan campaign. I told him I was confused, that I was hearing new details about the county's political system which cast doubt on the Carthan campaign.

"There are black officials all over the place here," I said. "How can criminal charges against one be seen as the white power structure systematically keeping blacks out of office?"

John referred me to Sheila's "Revenge of the Good Ole Boys." "It's all there," he said.

"What about all these black jurors? Did you know most of the jurors were black?"

"Find out who those black jurors owe their jobs to," John said. "There are lots of ways for the white power structure to intimidate."

"But how can you know that?"

John explained that the NCC and Global Ministries had a lot of experience in the Delta. Segregation and racism were as deep here as the incredibly fertile soil deposited by centuries of Mississippi River flooding, he said. A whole generation of church activists had cut their teeth fighting to overturn one of the most oppressive cultures in the country. A lot of people in the national church agencies knew very well how oppression could be disguised and rationalized here.

"We're involved in this because the local people feel there is a fundamental issue of black political rights at stake."

"Which local people?"

"The blacks."

"But what about all the blacks in office? I don't get the idea that a lot of them are jumping in behind you on this conspiracy claim."

"One possibility is that the blacks who have been elected are acting like whites," he said. "We're told that some of these blacks still have a plantation mentality. They don't have confidence to act in their own self-interest but always look to whites."

"Did you know three-fourths of the voters are blacks?" I asked. "They're electing these officials."

"An awful lot of the black voters have a plantation mentality, too," John said. "They don't understand what is best for them."

"So how do we know which blacks to trust? It sounds like the church is deciding which blacks are the real blacks and which ones are fake," I said. "Isn't that kind of dangerous, especially since we're a mainly white church?" John, like Sheila, was white.

"We support persons who believe there is injustice," John said. "We believe the gospel calls us to be on the side of the poor. That's why we are supporting Mayor Carthan. What more do you need to prove that the whites run Tchula than to know that it never had a black mayor until 1977? Or to know that Tchula and Lexington have segregated schools? The public schools are all black and the private academies are all white."

John advised me that I as a white person probably wouldn't be able to hear the truth from black people. They tend to tell white people only what they think white people want to hear and to be afraid to say what they really think, he said.

"Then why would they tell the truth to the white people in the missions agency?" I asked John.

"Because the agency had a lot of black staff people involved, as well, and because the whites who were working with this problem had a long history of dealing with these kinds of issues."

I hung up the phone and looked out the church window at the black and white but mostly black people walking about the square.

Now I really was confused. Maybe I was being foolish to think I could walk in here and get black people to talk frankly with me. Or for that matter, thinking I could get the straight story from whites. How could I believe anything I heard here if, as John had suggested, the majority of blacks lacked the courage or integrity to tell the truth in public or to cast a secret-ballot vote for a person of choice?

I decided to get some mid-afternoon lunch across the street and talk a bit with the black cook alone.

"I haven't followed this Carthan thing too much," she said.

"Do you know anything about this United League?" I asked.

"A good friend of mine is the wife of the United League's leader. I used to attend meetings, but I'm too busy with jobs now."

"Did you ever feel any pressure from your employers or anybody else because you were connected to the league?"

"No, nothin' like that."

With John Jordan's advice ringing in my ear, I wondered, *was she lying to me? Is that what she thought I wanted to hear?*

"Look," I said, "as I told you before, I'm working for a United Methodist paper in Texas. Our denomination is busy helping Mayor Carthan. We're trying to make sure black people in this county have the political power they deserve. Do you think most blacks around here feel the white power structure is trying to ruin Mr. Carthan?"

"Oh, I think the black folk that know much about it are about divided on it," she said. "Lots of us around here, though, just aren't that involved with it."

Once again I was confused. Somehow I thought a civil rights case drawing major attention from groups nationwide would be on the tips of the tongues of the blacks in the shadow of the courthouse where Eddie Carthan was framed.

Into The White Power Center

I walked to the square into the Barrett law offices. The Barrett family was as close to a power structure as you were likely to find. Two generations of lawyers. Old man Barrett had a reputation with the White Citizens Council that tried to fight desegregation in the '60s. During that time one of the sons, Don, had shot his mouth off as a college student about the inferiority of blacks. That was the period the Lexington newspaper had stood up for integration and endured a long boycott by the White Citizens Council which since had faded away.

The Barretts were United Methodists.

Don consented to see me and invited me into an office. He didn't sound at all like his college rhetoric. He tried to put forth an image of "the New South."

"We just don't understand how this could happen," Don said about the mission agency support for the United League and Carthan. "We don't want to fight the national church. We want to love it. But the Board of Global Ministries is so prejudiced against white Mississippians that they can only see us as bigoted rednecks." His eyes glistened.

What a fascinating concept, I thought, *prejudice against white southerners.*

Barrett continued, "Their information-gathering wasn't just faulty; it was designed to be faulty. They didn't *want* to know the truth."

"I just talked to John Jordan in New York. He said the board is committed to be on the side of the poor."

That set Don off. All the publicity about Eddie Carthan's poor roots was a laugh, he told me. "His family certainly isn't poor. His father owns 500 acres of rich delta land. That's easily $1,500 an acre. He's nearly a millionaire in assets."

"What about Eddie?"

"He was a successful businessman. He owns a grocery store. He had a liquor store before his conviction. And he has a fast-food restaurant. He had a convenience store in Durant, but it burned."

"When?"

"Back in 1975. Eddie was charged with hiring a couple of guys to do it. Our firm represented him, and he was acquitted. That jury was the whitest jury I've seen around here since the Voting Rights Act passed."

"How'd you win the case?"

"I really can't talk about it because of the confidentiality of an attorney-client relationship. But these outsiders are making Eddie to be some great leader of the blacks when the blacks of Tchula already rejected him and chose other people."

"How's that?"

"He was school board president and mayor for awhile. But even before his assault conviction, the voters voted him out of the school board position. And after Carthan was forced out of office in 1981 by his conviction, the black opposition aldermen were re-elected, but Carthan's black supporters were defeated. The national campaign literature that says the white power structure framed Carthan to deny the black people of their leader just doesn't make much sense when the black voters already had decided they didn't want him as their leader. On this latest charge, though, we're not taking the position that Eddie is guilty of this murder. I hope he is not. We've known each other a long time. But we're upset with what the national church is doing, because it is stirring this up as a racial frame-up. They're actively preaching racial hatred."

The young lawyer was surrounded by the conservative, paneled accouterment of attorneys' offices everywhere that give you a sense of the stability of law. But rapid change and perhaps fright—at least uncertainty—about how to deal with a drastically different world were starkly present in Don Barrett's conversation.

While he was growing up in Holmes County, the minority whites ran everything. The public order was as it had been for decades. But just as he entered adulthood to take his share of the reins, all the rules changed. The long arm of the federal government reached down from Washington and put Don Barrett in a situation his grandfather couldn't have imagined.

Once blacks got the vote, whites were outnumbered three to one. Don claimed to have adjusted to a situation he described as one in which whites had political influence primarily through black leaders willing to build their support on black and white voting coalitions.

Fewer and fewer elected leaders were white. He saw the time coming soon when virtually none would be white. That was OK, he told me, with a tone that was almost convincing. The early fears had subsided as he and the other whites had found that the black leaders didn't run roughshod over the white minority. Whites still were able to run most of the stores and enjoy more than their share of the little economic prosperity that was to be found in Holmes County. Blacks now owned approximately half the land in the county.

I left the office wondering: *Does that indicate that progress toward racial integration is marching inevitably, albeit slowly, forward? Or does it give a reason to suspect that Mayor Carthan's troubles are the result of panicked whites making one last grasp for political power before the black majority takes firm control?*

I walked across the street to the courthouse and began asking for various court records.

First, I found that the wealthy land holdings of Carthan's family checked out. Of course I knew that farmers could be rich in land and not have a cent for living expenses. Nonetheless, I figured I would keep out of my stories any of the national campaign's implications that Carthan was a man of the impoverished class.

Carthan, in fact, was a thriving entrepreneur—at least before his trouble with the law. In a 1980 pre-trial sentencing report, his net worth was listed as $261,000. He had a masters degree in education and had studied law.

Maybe, I thought, *that's the reason he would be targeted. If the other black political leaders were dependent on white economic leaders, maybe Carthan was a threat because his education and wealth made him too independent.*

Convenient Facts To Get Confused

I told Calvin Moore, the white circuit court clerk, "I'm looking for records about Eddie Carthan being convicted of assaulting a white man who took over the police department over in Tchula."

"It wasn't a white man," Moore said. "It was a black police officer."

"Black policeman that did what?"

"Carthan was convicted of assaulting a black policeman," the clerk of the court said.

Well, I thought, *wasn't that a convenient fact to get confused in the national campaign literature?* The Carthan supporters sure could play a lot better on people's images of how they think things are done in Mississippi by saying a black mayor was thrown into the clink for assaulting a white man. But sure enough, the records were clear. Carthan was convicted of assaulting a four-year veteran of the Tchula police department who was black.

I wondered how the National Council of Churches investigating team last month missed that fact. The clerk of the court, though, explained how some confusion may have arisen, "Eddie Carthan and the other six were charged with assaulting both a black and a white policeman, but after they were convicted of the assault on the black the other case wasn't pursued. Actually, they shot the white man."

"Shot him? I never heard anything about any shooting."

"Yeah, look at this."

Court testimony told a story of small-town political bickering that ended up looking like the Wild West. The court records told a sharply different story from the one recounted by Carthan and his national supporters.

Eddie Carthan was out on bail right now making a national speaking tour sponsored by the Methodists' Board of Global Ministries and a few others. He was reported saying in one speech:

> On May 1, 1980, seven of us were charged with assaulting a white man. What had happened was that our chief of police retired and I appointed someone else, a black, to the position. The only white on our board of aldermen at the time appointed someone else to the post, a white man, Jim Andrews, who had run against me unsuccessfully for the mayor's job. Andrews and some friends he deputized armed themselves and took over city hall.
>
> That's when the seven of us went to city hall to find out what was going on, and to straighten things out. Andrews was overcome and locked up for the night. The next day he went before a local justice court judge, who was his sister-in-law, and filed charges against me and the others, and in May we were sentenced to three years in the state pen.

Court records filled in a lot of blanks. They showed that the chief wasn't the only man who quit. In fact, four of Tchula's five-man police force quit in April of 1980 because they weren't getting paid. This was one of the results of the paralysis caused by the inability of Mayor Carthan and his board of aldermen to get along. The only policeman left was James Harris who was black. Carthan appointed another black resident, Johnny Dale, to be acting police chief on April 29.

But state law gave the real power over a town to the majority on the board of aldermen. In a special meeting the night of April 30, a white resident, Jim Andrews, was nominated and elected the new police chief by the majority of the aldermen. While Carthan to this day continued to claim a white alderman had taken it upon himself to appoint Andrews, court records showed that three alderman, two blacks and one white, made up the majority of the five-man board that elected Andrews.

Carthan ruled all actions that night to be out of order and warned that he'd better not see Andrews on the street with a gun. The three aldermen who comprised the majority stormed off and told Andrews, who had been the chief from 1968-78, to suit up and get down to the town hall to take over police duties.

A Shotgun Blast, A Pool Of Blood

I felt as though I was reading a soap opera. The incident was filled with petty and questionable tactics by all sides. But the testimony showed that Mayor Carthan changed the dynamics quickly from heated to potentially lethal.

Andrews arrived at the town hall about 10 p.m. and told Carthan's man, Johnny Dale, that he no longer was the acting chief. Dale immediately sought out Mayor Carthan. Carthan called five other people, including one of the two aldermen who always were in the minority on the board in supporting the mayor. He told them to join him and come armed.

A passerby saw the armed band gathering on the street about midnight and rushed to the town hall to warn Andrews. Andrews called the one policeman whom all sides recognized as legitimate, James Harris, and made an urgent appeal for help. The black officer came immediately. He was in the back room trying to radio Sheriff Huggins in Lexington for reinforcements when "the Tchula 7" burst through the front doors of city hall with rifles, shotguns and pistols drawn. People on the street said Carthan was in the lead.

Testimony varied on what happened next. Carthan said Andrews drew his pistol and had to be overcome; a "tussle" ensued and Andrews got injured. Andrews said Carthan and three or four others immediately jumped on him when they entered the town hall.

They were struggling when a shotgun was fired. Andrews was grazed on the side of the head. He lost consciousness for a short time and awoke lying in a pool of blood. Two black people outside testified to that.

In addition, Harris said he was called to come out of the back room with his hands over his heads. Just as he stepped out the door, he said, Mayor Carthan pointed a pistol at his head and pulled him around. Somebody then struck him twice, on the shoulder and the arm, he testified.

Rather than putting Andrews in jail, as Carthan was continuing to claim now, he had called an ambulance and had Andrews taken to the hospital in Lexington. The Holmes County Hospital emergency record indicated he was treated for a laceration on his skull that was six centimeters long, with a flap of two centimeters.

Carthan and Johnny Dale had driven the Tchula police car to the hospital. After Andrews was treated he was driven in the police car back to Tchula where he was "turned loose."

The state argued, and the jury agreed, that a mayor does not have the right to raise a small army to settle political differences with his board of aldermen. For acting in a reckless, improper and criminal manner, all of the Tchula 7 were sentenced to three years in prison. But Judge Webb Franklin suspended the sentences of all but Carthan.

I turned to the clerk of the court, "With Carthan being the only one having to go to prison, that kind of lends credence to the claim that the state was just out to get him, doesn't it?"

"There's no conspiracy in that," the clerk retorted. "Look, Eddie's trying to keep from going to the penitentiary. I'd holler racial discrimination, too, if I thought it would keep me from having to go."

Calvin Moore was not agitated as he spoke. Rather, he talked in the way you might visit about a neighbor you thought wasn't making sense in a neighborhood feud. "Eddie's going to prison regardless of this assault charge, anyway," the clerk said.

"How's that?"

"Why, he was convicted in federal court down in Hattiesburg for defrauding the federal government while he was mayor. Now you know the federal government doesn't operate in a racial way."

How many more times, I thought, *am I going to get tripped up with these new revelations about this supposed 1980s answer to Martin Luther King?*

"Where you headin' next?" the clerk asked.

"I thought I'd talk with the sheriff a little."

"You know, I used to be the sheriff," the white official noted. "After 12 years, I decided to do something else. Howard was my deputy. I supported him to replace me. I supported him against a white opponent."

Like about everything else I heard, that hit me two ways. Either it showed how integrated political power had become or it indicated that the black sheriff was a puppet of the white power structure.

"This Isn't 1965"

Sheriff Howard Huggins consented to see me in his office, a modest room at the front of a ramshackle jail.

He looked like a stereotypical rural southern sheriff ought to look: big, a substantial paunch, stern glare and firm words. But he was black. And somehow that just turned all my stereotypes on their head.

Like most sheriffs I'd interviewed, he didn't want to say much. So I ended up giving him a fairly long speech recounting what the national activist groups were saying about justice, conspiracies and his own role in it in Holmes County.

"This isn't the Old South of 1965!" the sheriff finally said. "That's what those people are acting like."

"What was it like in 1965?" I asked, figuring I'd pursue any subject the sheriff would bring up on his own.

"That was when Congress passed the Voting Rights Act. No blacks held office in this whole county. Not many could even vote. I was a cab driver. I never could of thought I'd be the sheriff."

"So when the Voting Rights Act passed, this county didn't start electing all black officials did it? I mean, three-fourths of the county is black, so they could have."

"Not at first. We kept electing mainly white people for awhile. But only whites were elected who went out and got the black people's votes. Calvin Moore, who's now the clerk. . . ."

"Yeah, I just talked with him over at the court house."

"Well, he came to me in 1968 and asked me to support him in his campaign for sheriff. I asked him if he was going to have a black deputy, and he said he would if I'd be the one. He won the election, and I stopped driving the cab. Then he supported me when I ran for sheriff."

I figured this was a good time to put John Jordan's speculation to him. "Some people say you wouldn't be in this position unless the white power structure decided you were their tool."

"I wasn't elected because whites put me here." He dominated the chair in which he sat, and he leaned back just enough that when he spoke it was if he was raring back and throwing his words out. "I was elected because the people, black and white, wanted me. If the white people in Tchula run everything, how'd Eddie Carthan get elected in the first place?"

I told him the United League of Holmes County was telling outside groups that the sheriff was helping the white conspiracy against Carthan.

"I'm only doing my job. The grand jury indicted him. It was my job to arrest him. I do what's right. I walk straight. The United League doesn't represent blacks in this county. Those outside groups are wrong when they say the United League is the voice of the blacks."

"Who is the voice of the blacks?"

"The people the blacks elect."

"I'm told by outside people with experience in civil rights in the Delta that black people around here have been off the plantations for such a short time that they still are easily intimidated by whites. And that's why a minority of whites can still run things. The plantation mentality keeps them too scared to tell the truth."

The sheriff shook his head like he'd heard something bewildering. "Years ago, blacks here were afraid of whites. That ain't true no more. They'll speak straight."

"You know your version of what it's like around here just doesn't match the word that the National Council of Churches and United Methodist mission board is putting out?"

"That's because the reporters and the outsiders get only the United League story," said the sheriff, a Baptist.

"I understand you got some telegrams when you arrested Eddie Carthan."

"I got about a dozen of them and no telling how many phone calls. They were worse than the telegrams. They don't make you feel good."

"Did you answer them?"

"No. They say, 'We're watchin you.' Why do they want to watch me? I've done nothing to nobody. I'll stand up for what's right. I'm not afraid to lose my job. I like this job, but I can retire today. I'd say it if I thought there was a miscarriage of justice."

"A lot of people around the country think there was."

"That's because the United League is duping them. The United League knows that the people out there know how Mississippi used to be. And they know the northerners believe that's still true. So they take advantage of them. But I tell you, this isn't 1965."

White Nuns And Black Problems

I didn't have any luck obtaining an interview with Eddie Carthan or with any of the black leaders of the United League. But I got an invitation for later in the evening to drop by the house of the United League's three white nuns that I had heard about all day.

At night the nuns' house seemed overgrown and a little mysterious. I parked on the side where one of the nuns came to a door and invited me in. The three gathered in a simply furnished room. There was a hint of a '60s commune. The nuns were dressed casually, perhaps giving them an especially young look. I was surprised by how young they seemed. They acted very suspicious of me. I handed them a couple of copies of the *National Christian Reporter* and *United Methodist Reporter* to give them a better idea of who I was.

"Do you know Sheila Collins?" one asked.

"Yes, with the Board of Global Ministries."

"Are you connected to it?"

I explained that we were independent of the church but had a half-million circulation. "Do you know the *National Catholic Reporter?*" Their faces seemed to light up. Oh, yes, they knew it.

"We're sort of like them in that we are members of the church and write about it but aren't controlled by it," I explained. I decided to begin straightforwardly by telling them that everybody local whom I'd talked to today belittled anything suggesting a conspiracy by a white power structure.

The nuns proceeded to tell me a long string of horror stories during their years here. The stories came so fast and with no apparent connection to the present-day situation with Carthan that I didn't get notes on most of them. They spent their time with the poorest and least educated blacks of the area. After a decade of fighting for their political and economic betterment, the nuns said they didn't see much improvement in anything. They added that it would not be surprising if I met a lot of blacks who didn't join in concern about the white conspiracy.

"The plantation mentality dominates among the blacks here," one of the women said.

"They're very fearful and poor," another added. "They don't have a healthy self-image."

Back and forth, the nuns described the pitiable people they were fighting for. "Whites buy their votes. The blacks sell their votes for groceries."

"I know some cases where just that happened," said another.

"Usually, when there's an election there's a big free meal to buy their votes," the third chimed in.

I interjected, "But with 75 percent of the population black, don't you think blacks are capable now of electing blacks they really want?"

"They're afraid to. This is the tenth poorest county in the nation. People are easily threatened. I know officeholders who threaten to pull food stamps if blacks don't do what they want."

"We've got over half the people in this county on some kind of welfare. There's a lot of entanglements and favors tied in with the old white structure that is an invisible web controlling the blacks."

"But," I said, "there are more than 30 black elected officials in this county. Are you telling me that none of them are responsive to the black population's needs and that all of them are controlled by whites?"

"Almost all of them." The nuns discussed two or three names I didn't recognize of black officials who might not be Uncle Toms. The black leaders who really cared about blacks were in the United League, they said.

I said I'd like to talk to some of them. They said that wouldn't be possible but that maybe I could talk to Ken Lawrence, a key activist in Jackson running the National Campaign to Free Eddie Carthan. They said he might be coming to Lexington tomorrow. One went into the next room to call.

"What about the NAACP and the other civil rights organizations around here?" I asked the two remaining in the room.

"Most organizations like that are supporting the national campaign for Mayor Carthan quietly."

"I talked to Sheriff Huggins this afternoon," I said. "He contends that those days of blacks being intimidated by whites are over."

"The sheriff is awful. He's running a terrible jail. He favors the whites. After 10 years, I'm still shocked at the way the white power structure uses blacks in office."

I suggested, "Maybe the black officials are just trying to be leaders for all the people, regardless of race."

Not possible, the nuns indicated. They explained that their goal was to persuade state and federal officials to drop all charges against Eddie Carthan and pardon him of past convictions, so he could go back to leading his people.

Returning from the phone, the one nun said Ken Lawrence would meet me tomorrow morning, a Saturday. I was to call them at 8 a.m. to arrange where to meet him.

She then went into the next room, and I could barely hear her talking, apparently on the phone again. It sounded like she was describing me. The thought went through my head that she might call Sheila or somebody else in the Board of Global Ministries. If so, my reputation from the South Africa conference story might cause me trouble.

She came back into the room, and I resumed, "I suppose the black juries that convicted Mayor Carthan were bought off," I said.

"They were confused," one nun said.

"Two of them are saying now that they wouldn't have found him guilty if they'd known he could be sent to jail."

"Some of them said a white man on the jury misled them. If you get one white on the jury they can threaten everybody else because the blacks know the white can tell all the other whites how they voted."

"I had one juryman say about the Tchula 7, 'Those were seven innocent men,'"

"Calvin Moore seats only the old plantation blacks on the juries."

The phone rang, and the same nun went to answer it. I thought I heard her say something like, "Oh. . . .He is?. . . .OK, I will. . . ."

When she came back we were talking about the First United Methodist Church of Lexington and the members' concern about thinking the mission board should be more involved in conciliation instead of stirring things up.

"I get sick of hearing people talking about the church being a conciliator," one nun said. "The church needs to be the advocate. It needs to be the one creating tension by speaking for justice. Let somebody else do the mediation."

Depressed Confusion

It was late. I felt as though I stumbled out of the nun's house. My head had just been jerked another 180 degrees. Talk about confusing! I had white nuns saying they spoke for the blacks of the county and that the black sheriff spoke for the whites. Each said the other could not be trusted.

Lexington had no motel. I had another late night drive through the trees back to the motel at Durant.

Tonight it wasn't a sense of impending malady that weighed on me, but rather a sense of futility. I was depressed at the inability to pin things down because everybody was accusing everybody else of the inability to tell the truth. I was really depressed by the lowly descriptions of Holmes County blacks as given by the nuns and the outside activist groups. Ironically, the only positive descriptions of the black population in general had come from people the outside activists labeled white conspirators.

I didn't feel any better about the facts that I basically had nailed down. Nearly all of them showed national church backers of the Carthan case to be distorting or lying. I could distinguish the truth tonight no more clearly than the individual trees enveloped in blackness on either side of my car as I sped toward Durant. The nuns had loaded me down with accusations that were going to be hard to track down and try to prove. How was I to be sure enough of anything to write it for next week's paper?

I quickly fell asleep in the Bates motel, mentally and spiritually exhausted.

My travel alarm went off at 7 a.m. Saturday so I wouldn't miss my 8 o'clock contact with the nuns. I showered, dressed and sat on the bed reading over my notes from yesterday. I felt just as confused as I had last night. I tried to focus on what I needed to learn today to sort out some of the issues and facts. My mind had that kind of aching which develops when it just can't handle what's clashing around inside. Discouragement filled my soul. I was having trouble seeing any hope or goodness in Holmes County. The nuns' description of a society where evil prevailed everywhere was dominating my spirit.

Despite more than a decade in the news business spending a disproportionate amount of that time with mistakes of society, I rarely approached life or my job from a cynical view. As a reporter and as a Christian, I always had believed it wrong to view humankind as merely a collection of individuals motivated solely by their selfish interests.

I thought about a tough city editor from East St. Louis who once told me that there was no place for cynics in journalism. He'd seen some of the worst of human behavior. He'd run gutsy crusades against corruption that had sent public officials to prison. But G. Thomas Duffey sternly told me, "If you distrust all human nature and motives and don't believe things can be better, you have no place in journalism. A journalist provides information in the belief that when you put it in the hands of the people something will be better because of it."

That's not dissimilar to the message of Jesus. While acknowledging the existence of an evil that must be fought, Jesus stressed the sacred worth of each individual and the ability of each to be redeemed as a child of God.

Where's the redemption and the good in this county? I thought. *How can I sort it out?* In a kind of a slump not controlled by cognitive faculties, my body slid off the bed to my knees. I buried my face in the frayed, musty bedspread and prayed over and over, "Help me to understand. Help me to understand."

After awhile I began to think on an incident back in the spring of 1980. That was three months before the unexpected contact from Spurgeon Dunnam that brought me to the *Reporter* newspapers. In the spring I had told my pastor in Cincinnati that I felt some kind of a call to take a couple of years off daily newspapers to work in the church. He suggested I drive up to Dayton where the United Methodists had a seminary and a communications center.

In Dayton I talked to one of the seminary professors who reviewed with me the large number of religious magazines available. Knowing my commitment to Christian justice, he talked quite a bit about thought publications and advocacy magazines like *Sojourners*. What I liked best about journalism, I told the professor, was diving into a controversial issue and lifting out new information. He thought on that awhile and said, "You know, the church is full of people analyzing and commenting on the issues. What we're probably short of is people providing new data and sorting out the facts to keep all the analyzing and commenting fresh and related to the truth."

Here in Durant, Mississippi, I felt encouraged by that memory. I didn't have to understand everything here. There were plenty of people around the country who thought they could analyze. But it already had become clear that most of them were sorely lacking in the fact department. It wouldn't be easy, but I at least could come out of this trip with some dependable facts and some new impressions to add to the discussion.

At 8 o'clock I called the nuns' house, and Sister Beverly answered. I asked, "Did Ken Lawrence get in touch with you this morning?"

"Yes, but he says he can't see you. He's too busy."

"But I don't need a lot of time. I really want to talk to him. It's important for my story to be balanced."

Sister Beverly was curt. I couldn't talk to Ken or anybody else in the United League today. I was suspicious. I couldn't shake the feeling that the phone call she got at the end last night was somebody suggesting not cooperating with me.

As I ate breakfast in the motel diner, I glanced at a man at another table as he folded the morning paper to look at the back page. That turned the front page toward me. My eye caught on a headline about a sheriff of another county being indicted. I squinted to see the picture. It was a white man.

Black Subdivisions

I drove on through Lexington to Tchula. The sun shone brightly. Tchula made run-down Lexington look like boom-town Dallas. The excuse for a commercial district was typical of the tired brick buildings in little agricultural hamlets that long ago became anachronisms. Unlike a town in a recession where repairs and modernization are put off for a few years, commercial and public buildings in villages like Tchula haven't had prideful attention in decades. They get attention only to keep the rain out.

The dusty streets, wide enough for major commerce, were filled with listless-looking people trudging through life. The neighborhoods were strictly segregated, with the blacks, regardless of status or income, across the railroad tracks. Newly built brick homes of the black teachers and government workers sat among the shanties that housed the 30 percent of the town's workers who were unemployed. The neighboring shacks and the universal lack of landscaping almost hid the fact that some of the houses were new.

Jesse Banks had one of those nicer houses on the black side of the tracks. A "proper" woman in attire and manner, she invited me in when I knocked on her door. She'd just been to the grocery store and was unloading the sacks.

"May I get you a drink? I have some Cokes in the refrigerator." She brought the soda to me in a can, but with a crocheted doily wrapped around it so it wouldn't sweat in my hand.

Jesse Banks, after spending most of a lifetime as a respected teacher, became one of the two aldermen who steadfastly backed Mayor Carthan during his tumultuous time in office. If Carthan and his supporters had an image as a roughshod band of semi-outlaws who might have made good leaders out on the frontier, you had to rethink it all through again when you met Miss Banks.

She talked about "Eddie" like a student who had grown up to be the shining star of the community. Nothing but a white conspiracy was behind Eddie's troubles, she said. "I'm a religious woman. If I thought Eddie was guilty I wouldn't support him. Before I became alderman I had a lot of so-called white friends. But they dropped me when they didn't agree with my situation. White friends who sat right where you sit voted against everything Eddie proposed. They said he was going too fast." Miss Banks had fallen with Eddie. The black voters had thrown her and Carthan's other alderman supporter out of office the election following Carthan's assault conviction.

Tchula's blacks were deeply divided. Not far from Miss Banks' house was another nice one owned by Nona Granderson who was as convinced of Carthan's guilt as Miss Banks was that he was being unfairly persecuted. Nona was the beautiful young widow of the man Carthan was accused of having murdered. She continued to maintain a year later that Carthan arranged to have her husband killed because of his years-long opposition to Carthan.

Roosevelt Granderson had been the basketball coach at Tchula's school where Nona also taught. He represented a slower, more accommodating approach to black politics than did the much more aggressive Carthan. On the board of aldermen, Roosevelt joined another black man and the board's only white man in almost continuously blocking Mayor Carthan.

In his other capacity as school board president, Carthan was behind the firing of Granderson. But a court order reinstated the coach.

Everybody in Tchula agreed the blood was bad between the two. When Carthan was forced from office in spring of 1981, he was well aware that the assault of which he was convicted wouldn't have occurred if Roosevelt had been supportive of Carthan's leadership.

Roosevelt became acting mayor to fill Carthan's term.

A month later, while Roosevelt worked his moonlight job at a convenience market, two out-of-town gunmen robbed the store, forced him into a storage room and shot him twice in the back of the head. In his widow's way of thinking, the national church and civil rights groups supporting Eddie Carthan were not standing up for Tchula's most popular black leader like they claimed. Rather, they were supporting the murderer of Tchula's most popular leader.

Adding to the difficulty in easily assessing the good guys from the bad guys was Herbert Granderson who lived near Nona. The two did not speak to each other. Herbert was Roosevelt's brother but through the years sided with Carthan. Herbert said his brother had too much of the mentality of the plantation where they'd grown up, too easygoing and intimidated by white power. While Herbert didn't agree with Carthan's contention that Roosevelt was killed over a drug deal, he insisted on Carthan's innocence.

I called James Johnson, a black member of the county's most powerful body, the County Board of Supervisors. Jessie Banks had told me he was "about the only black officeholder that's independent and doesn't have a plantation mentality." Johnson said he didn't know what to think about the murder. But about the storming of the town hall that first made Carthan a criminal, he said he didn't think there was an innocent person in the whole bunch on either side.

He agreed that in some cases the white economic powers used black people to do their bidding. "But I wouldn't say all or even most of the black elected officials in this county have a plantation mentality. Some blacks are still a little nervous about voting how they feel but I think most blacks understand that the ballots are secret now. A majority of blacks still don't vote like I think they ought to. But that's not because whites are intimidating them. It's just because that's the way they think."

Hired Arsonists

It was time to go to talk to Tchula's most visible white power, Mayor Lester Lyon. He was the incumbent mayor whom Eddie Carthan defeated in 1977 to become the county's first black mayor. And he was the one who beat Herbert Granderson, Carthan's choice, in 1981 to replace Carthan and put a white back in the office. Lester Lyon was an active member of the Tchula United Methodist Church and the man who represented the South's most celebrated, "prototypical" shift from black power back to white power.

The white power figure was a surprise. Lester Lyon was soft-spoken, thoughtful, unassuming and frank.

Mayor Lyon owned an appliance store. I had to wait for him to get off a tractor over by his house and come into the store, dominated by the smell and sound of old, unvarnished hardwood floors. A youngish, middle-aged man, he had a red neck for sure, easily seen under his open collar, and a well-tanned, firm face and head topped by a brush cut. He suggested we walk on down to the town hall and talk.

The national church and civil rights leaders were right that a lot of racism was behind some of the white reaction to their activism for Carthan, Lyon said. White solidarity was a reality, too. "Whites tend to stick together on everything because they are such a minority here, but there's no white conspiracy. I'd know about it if there was."

Lyon agreed with Carthan supporters that a lot of blacks in Tchula still had a plantation mentality. "But to think that white folks can make sure that only Uncle Toms are elected seems impossible." Blacks had been badly abused but had "really improved themselves through their own hard work and education," he said, noting that Roosevelt Granderson's philosophy had been, "Let's go on from here."

Lyon also had "problems" with the believability of the testimony of Andrews and Harris that helped convict Carthan in the assault case, but he thought it ludicrous that there now was a national crusade painting Carthan as leader of blacks, deposed by a white conspiracy; Carthan had deposed himself.

"Eddie was capable of being a good mayor. I think his personal ego and greed ruined it for him. People turned against him when they thought he wanted the whole government to be him."

I asked, "You don't think he could win an election here?"

"I don't see how he could ever get black support here. He doesn't draw anybody here. They had a Tchula 7 appreciation night the other day; there weren't a half-dozen cars."

At one corner the mayor pointed out an old man across the street and said he was the father of one of the two young men who said Eddie Carthan paid them to burn down Carthan's store over in Durant because the business was failing.

"Don Barrett told me about the trial," I said. "He said the jury found Carthan innocent."

"Did he mention the federal trial on the same case?"

"No. There was another trial?"

As it turned out, the insurance company that had compensated Carthan for the loss of his previously failing business took Carthan to federal court. Based on confessions and testimony of both arsonists, a girl friend and family members, the federal civil court jury rendered a verdict that Carthan "arranged and participated in the destruction by fire" of his store. It ordered Carthan to pay back the insurance money. That ruling came during Carthan's second year as mayor and added to growing disenchantment with him, Mayor Lyon explained.

Lyon said Mayor Carthan's form of rule had fanned a mood of frontier lawlessness. He said he ran for mayor again, with the support of Tchula's blacks, because the town had just gone crazy the last couple of years. For instance, as Roosevelt Granderson's coffin was being lowered into the grave a year ago, Tchula's main street erupted in a machine gun shoot-out, including a hand grenade explosion. Regular meetings of Lyon and his newly elected board of alderman were posted with guards armed with rifles.

As he talked, Lyon began to shoot down almost every claim made by the national Carthan campaign. And various records later backed Lyon. The cutting of Carthan's salary from $600 to $60 a month needed to be seen in the light of his having raised it from $60 to $600 when he took office. He left Tchula's social programs for the poor in a mess, Mayor Lyon said.

"Social programs?" I asked. "Wasn't the reason Carthan had so much political trouble because people resented how fast he moved in bringing in programs for the poor?"

"Like what?"

"Rehabilitating the housing of poor blacks, for one."

"Actually," Mayor Lyon said, "we got that grant before Eddie became mayor. "But Carthan had administered the $150,000 housing grant badly.

The federal Department of Housing and Urban Development found that houses outside areas approved by HUD were remodeled, giving the indication the money may have been used for political favors and friends—or kickbacks. Poor black citizens who were listed in records as having received help were left with shoddy and even dangerously incomplete projects in their homes. Others listed as having received repairs said they'd received none.

Carthan "lost" $92,000 of the grant money. Federal investigators never discovered where the money went. HUD officials still believed graft was involved but couldn't prove it, they told me.

The chaining shut of the town hall by the aldermen had occured when Carthan refused to show them the town's financial records in the midst of the housing scandal.

"The really rough thing for the poor people of Tchula," Mayor Lyon concluded, "is that they didn't get the aid, and the federal government now refuses to give us any more help until we pay back the money. Well, there's no way a little, poor town like this can ever do that."

I was thinking about all the people around the country who were hearing Eddie Carthan speak and who were reading the national literature describing him in terms as if he were the new Martin Luther King Jr. come to save the poor.

Another Look At Accomplishments For The Poor

I couldn't believe a whole national cause had been built on so many lies and distortions. Every time I turned around another so-called fact was being proven false. The health clinic he "initiated" actually was initiated under Lyon before Carthan was elected in 1977. Carthan's great help to Tchula's unemployed in bringing in federal Comprehensive Employment and Training Act money also was tainted. The Mississippi Office of Job Development and Training found Carthan spent $12,000 of the money without documentation.

"We're just now getting that cleared up," Mayor Lyon said.

Attributing to Carthan a 50 percent foundation grant for a public library was twisted in more than one way. First, the library project and the securing of outside money had begun under Carthan's predecessor's board of aldermen. Carthan, however, did secure a pledge for $20,000 from a foundation in 1979. But in early 1981, Carthan wrote the foundation and asked it to "re-channel" $10,000 of the grant to pay Carthan's legal expenses in dealing with HUD's investigation of the missing housing rehabilitation money. The foundation withdrew the grant offer altogether. The library wasn't built.

The day care center credited to Carthan was a bigger mess that newspapers around Mississippi had been reporting for three years. Trouble started when the board of aldermen paid for an option to purchase the building for the day care center. When it came time to buy it, the aldermen were shocked to find that Carthan had organized a new development company and bought the building out from under them. So when the day care center started, it had to pay Carthan's company $450 a month rent instead of having to pay only for utilities had the town bought it. Carthan originally tried to get $750 rent.

State welfare officials noticed problems immediately, as did some of the workers at the center. Despite the infusion of considerable money, inspection visits found the kitchen empty and supplies not bought. The center's van seemed always to be with the mayor. A federal court finally found Carthan guilty of being involved in a kickback scheme related to the purchase of equipment for the day care center.

I had plenty to think about as I drove back to Jackson to catch a plane back to Dallas. Goodness knows, I was aware of how a person could get a fact awry here and there. What newspaper reporter hadn't been guilty of that? But the wholesale distortion by the National Campaign to Free Eddie Carthan and its religious and civil rights supporters was too grand to be anything other than intentional. The United League appeared to be the chief culprit in this scheme. Somehow it had fed its vastly edited and partly fabricated version of the life and times of Mayor Eddie Carthan to a national network of presumably well-intentioned people and groups.

I thought of all the things I'd heard in the last 44 hours and decided Sheriff Huggins had the best explanation. No deception so grand could have taken place without a massive eagerness of others to believe a story that fit the negative stereotypes of Mississippi.

Don Barrett may have had a point when he said what was involved here was prejudice against white southerners. But even worse than that was a prejudice by outsiders against all of Mississippi, especially the average black citizen who was supposed to be too dumb and weak to distinguish between rhetoric and deeds. And to my embarrassment, I'd succumbed to the prejudice myself.

As I drove through Yazoo City and thought of the images that name conjured, I realized how I had blown the brake fluid incident all out of reality because of my base negative expectations of Mississippi.

I'd been thinking about the brakes and thought I'd figured out an explanation other than somebody being out to get me. The previous renter of the car probably had some brake problems because of the leak. He or she might have stopped at a self-serve station and bought some extra fluid. He might have marked up things with a screwdriver or some other sharp object, not knowing quite how to get the cap off, and he may have failed to put the cap back on securely. The rental car people wouldn't have noticed a problem if the renter failed to report the leak when he turned in the car. Then I picked it up, and the cap jiggled loose. By the time I got to my fateful curve Thursday night the break fluid was gone.

It was a convoluted explanation but much less so than trying to figure out how, who and why some Mississippi ogre deliberately did it. Starting with Mississippi mythology, it was easy to believe just about any conspiracy explanation.

But on a rational level, the State of Mississippi and the grand jury had a fairly logical reason for thinking Carthan should be brought to trial on the murder charge. First, two gunmen had said Carthan paid them to do it. Second, Carthan already had proven himself in federal court, in the arson case, as capable of paying people to commit a crime. And third, a state court had convicted him of resorting to guns in another incident to settle a political problem. Fourth, the murdered man was a long-time personal enemy. These were four reasons for indictment, none having anything to do with a white conspiracy.

On the other hand, I thought, Carthan had a prime profile for a person who could be erroneously convicted of murder. He obviously had been such an impetuous young man, lacking the maturity to handle the responsibilities that came so quickly and easily to him, that he established himself in the eyes of many as a scoundrel. His record of scandals, corruption, mismanagement and malfeasance made him susceptible to false charges from a criminal seeking to plea bargain. He indeed might be in desperate need of special help in his legal defense to ensure a fair trial.

I figured that after I wrote my stories, the national Carthan network, at least the religious part of it, would adjust its campaign to more accurately reflect the true situation in Mississippi. I figured they wouldn't abandon Carthan but would end up bolstering his defense team while dropping all the white conspiracy and Martin Luther King-reincarnated stuff.

I figured wrong.

6

Sad But True

Dudley was more worked up than usual. "Can you believe what they've done now!" he exclaimed through the phone as soon as I answered. It was late October, five months since I first talked with the Rev. Dudley Brown in his office at the First United Methodist Church in Lexington, Mississippi.

Virtually nothing had been settled since the 44 hours I spent in Holmes County in May or on return visits. An ecclesiastical war had broken out between Mississippi Protestants and the New York City staff people of national church agencies. A lot of other people were picking sides. Dudley had called me probably an average of once a week since May to keep me apprised of the local situation. I'd averaged writing a story every other week.

"Hi, Dudley. News from New York has reached you again, I see." I threw my feet up on my Dallas office desk, leaned back in my chair and settled in for what I knew would be an interesting conversation. "How's the trial going?"

Across the street from where Dudley was talking, Eddie Carthan was in his second week in the Holmes County Court House on trial for murder. The black former mayor of Tchula hadn't been making any church-sponsored national speaking tours lately. Rather, he'd been taking his meals and sleeping in Sheriff Howard Huggins' jail since the end of the summer. That's when the Mississippi Supreme Court rejected Carthan's appeal of the three-year prison sentence for assaulting a police officer.

The nine judges unanimously ruled in a lengthy opinion that the conviction and sentence were reasonable, based on the severity of Carthan's and his six cohorts' armed assault on the Tchula Town Hall. The judges remarked that the jury had convicted them of lesser offenses than the state had charged and that the judge had not handed down the maximum sentence.

National Carthan supporters and the United League of Holmes County were undaunted in their cries of unfairness. They merely widened their ever-larger pool of alleged conspirators to include the Supreme Court justices.

"You should see all the people on the lawn of the court house," Dudley said. "It was a carnival at that first rally." He was cackling again. "While the civil rights people were singing on the court house square we had a bunch of white Lexington residents conducting a protest of the firing of five black sanitation workers. They brought garbage sacks and left them all around."

"How many people do you have in the Carthan support group?"

"Maybe 300 at the rallies. A few dozen are there all the time. Every time the poor jurors walk in or walk out of the court house it's like a gauntlet with the Carthan supporters on both sides whoopin and hollerin and singin. They're not concerned about a fair trial. They're trying to intimidate the jurors into finding Carthan innocent. They've got the whole walk lined with huge African flags on small sticks they've stuck in the ground. They've got posters and banners."

"How many blacks on the jury?"

"They're all black. And I don't envy them. They hear the threats coming at them from the United League."

"I heard that somewhere else," I said. "I talked to a long-time civil rights activist who attended one of the Carthan rallies there in Lexington. He was really disturbed and said people there were pretty open in putting the word out that the jurors would suffer in some way if they voted a conviction."

"That's what the Carthan people want. They scream conspiracy here, but you notice Carthan's lawyers never once asked to move the trial to some place where he can get an impartial hearing. They know they can't intimidate people in other counties like they can here."

"That's not a good situation, Dudley. Are our national church groups involved in this?"

"They sure are, through the United League. And that's what makes this latest fool action from the Board of Global Ministries that much worse," Dudley said, getting back to the reason he called. "I just can't believe after all the information that has been supplied them, they'd come out for the United League again like they did."

"I was surprised, too, when Sharon Mielke called me from the directors' meeting last week. We've got her story in this week's paper." In "Agency reaffirms support in Carthan case," mission agency directors said they were re-endorsing the United League as an illustration of the principle of supporting justice ministries. "Have your people in Holmes County heard about the new support?"

"Oh, they all know. Most everybody I talk to today, Roy, wants to just quit the church. It's worse than what I thought could happen. And what hit them so hard was the way they just ignored the peace committee work."

League Storms Church Doors

The peace committee was set up after both Mississippi annual conferences (including a black membership of about 13 percent) in June almost unanimously blasted the national missions agency and demanded it stop its support for the United League. Congregations throughout the state began boycotting offerings to the mission agency. Mississippi's Bishop C. P. Minnick and the Board of Global Ministries in New York each appointed a team to the peace committee to study the situation in Holmes County.

With my coverage to our million readers nationwide and with the national Carthan campaign in full swing, this was far from a local matter anymore. National church leaders were concerned about the spillover of the constant hammering of the headlines over my stories in the *Reporter*.

UM agency chief apologizes / Churches not consulted in racial case—May 28, 1982.

Mississippi dispute spreads / UM agency conducts massive mailing to clarify role in local criminal cases—June 4.

UM staff cite "compelling" basis to aid convicted mayor / Is Mississippian a martyr for the poor or unpopular corrupt mayor?—June 11.

"This isn't Old South of 1965!" / Some claim church agencies base actions on outdated concepts, incomplete information—June 11.

Official votes urge end to help for convicted Mississippi mayor—June 18.

Aftermath of Mississippi case / Mission unit tightens consultation—July 2.

Hallway confrontation interrupts attempts to hear race issues—Aug. 13.

Mississippians testify national agency broke UM law / Missions execs counter that consultation not required for two grants—Aug. 20.

"Mayor" jailed, Mississippi episode continues / Church leaders broach idea of pressing for pardon—Sept. 24.

The "hallway confrontation" story was a dramatic example of the peace committee's difficulty. I thought the missions board as a whole would have seen at least some cause for caution after their representatives encountered firsthand the United League's operating style. Fifteen members of the dual committee had gathered from around the nation and the state in Dudley's church. They invited a long list of local people, including United League leaders, to come individually to tell their version of what was going on. It was the kind of thing that should have been done in the first place. And it was another form of what I tried to do during my May visit.

Alas, true fact-finding was not to occur that day. About 50 United League people burst into the church, down the hallway and stormed the doors to the room where the peace committee had begun interviewing. The committee wouldn't let them in ahead of their place in the schedule. Somebody witnessing the commotion from the outside ran for help. Sheriff Huggins and four black deputies arrived and returned a degree of order to the church.

The United League demonstrators were demanding to be present to hear everything that anybody said about their organization so they could counter any lies told about them. The committee deliberated an hour before deciding to allow three United League people to sit in on all sessions. Also present for the interviews were the New York staff members who had been long-term supporters of the league, including Sheila Collins and John Jordan. That effectively cancelled appearances by most black elected officials and black church leaders in the county.

"I love my life too much to appear in front of those United League folks," one black leader said.

"I couldn't go into any confidential stuff with the league in there," said the Rev. Tom Hawks of the white Durant church. "I didn't want any more threats against my family like I've been getting all summer."

Many of the leaders who had gathered to talk to the committee lost their nerve and left. Others just didn't show up. The Rev. William S. Evans II, chairman of the mission agency directors there, said it was obvious the league had badly intimidated many of the witnesses.

At the end of the summer the mission agency members on the committee agreed with the Mississippi members to a statement that recognized "growth in race relations" in Holmes County and said the denomination must be involved in justice ministries in the county in order to carry out the mandate of the gospel. But the joint committee also agreed that the United League was a divisive group. No reconciliation between local United Methodists and their national mission agency was possible as long as an official connection with the United League remained, the two groups agreed.

"We were really hopeful something positive was going to come out of all of this after that peace committee recommendation," Dudley now was saying in October. "But obviously, some of the rabble-rousers on Global Ministries' board of directors got together with the radical staff and shot down a chance to deal from a truthful basis."

I broke in, "Sharon's story says the mission agency directors pledged themselves to promote Carthan's cause as indicative of larger national issues of racism and political repression. Let's see, there's another good one in this story. . . .Here, the resolution says, 'Truth is not determined by a majority opinion. We encourage the National Division to its fidelity to the principle of human development and justice in every quarter even when that denies a dominant point of view.' What do you suppose that means?"

"It means that no matter what most reasonable people can tell is the truth, New York is going to slap at us anyway."

"Dudley, I'm afraid that's sad but true. When you're so busy trying to be right, truth just kind of gets in the way."

I was amazed that with all the information now available on Eddie Carthan's background and the far less than unified local black support for him, the national church leaders continued to see everything as simple black and white.

Even with the knowledge of Carthan's finances and political failures, if not crimes, the United Methodist mission board said its support for Carthan and the United League was because of Jesus' call to bring "good news to the poor. . .release to the captives. . .to set at liberty those who are oppressed." Officials of other denominations were taking the same stand.

Lazy Literalist Fundamentalism

I saw no reason at all for wrapping the issue in such gospel absolutes. Increasingly I was bothered by what I saw as a lazy scriptural fundamentalist approach to social issues from mainline Protestant leaders. Too many Christian activists felt they could cite a passage of Scripture, suggest its applicability to a specific situation and act as though that settled everything without any need for the use of reason in interpreting the Scripture or assessing the full facts of the situation.

Obeying Christ's call in his innaugural sermon required determining in any given situation the identity of the poor, the captives and the oppressed. Was the United League the oppressed or the champion of the oppressed? Or were the poor blacks who said they were intimidated by the United League the oppressed? Was Eddie Carthan the oppressed? Or was he the oppressor of poor blacks in Tchula? Or was he both the oppressed and the oppressor? As for captives, I couldn't believe that the mainline leaders were a kind of biblical literalists who believed that Jesus intended for all prisoners to be released from jail, no matter their crime. Yet literalist fundamentalism, with scant regard for reason or facts, seemed to be prevailing.

I thought the national leaders might see a reason for nuance after the statement from Rev. Theo Tripplett, who was the black chief of a standing Mississippi church commission that monitored the United Methodist Church there for racism. He said the United League had asked his commission for aid three years earlier, but it had rejected the request because the league was too divisive.

And a black United Methodist district superintendent reported that as much as he loved the national mission board, he had to say it had made a mistake linking with the United League. The league's radical approach "does not represent my Christian conscience," the Rev. Merlin Conoway said.

Hazel Brannon Smith was giving similar advice but with a greater sense of urgency. She was the eccentric, white, Pulitzer-Prize-honored editor of the Lexington, Mississippi newspaper. She stood up for black rights for nearly 30 years while the White Citizens Council boycotted her paper.

"There's a power play going on in the black community here," she explained when I told her of my deep confusion. "On the one side of the fight are the black leaders who broke segregation and have been getting elected. On the other side are some blacks who don't have power and have aligned themselves with this radical United League." She couldn't understand why the national church groups had chosen to take sides in the black civil war and especially to take sides against the traditional civil rights leaders.

Robert Clark had appeared to be on his way to becoming Mississippi's first black congressman since Reconstruction but now was in trouble because the United League was undermining him, the spunky editor told me. "These three white nuns are keeping this going. If the nuns would leave the county, the black people could pull themselves together and work together. But they're getting all this outside help now for the United League. The league is tearing apart the black community the way the White Citizens Council did the white community."

At the *Reporter* we were baffled by supposedly liberal church people's actions against the wishes and apparently the self interest of so many black Holmes County residents. When the Supreme Court sent Carthan back to jail, the National Council of Churches issued an urgent appeal for money to fight the "white conspiracy." The NCC also organized massive letter-writing to Mississippi Gov. Winters, asking him to pardon Carthan.

"People around here wouldn't make a big deal," Dudley observed, "if the outsiders were just helping with Carthan's legal expenses to help him get a fair trial. But constantly slapping at our courts, our elected officials, our blacks, our whites, our churches and saying they're part of a conspiracy is killing us."

Liberal wings of the church were jumping into the fray, even criticizing the national agencies for not being tough enough with the Mississippi "racists." My *Reporter* colleague, Garlinda Burton, felt herself pushed beyond patience when she covered a summer meeting of the Methodist Federation for Social Action. It unanimously voted after almost no discussion to support the campaign against the white conspiracy in Holmes County.

Intensely proud of being part of the black community, Garlinda found the liberal group's action frightening, given the fact that so many blacks were on the other side of Carthan. She wrote:

That any group would assume discrimination and cry "racism" in a case as muddled as this one appears to me to be a classic case of knee-jerk white liberalism. As a black Christian, I have known the reality of racial injustice and laud any group which seeks to wipe out all remaining evidences of it. But racism's hard shell covers many un-suspecting hearts—perhaps even some of those who refer to themselves as liberals. . . .Christ calls us to act, but also to weigh the merits of our actions in light of his teachings.

When the national youth organization of United Methodists met in early August, they were provided only the Carthan side of the con-troversy, including linking him to Martin Luther King Jr. The youths sent official letters to various parties encouraging continuation of Global Ministries' advocacy efforts in a situation they said obviously was a "violation of justice and a racist action."

When the news story crossed my desk, I threw my pen down in disgust. What an undermining way to provide guidance to youth about the intellectual dimension of Christian discipleship!

Dudley's Heart

I'd made a couple more trips into Mississippi. But I had the ad-vantage of being far removed when I sat down nearly every week to try to put out a story that dispassionately gave every side's claims.

Dudley was in the maelstrom and it was beginning to show in this late October call. "My church is deserting the collection plate," he said.

"You're still putting funds for the national benevolences in escrow?"

"No, I mean they're deserting everything. They've just quit giving."

"But that's like punishing you. I thought you'd been their cham-pion in all of this."

"I'm trying to keep them in the church and reaching out. I had hoped to build some constructive dialogue between whites and blacks. Every other church I've had, I've got them to come back into the sys-tem. Always before I could smooth things over."

"Sounds like you feel caught in the middle."

"My people are chewing me out over what the board just did, and people connected to New York are saying I'm a racist."

I had done research on Dudley. Although he'd always proven trustworthy as an information source, I'd wanted to know if he was a force for improvement or for the racial status quo in Mississippi. Black and white sources vouched for his long-standing support for racial improvement. But he was a quiet leader, not an integration firebrand. Some said Dudley had suffered a great deal for his often-conflicting commitment to justice for blacks and his pastoral obligations to his white flocks.

"He's had a lot of heart problems," a ministerial colleague in another part of the state said. "I worry about him now, bottling so much up, being in the middle. Here's a man who did far more in local chuches on this racial battle than the majority. He's spoken for the dignity and rights of all people, even to the point of sacrificing his salary."

Dudley's sacrifice involved "apportionments." Each year every one of the 38,000 United Methodist congregations in the nation was assigned a "fair-share" payment they were expected to make to a huge denominational fund for agencies and benevolences. Cutting back or refusing to pay that "apportionment" was a prime way for a congregation to protest something the national agencies had done or to tweak a bishop for the assignment of a preacher.

During and after the denomination's heavy involvement in the '60s civil rights movement, white Mississippi churches barely paid any apportionments. Dudley, I was told, went into one church after another and got them to start being real churches again, involved in social outreach and mission. One congregation had been especially resistent; so Dudley pro-rated his typically low pastor's salary to the members' payment of apportionments. For every seven dollars the members fell short on paying apportionments each year, he took three dollars off his salary. He did that five years, and the congregation's love for him caused it to pay the apportionments in full.

During the two months after the Carthan murder trial, Dudley would be hospitalized twice with serious coronary problems and for surgery. By the time this whole episode was over, he found himself isolated in the middle, with his congregation and church leaders on either side suspicious of his true motives.

Within a couple of years, Dudley Brown would leave the ministry

This second week of the murder trial, however, Dudley was in the middle of a whirlwind of activity. He called me again later in the week on Thursday night, October 28.

Discovery On The Square

Dudley had made a discovery up on the square; some of the pro-Carthan people who were harassing the jurors had been sent by the Board of Global Ministries. The mission board had bought their tickets from all over the country.

I was shocked. It seemed to make mission board officials into liars. The board's continuing support since May had been only in the form of verbal endorsements and allowing the United League access to the board's group health care plan and training events. After the initial outcry against its activities, board officials repeatedly sent mailings and gave pledges that no new money was "in the pipeline" to come into Holmes County. Rene Bideaux didn't rule out new money but said none would come until after substantial consultation with local people. No consultation had occurred on this latest expenditure.

What Rene didn't know until Dudley tipped him this week of Carthan's trial was that Sheila Collins of his staff had held a meeting in September with representatives from the 23 grassroots organizations, including the United League, that were part of her network. Another missions staffer, William Rollins, also was present when they decided to pay for about a dozen network people around the country to travel to Carthan's trial. Rollins and missions executive John Jordan signed the travel vouchers without mentioning them to agency superiors, let alone to Mississippians. Rene Bideaux had made a big deal in the summer with a mass mailing telling of a new agency rule that guaranteed that a staffer's signature on a voucher meant the necessary consultation had taken place.

When staffers the end of October were persuading mission directors to adopt the aggressive resolution favoring the United League, they didn't tell anything about the new expenditures. Yet at that very time, the Global Ministries-funded protestors already were on the Holmes County Court House lawn helping form the gauntlet for jurors.

Dudley called me about this on a day I'd spent in Louisville covering the United Methodists' supreme court. The court ruled on Global Ministries' previous contributions to Carthan and the United League and said the agency definitely had violated the church law that required local consultation.

Outrage, Then Suspensions

Bishop Minnick expressed outrage at the latest breach of trust. A liberal, social-conscience minister elected bishop out of Virginia just two years earlier, Minnick told me he felt his ministry in Mississippi was now nearly ruined. Through the public media he had begun an effort to lend heavy leadership to racial progress in the state. But you can only ask people to trust you so many times when your word gets broken by others, he said.

Roy Lawrence, Mississippi Methodists' editor, said the bishop and others had been badly hurt by trying to defend or at least counsel understanding of the national agencies. "Our leaders down here have been humiliated," the veteran editor said. "We've tried so hard to smooth this situation and to move our church farther into justice ministry. But it's really frightening about Global Ministries' directors. There's over 150 of them from all over the country. To see them adopt that document last week based on such one-sided and biased views makes you wonder. If they're that easily swayed, you wonder about all their decisions."

On Friday, the three agency staffers were suspended temporarily.

The *Reporter* and I were getting quite a bit of hostile mail for our coverage. A few of the writers were Mississippians who thought I was being way too hard on them, but most of the writers, particularly various ministers around the nation, accused us of being co-opted by the Mississippians. They said we were being legalistic Pharisees and making church law and consultation more holy than justice.

But consultation was about justice, I argued. The requirement of consultation was an effort to be certain crusaders from far away tried to ascertain the facts before rushing in. How could justice result from operating on erroneous information?

I recalled stories I'd heard about medieval crusaders committed to driving out infidels from the Holy Land and reclaiming the sacred ground for Christians. Among the people they slaughtered were large numbers of Arabs whom the European crusaders hadn't bothered to find out were Christians. Mayor Lyon and others in Holmes County had told me that they made requests for the early teams from New York to talk to them but never were contacted.

Meanwhile, reports from the murder trial were of the two Granderson killers testifying they met with Eddie Carthan in Chicago and Atlanta to plot the assassination. A woman also testified she saw Carthan at the Atlanta meeting. Carthan said he never met any of them. The defense brought in information about Granderson and drugs.

A week after the staff suspensions in New York, the Holmes County jury deliberated less than an hour and returned a verdict of not guilty. Carthan went back to jail to continue serving his sentence for assault of a policeman.

Ironically, the judge who sent him there, Webb Franklin, was the chief political beneficiary of the tumultuous rallying behind Carthan in the murder trial. Discouraged by the civil war between Carthan/United League supporters and other black leaders, black voters turned out lightly at the polls. And white Republican Franklin narrowly became the U.S. congressman over black Democrat Robert Clark. Like a Faulkner plot, the tangled tale would continue.

The next week, the *Reporter's* board of directors met for its annual meeting in Dallas. As with the year before, the first night was spent with me and my reporting on the hot seat. Some of the annual conferences had sent their representatives with deep concerns about my "negative reporting" that had helped put national agencies in such a bind. The fact that the church's supreme court had said the agency people put themselves in the bind didn't deter some criticism. Other people simply thought we'd devoted too much attention to the controversy. The discussion was healthy and rational. In the end, the news judgment of us at the *Reporter* was not censured.

In addition, Spurgeon attempted to shift my growing negative image by making a little speech about all the "positive" stories I'd done during the year about the impressive work of churches throughout the Rust Belt in dealing with the massive unemployment in the steel and auto industries. He also cited the time I'd put into lifting up annual conferences north of the Sun Belt and reporting how they'd managed to turn the tide to have membership growth the last year.

Still, I knew doubts about me remained. I recognized from the beginning that if I reported the disconcerting facts I discovered in Holmes County I would seem to be setting myself against an incredibly large slate of racial-justice activists. Dozens of mayors, state legislators, churches, denominational agencies, congressmen and civil rights groups all over the country were listed as endorsers of the national campaign against the "white conspiracy" in Mississippi concerning Eddie Carthan.

I doubted even a tenth of them had any idea what was really going on. But with all those good people making their claims, how could my reporting of a very different view possibly be right? That was the attitude of some journalists in the ecumenical press who chastised me for undermining some of Protestantism's finest fighters for justice and for being "obsessed" with church legalisms.

Most critics, however, never got down to the fundamental level of ascertaining the facts upon which to judge the case. Rather than start at the level of presenting opposing philosophies for people to choose in the controversy, I had worked throughout the year to present facts. But when people already had chosen sides based mostly upon philosophies, the facts couldn't budge them.

Many church liberals often seemed like a mirror of the Reagan administration they hated so much. Preference for ideology and casualness with facts were frequent attributes of White House action that most infuriated those church leaders. It certainly infuriated me. Yet religious leaders seemed often to fight back with the same methods.

Two Streams Of Affirmation

I sorely needed the affirmation I got the last night of the *Reporter* board meeting. It was a social evening at Sharon Mielke's rehabilitated three-story Victorian home in the heart of the illegal-Mexican-alien and recently-arrived-Asian-refugee inner city of Dallas. Just as the directors were gathering at the door to load up in vans, the phone rang. It was Garlinda Burton, who was representing us in Nebraska at the United Methodist Association of Communicators.

Sharon took the phone and waved for everybody to be quiet. Nebraska journalism professors and practitioners had judged all the entries. "It's Garlinda, and the best news coverage of the year," Sharon said as she repeated each phrase from the other end of the phone, "is for Tchula, Mississippi." The directors standing in the big foyer cheered, and some surrounded me, slapping me on the back.

"Wait, there's more. And the Communicator of the Year is. . .Roy Howard Beck!"

The judges had taken all entries in all categories and judged which person's cumulative entries were tops over all. I indulged myself with a sweet sense of temporary satisfaction when I heard the judges' comments.

The Award of Excellence for news coverage must go
to the stories set in Mississippi because they escalated into
a national issue, or demanded national attention, and because of the continuing nature of the story. . . .Beck did an
exhaustive job of gathering facts, checking them out and
playing them back to the reader in a meaningful way.

The Communicator of the Year was based not only on the Mississippi work but the coverage of the conference on South Africa, my
filings from Cuba and my breaking of the story last spring of the underground railroad bringing El Salvador refugees illegally into this
country.

The judges noted that my closest competitors were my colleagues
at the *Reporter* and added:

It is refreshing to see in the *Reporter* a willingness to
tie into the controversial, difficult and risky (to the reporter
and paper) social issues that could easily be sloughed off
or be covered only superficially.

Roy Howard Beck's entries involve investigative
reporting and go beyond merely recording something that
transpires at a given setting. He exhibits the drive, initiative and persistence characteristic of the best reporters in
commercial print media, qualities not observed as often in
the institutional press.

I wasn't the only one being affirmed in this episode. Sheila Collins, John Jordan and William Rollins were drawing wide support from
a number of social action organizations which condemned Global
Ministries for suspending them.

The National Council of Churches' Governing Board met in
November and gave a resounding endorsement to all of the work to
combat the "white conspiracy" in Holmes County. It commended its
own fact-finding delegation of last April for its "courageous witness,
in particular, Sheila Collins who first highlighted the issue for Christian churches." The NCC called for Sheila to be congratulated, commended and supported.

The Methodist Federation for Social Action "deplored the harsh
and punitive measures" against Sheila, Bill and John. It saw the attack

on the three as an attack on the "church's overall missional stance throughout the world." The suspension not only demoralized the mission staff but gave "comfort to those who are attacking the mission of the church."

James Lawson, the highly talented pastor of a large, vibrant black church in Los Angeles and former associate of Martin Luther King Jr., came to the three suspended workers' defense by firing a salvo at Rene Bideaux and Bishop Minnick. In an open letter, he said Rene's disciplinary action had been an historic racist procedure of "isolating, driving out and destroying the nigger lovers." Rene had capitulated to "racism and to those voices" in Mississippi United Methodist churches who speak for the "demonic in our society," Lawson said.

Truth A Continuing Casualty

For his role in stressing church law on consultation and not supporting Sheila Collins and her associates, Bishop Minnick was accused of "racism, the vicious kind of racism which permeates our land today and surely is the greatest sign of spiritual death."

The bishop was stunned. Like so many other people caught up in the affair, he was weary of the inability to stand for truth and at the same time to seem to care about justice.

Rather than taking the customary second four-year term over the state, Bishop Minnick would move elsewhere when his first term ended in 1984.

Truth continued to be a casualty through the winter. The national church/Carthan network was widely distributing charges that a couple of the jurors who acquitted Carthan had lost their jobs because of it. And the United League supposedly was harassed in its insurance because of its Carthan support.

I checked out every claim as it came. None could be substantiated. In each case people in other states had made the decision based on routine procedures of their companies. The jurors were caught in larger layoffs based on criteria previously established and later were offered their jobs back. The insurance was cancelled because it had been obtained under false pretenses. Yet, the claims continued to be repeated in New York church agency-supported literature for months.

Dudley was furious. He fired off a letter to the New York executives, inquiring why they had not sought to check the validity of the charges before repeating them.

In such serious matters as this, we must stick to facts and not let our imaginations run wild. . . .It may be too late for you to use the information I've given. You can, however, be reminded that there are right ways and wrong ways to do things. You can flog the public, slap out at whites, spread truth and half-truths to reach your goal, or you can follow decent procedure.

The source of our controversy from the beginning has not been over your good intentions to work in a justice ministry. . . .But you have chosen methods for use without regard to their morality. . . .The methods chosen for use were not those ordinarily accepted in our Christian society.

A lie is a sin, and a sin is a sin even when sponsored by the church. . . .In my opinion, the day has not come when it can be an acceptable tool for carrying out the Gospel.

The literature containing the severely distorted information, if not straight lies, continued to be distributed. I was in the big multi-church headquarters building at 475 Riverside Drive in New York City in March and saw posters hanging in the church offices containing the same misinformation, with a picture of Eddie Carthan against a backdrop of an image of Martin Luther King Jr.

Wave Of Indignation Against Corruption

Dudley was sneaking calls to me from his hospital bed. "It's picking up again. The papers are full of the new pressure to get Eddie Carthan relieved of his state and federal prison sentences."

"What now?"

"The Presbyterians' New York people agreed to donate $10,000 more to the Carthan and United League people. And $5,000 was pledged from the Lutheran Church of America, $1,000 from the United Church of Christ. The National Council of Churches put out an appeal to raise $100,000 in all to get Carthan out of jail. And Global Ministries people have been making contacts here that are supposed to be the start of a consultation process about donating $10,000 more."

"What's the rationale? Does it not matter how many courts confirm his convictions?"

"They're saying he's been selectively prosecuted for the kinds of political shenanigans that white elected officials get by with all the time," Dudley said.

I was beginning to think they might have a point when I had a conversation with the Rev. Edwin R. King Jr. in Jackson, described to me from various sources as something of an icon of the stormy Mississippi civil rights movement, during which he spent considerable time in jail.

"These national church groups don't understand what is happening down here at all," said King, who continued to devote time to civil rights. Before the white and black Methodist conferences merged in Mississippi there was an effort to get some black preachers into the white conferences. When they refused, King, a white man, joined the black conference until the merger occurred. "We're in a wave of public indignation in Mississippi against political corruption," he said. "Carthan just got caught in it."

"Are they mainly going after black officials?"

"Not at all. Probably once a month, a prominent politician is indicted. Almost all of them are white. They got the white tax assessor here in Jackson County. They got the governor's top white administrative aid and a white state senator."

A special federal grand jury was started in 1979 to explore the public corruption across the state. It conducted 250 investigations and finally prosecuted 17 public officials. Included besides the one Ed King mentioned were the white former director of the highway safety program and several white county supervisors.

There also were many convictions of people for corruption involved with federally funded nutrition, daycare and Head Start programs. Eddie Carthan was one of the people unanimously indicted and later convicted for undermining those programs for the poor by seeking his personal monetary gain.

"It is true," King said, "that blacks have come into power at a time when the public just won't stand for political corruption any longer. Surely the church isn't going to argue that blacks ought to have their chance to be corrupt. But clearly, whites are the main targets. A prominent white banker and one of the governor's white aides were convicted in the same case that got Carthan."

"If there's no racism behind his being in jail, why haven't you Mississippi civil rights people said that?"

"We have. I'm in the state American Civil Liberties Union. We looked at the Carthan case and voted unanimously that there was no civil rights issue involved."

"So this thing about a white power structure in Holmes County is just fiction."

"Oh, there's a white power structure there that will make every effort to keep blacks from having power. But it's not the cause of Eddie Carthan's problems. We no longer need outsiders helping us like we used to. Blacks and open-minded whites have the power in Mississippi now. Almost all the people involved in this Carthan case are from out of state. They don't understand."

I interrupted, "They're more convinced now than ever that they're deep into the most important civil rights crusade of the decade. Have you seen what the National Council of Churches is doing now?"

"Yes, and the NCC was tricked."

Tricked By The Investigating Team

"Tricked?" I responded.

"I helped the NCC fact-finding team when it came here a year ago," Ed King said. "All of these church groups have gotten onto this issue because of the team's report. But the report tricked the NCC and everybody else. They misstated my offering and much of what they heard. That report is a very damning thing for them."

"I've read the report." I pulled it out of a drawer in my office.

"Do you see how it's filled with images of people spying on them and a sense of secret power plays?" he asked.

"Sure, here's one. This subsection has a heading called 'Jackson—The Climate.' I'll read some of it:"

> Upon arrival at the Sun-N-Sand Hotel, some members of the delegation became aware of a number of law enforcement cars at the hotel. After close examination and inquiries, members of the delegation were told that a law enforcement convention was being held at the hotel. The delegation noted that little visible evidence of such a convention was present.

I had noticed when I read this the first time that throughout the report there's this constant sense that people are out to get them. This sounded so much like my paranoia the night my brakes had gone out last year.

"The part about all the policemen," Ed said. "There really was a police convention. They made no effort at fact-finding."

The team failed to talk to the black elected officials or old-line black civil rights leaders or white and black United Methodists in Holmes County who could have given them an entirely different story than the one they so obviously were wanting to prove. "And by doing what they are doing, they're all going to discredit the true needs of the people and the real struggles that need support," Ed said.

Finally, I felt like I had some understanding of the NCC investigation that came out so totally different from my own. I'd tried to talk to some members of the team in the past but not gotten much other than platitudes about justice.

The NCC/Carthan campaign continued like a perpetual motion machine running on a fallacious source of power. When Eddie Carthan was moved from Sheriff Huggins' jail February 1, to finish serving his sentence in the state prison, the NCC joined in a "National Day of Prayer" for the mistreatment of Carthan. The NCC, Global Ministries and several other New York church agencies sent representatives to Lexington to participate in a special prayer exercise on the courthouse lawn.

"I counted about 125 people there," Dudley told me. "About 100 of them came in vans from New York, Maryland, Ohio, Wisconsin, Virginia and cars from Ohio, Michigan, California, Minnesota and Tennessee."

Dudley called me again during the same period with news that members of the United League had occupied Sheriff Huggins' jail in protest of Carthan's transfer, which they said was obviously a racial conspiracy to deny him access to his supporters.

"Nine were arrested, including two of the nuns, when they refused to leave. And get this, the New York Annual Conference Methodists are sending a van of freedom riders down to check things out. Now I ask you, if you were convicted of a state crime and sentenced to prison In New York and you lost your appeal in the Supreme Court, where would you be?"

"In prison?"

"Of course. I don't know what people think ought to be happening here."

Once again the Carthan supporters were labeling as racist something supported by other civil rights groups. The rights groups for a long time had pushed for routine sweeps to get state prisoners out of inadequate county jails into the federally supervised prisons.

I checked with the office of Federal Judge William Keady and found he had ordered the prisoner transfers of many people the first of February and that Carthan just coincidentally was involved. The judge had taken control of the prisons years before and was known as something of a radical advocate of civil rights. That didn't stop the national church and United League protests against his action.

A Revelation About Ideology

It was around that time that I and the million readers of the *Reporter* got some additional insight into what was so unique about the United League and why some people might choose it over the other black organizations and leaders: United League leaders were guided by Marxist-Leninist tactics and analysis.

When I came upon that, I thought, *Oh no, not another trip through red-bait city.*

But the evidence was indisputable. One of the nuns, Sister Loretta, and United League president Arnett Lewis were presidential electors on the 1980 Holmes County ballots for Deirdre Griswold. She was running for the U.S. presidency on the Workers World Party ticket. Griswold described the party to the news media as Marxist-Leninist. And, perhaps coincidentally, Eddie Carthan, during one of his times out on bail, had done some speaking in tandem with Angela Davis, vice presidential candidate for the Communist Party U.S.A.

I had no idea just how ideologically committed and sophisticated the United League people were in Marxist-Leninist thinking. I certainly had no concern that Holmes County was about to become the next Afghanistan, although Mississippi gave the Workers World Party its second largest vote in 1980. But that information helped put a lot of the United League's actions in perspective: The championing of the cause of the poor, while totally belittling the poor's ability to think for themselves. The assumption that they knew better what the poor needed than the poor did. The undermining of people, like black leaders, that they should have had sympathy for. The preference for confrontation and polarization.

I could only speculate because the United League blacks and nuns never answered my questions and seldom answered my calls after that one night at the nuns' house.

So I understood what was unique about the United League. I could not understand, and hated to speculate, why the national church professionals of several denominations in New York chose to align themselves with the league.

Black Leaders Fight Back

All of the events finally pushed much of Holmes County's black leadership over the brink. A new coalition of seven black organizations, including the NAACP and the Freedom Democratic Party, that claimed 3,000 active members in Holmes County formed to "stage a campaign to let the world know" that the United League and its supporters did not speak for Holmes County blacks.

"The Board of Global Ministries, the NCC and all these other outside groups are part of a conspiracy, either out of ignorance or intentional, to replace the black leaders of this county," a coalition officer, Mary Hightower, told me.

The new black coalition had begun to meet somewhere nearly every night to strategize on how to combat the threat from the national church groups who claimed to care about blacks, I learned from Mary.

"Why have you waited so long to make your feelings public? I thought this was the way you felt, but I always heard it kind of indirectly," I said.

For one, the black leaders thought the controversy would blow over, and they didn't totally disagree with focusing some attention on the still unresolved racial problems. But the national campaign behind the United League was fostering a climate of lawlessness in the county and a disrespect for elected leaders, most of whom were black, Mary Hightower said.

"We want the law to be taken seriously. It allowed blacks to progress to where we are. I don't like to say this about religious groups, but a lot of these activities have been staged. People's conduct is not becoming of people fighting for justice, for the poor and for black people. It gives racists an excuse to say they were right about blacks."

Robert Cooper Howard, one of the founders of the Freedom Democratic Party in Holmes County in 1963, said the black leaders were prepared to fight the national church organizations. "I'm really upset that the ministers they send down here do not respect the black leadership enough to consult us and support the gains we've made."

"To say that we black folks don't have anybody to speak for us, that's a lie," Mary said. "Our method has been effective. We've got more black elected leaders than any county in Mississippi."

"But the national church agency people say you all have a plantation mentality and bow to the whites," I said.

Mary was agitated. "It seems like these church outsiders want us to discriminate against whites like they did to us when they were in control. We're proud of our good communications with whites. We don't want an all black county. It's all right to elect some white leaders. It's the white nuns that have caused the problem over at the United League. They say they will help us if we will follow them. We have our black leaders. We don't need white nuns to speak for us," she said.

"What about the national campaign that says Eddie Carthan is in prison because of a conspiracy?"

"In order for the conspiracy to work against Eddie, lots of blacks had to be involved. And that's a lie. We don't appreciate these people coming in here and blasting our black jurors, blasting our black superintendent of education, blasting our black sheriff, blasting our black state representative!"

I felt sick. Since my 48 hours in Mississippi last May, I had suspected that some of what this new black coalition was saying had been true. How could this have happened? The crusaders appeared to be slaying the Arab Christians again. I reported the new black coalition's manifesto and the United League's Marxist-Leninist connections and waited to see what happened.

In April, the Board of Global Ministries directors met again. Their reaction to all the additional information from Holmes County?

The members voted an additional $10,000 to continue the national publicity campaign portraying Eddie Carthan as a victim of racism.

Absolutely incredible! There wasn't a word or gesture to acknowledge even any complexity to the issues in Holmes County. Not a sign that anybody cared or even noticed the black Holmes County residents who were asking the mission directors to relate to the county in a different way. G. Thomas Duffey would have to forgive me, but I was becoming cynical about the power of information to affect anything.

Carthan by that time had been paroled by the Mississippi governor and was sent to a federal penitentiary in Alabama to begin his federal sentence for corruption.

Rick Abraham, a white racial and economic justice advocate who was working with farm worker problems, probably had the best explanation for how things had gotten into such a mess with the church organizations.

"A lot of the groups that got involved at the beginning needed an issue as much as Carthan needed their support." Rick knew the groups well. He was part of them. Among his jailings for activism throughout Mississippi since 1968 was a stay in the Holmes County jail where he helped boycott white merchants a few years back.

He said the rights groups needed a dramatic issue that could generate a lot of publicity and fundraising. "They were successful because they appealed to the legitimate concerns of people. But the appeal was based on inaccurate and misleading information."

People were refusing to let go of this issue because they were so hungry for clear good and evil issues like they enjoyed during the 1960s civil rights movement. Because Rick felt the Carthan campaign ultimately would undermine support for legitimate justice causes, he had been working for months to persuade various groups to dislodge from the campaign. He compiled an extensive collection of court records to back up his pitch.

"By now this conspiracy your church people believe in has to include the U.S. Department of Justice, the FBI, two U.S. District judges from different districts, a panel of judges on the U.S. Fifth Circuit Court of Appeals in New Orleans, the U.S. district attorney, the state attorney general, the governor, a predominantly black Holmes County jury, a State Circuit Court judge, the nine members of the Mississippi Supreme Court, the Holmes County sheriff, the U.S. Department of Housing and Urban Development, the U.S. Department of Agriculture, the State Welfare Department, the State Department of Education, statewide newspapers, journalists, local church people, local officials and numerous citizens."

Once again, I decided people could believe the conspiracy because they weren't interested in facts. At a press conference in the spring, a reporter asked a high Global Ministries executive about some contradictory "facts" concerning the Carthan case. "Carthan's guilt isn't the point," he responded. "It's the symbolism."

In May Sheila Collins lost her job during another altercation with her boss, Rene Bideaux. In June, Rene, on the basis of a study by a special committee, cut the link between the United Methodist Church and the United League of Holmes County. The NCC and other church groups just quietly stopped mentioning the case.

It was like the way Ed McAteer and the Religious Roundtable had resisted seeming to back down in public but finally readjusted to the facts.

I thought back to a year earlier when I buried my head in the musty bedspread of the Durant motel and prayed for understanding. You have to believe that putting reliable information in people's hands ultimately will make a difference.

You have to believe in patience, too.

7

Squeezed From
the Nestlé Crunch

Thankfully, not all Christian social action I reported was bumbling. A master case in point was the Nestlé boycott affair.

For three years I was like a fly on the wall of Nestlé-related proceedings that undergirded my belief that collective Christian efforts really can further the cause of systemic justice, putting action to the prayer for "thy Kingdom come, thy will be done on earth as it is in heaven."

Because of the intellectual and moral clarity with which key individuals approached the issue, I witnessed one of those times when Christian concern combined with Christian action and broke through wordy deadlocks with transforming results.

The issue at hand was a deadly serious one concerning infant formula, multi-national corporations and infant malnutrition in the Third World. American Christians' way of dealing with it was like a whole new Prohibition movement in the '70s and '80s.

Presbyterians had embraced the new Prohibition in 1978. Since then, a descendent of John Knox who could not control the urge for a cup of Tasters' Choice coffee likely had to slip out the back door to take a snort. The brew was banned from fellowship halls.

Nestea was forbidden at United Church of Christ potlucks, and Nestlé hot chocolate mix was a taboo at Disciples of Christ retreats.

Respectable United Brethren were careful not to be seen entering a Stouffer's hotel; American Baptists were admonished not to yield to temptation when they passed the Stouffer's frozen foods at the supermarket. The youth of those denominations generally were protected from having to eat Libby's-brand canned vegetables at camps. And the sight of a Nestlé's Crunch candy bar was enough to send them all in search of a Mr. Goodbar.

Welcome to the Nestlé boycott, an effort to change the behavior of a multi-national corporate goliath. All those brands and more were products of the Nestlé Corporation of Vevey, Switzerland.

For a decade, church and other activist groups around the world had tried unsuccessfully to persuade Nestlé to halt aggressive marketing of infant formula in Third World nations. Nestlé used billboards, print ads, posters in health clinics and sales people dressed in nurse-like uniforms to promote infant formula as the modern way to feed babies.

Nestlé was accused of "hooking" poor infants on free samples of infant formula until their mothers' breast milk dried up. Then when the mothers found they couldn't afford to continue the habit, they over-diluted what formula they could buy with water that seldom was pure. The result was said to be a lot of malnutrition and death of infants.

As Americans rediscovered the health superiority of breastfeeding their own babies, they joined with scientists and nutritionists in promoting the natural way for Third World people as well.

In Vevey, Switzerland, Nestlé officials seemed unprepared for the corporate responsibility movement that had enlivened U.S. businesses' annual meetings for years. Nestlé reacted clumsily and arrogantly, basically ignoring the protesters.

INFACT, a Minneapolis-based organization, plus a group of nuns began a boycott of all Nestlé products to get the company's attention. When Nestlé did not respond, the list of endorsers grew rapidly to include many unions, universities and, most importantly, entire denominations.

"Boycott the baby-killers," the literature proclaimed. Church groups passed out little cards with a list of all the many Nestlé products. Shoppers carried the cards to the supermarket to help them avoid purchases that would support a callous baby-killer.

My family knew all about this. We carried the cards.

We were introduced to the issue in Cincinnati through Shirley's participation in the local United Methodist Women's group. We kept the Nestlé product list taped to the inside of one of the kitchen cabinet doors. I had worked with the issue as a member of our Cincinnati congregation's commission on Christian social concerns.

The national United Methodist Women organization had been among the first to endorse the Nestlé boycott, but the 1980 denominational General Conference had voted down an effort to put the entire United Methodist Church behind the boycott. Paul Minus, an Ohio seminary professor, had argued that the boycotters and Nestlé had reached a polarized standoff that needed a new player to shake loose a solution that truly would benefit poor Third World babies.

So the top legislative body for United Methodists, whose ancestors were in the lead in pushing for the Constitutional Prohibition early in the century, declined to encourage abstinence from Nestlé-brand purchases. Instead, it formed a task force to make one last effort to persuade Nestlé to change its infant formula marketing.

Seldom has a committee truly inspired me, but watching the members of this task force operate was a spiritual blessing. Some of the step-by-step work of the task force made an excellent case study for how morally concerned individuals can make a difference.

How a reconciling solution came to be squeezed from the Nestlé Crunch impasse could be seen in the headlines as they ran in the *Reporter*.

Infant formula studies
begin at ground floor
—Reporter, Oct. 31, 1980

Of course the task force said it was going to begin at the ground floor. Nearly all study committees claim that. But few do, because their members are so set in their own ideas.

This task force's members brought with them strong opinions on different sides of the issue. But under the chairmanship of Phil Wogaman, the task force set an agenda that really did leave room for people—members and those called before them—to be changed by the study. Wogaman, a noted Christian social ethicist, ran the task force like a laboratory.

Years later, the seminary professor confided to me that he had taken the job with the task force with the expectation that the group would study and negotiate for a year and then ask that the 9.5-million-member denomination be pledged to the boycott.

But Wogaman knew that a church pronouncement doesn't mean much of anything to members unless they know how it is formulated and have faith in its integrity. Fortunately, I found, he was concerned not with just the appearance of integrity but with real openness to hear, with hearts as well as with ears, from every point of view in the first meetings of the task force.

Nestlé officials, apparently weary of being labeled as demonic forces, began to show interest in dealing with this new player.

'Unethical campaign' charged; infant formula issue said 'clouded'
—Reporter, Feb. 6, 1981

After meeting with boycott leaders, the task force strongly criticized Nestlé for paying a Washington foundation which hired a writer who discredited Nestlé boycotters in a *Fortune* magazine article.

The article accused boycott leaders of being more motivated by Marxist-tinged hatred for multi-national corporations than by sincere concern for Third World babies. Such a charge was worthy of consideration, but it didn't have a lot to do with the question of Nestlé's behavior. Regardless of who raised questions about Nestlé or for what reason, those questions deserved straight answers.

The task force wisely saw that their primary job was to look at the infant formula questions, not the ones raising them.

Nestlé faces economic push on formula policy
—Reporter, May 15, 1981

By May the years-long grassroots boycott had pushed the infant formula issue into the top reaches of the World Health Organization. WHO was considering a code for marketing infant formula. The code was helpful because it would give an internationally agreed-upon standard rather than an arbitrary demand to use as a goal for Nestlé.

The Methodist task force was a johnny-come-lately on this. But its parent body, the United Methodist General Council on Ministries, lent encouragement to the effort. It sent a letter to Nestlé that it would cancel its fall meeting at Dayton's Stouffer's Hotel if Nestlé didn't agree to follow the WHO code. It was a small gesture to indicate that the denomination had the will for a full-scale boycott if necessary.

The United States was the only nation in the World Health Assembly to vote against the new infant formula marketing code, sticking with the multi-national corporations.

Infant formula code
wins world approval
—Reporter, May 29, 1981

Wogaman was there in the galleries, running back and forth to, and allowed into the confidence of, both the international boycott leaders pushing the code and the formula companies opposing it. He discovered that people on both sides "demeaned" their cause by excessively challenging the integrity of the other.

When he visited a top Nestlé official in Switzerland to personally deliver the Methodist council's ultimatum on its meeting site, the official seemed frightened about what that might mean about one of the world's largest denominations.

UM task force's Christian
faith is visible in its work
—Reporter, July 3, 1981

It was face-to-face with the "enemy" at the task force's mid-June meeting at a hotel near the Indianapolis airport.

Members met with representatives not only from Nestlé but from the three major U.S. infant formula manufacturers. In three- and four-hour shifts over two days, each company had a chance to size up and be observed by the new players in the grassroots activism.

It was supposed to be a Christians-vs.-the-lions affair. But I immediately saw that the two sides couldn't agree which was which.

Most of the businesswomen and men were Christian lay people who had very definite ideas about their own discipleship and saw themselves as following highly idealistic goals in their jobs. They were scientific and technical experts in Third World health matters. Some of the business people revealed their own distrust born from a lot of previous encounters with religious critics. Nobody was more pointed than Gary W. Mize of Bristol Meyers. He was scathing of the critics' tactics, "For example, they use a 10 million figure for Third World babies dying from improper use of infant formula. They pull that out of thin air. There is no basis for the claim. When groups in the name of Christ operate like this, it's not distorting but lying. Championing the cause of Christ and human health on a foundation of lies raises serious questions. It's morally wrong."

Mize suggested that companies like his were doing far more to battle infant malnutrition than the religious critics who had succeeded in getting the public to view the infant formula companies as profit-hungry villains.

"It's easy to sling eggs, but it's not so easy to clean up," he said. "I don't think Christ would condone this kind of behavior. And I say that as a God-fearing, compassionate Christian individual. This boycott movement diverts important attention and money away from important core issues on infant malnutrition."

So the church representatives' first task in negotiations seemed to be to convince that they really did seek the Spirit of Christ in the issue and shared a common faith with the Christian corporate people.

The uniquely Christian qualities of this gathering came through quickly. As soon as a corporate delegation sat down, they knew they were not dealing with just another social action group. The women members in particular made it clear that a boycott was not the foremost issue on their minds. Mothers and their babies were what counted.

And each time before launching into a three- to four-hour session, Wogaman set the ground rules for the discussion. "We've been asked by our General Conference to be a catalyst, to move the infant formula issue beyond polarization. . . . We do not come into this entirely neutral. Our loyalty is to God, through his Son, Jesus Christ. . . . Ours is a global church. We perceive God as being above nationalism or any economic ideology."

When company representatives wandered into an argument based on a defense of the free-enterprise system or the United States' self-interests, Indiana Bishop James Armstrong was the one who usually gently interrupted and reminded them that "we are not a U.S. church. And remember, we are most concerned about the infants of the world."

Task force members prayed with company officials at shared meals, one time asking one of them to offer the prayer. The task force showed respect for the corporation representatives' depth of working experience in the Third World

Group endorses code
Nestlé shows different face on formula issue
—Reporter, June 26, 1981.

I talked with members of each company as they departed the hotel. All commented on the sincerity of the task force members. Company officials acted surprised as they said they believed the task force really was motivated by a Christian concern for Third World infants and not by some anti-corporation agenda.

The biggest surprise at that June meeting was that Nestlé officials didn't act anything like they'd been expected to. I had a vague sense that I was witnessing one of those events of transcendence, of God breaking through the membrane of history to touch a physical situation. And the vehicle seemed to be the Christ-like spirit and loving intentions of the task force members.

As it happened, Nestlé had assembled a new team that was prepared to be receptive to just such a spirit. The Nestlé people indicated some of the change resulted from the shuttle diplomacy of Wogaman and Armstrong.

They acknowledged their company had fought passage of the WHO infant formula marketing code because of some technical problems they saw. "We fought the good fight to the end, but now we accept the verdict," said the team leader, Rafael Pagan. He said Nestlé would abide by the code in any nation that adopted it as its own. In nations that didn't, Nestlé would follow its own code, which now included about three-fourths of the WHO provisions.

I sat in the corner noting the irony of sending a man named Pagan to make peace with the Methodists.

Robert J. Kegerreis, the wry president of Wright State University on the task force, interrupted Pagan (pronounced puh-GAHN) during one of his non-combative discourses. "I have to confess that I am skeptical of you," Kegerreis said. "Your stance today is very amenable and relaxed, but that doesn't square with all the other impressions I've gotten about you."

"We are different than two years ago," Pagan said. He admitted that Nestlé for years had bungled its handling of the controversy. But a lot of company personnel had changed.

Nestlé had been persuaded that some marketing practices were inappropriate, just like the boycotters said, and had discontinued those, Pagan continued. "Our company was too unresponsive and inaccessible in the past. But there is no reason for the boycott of our products to continue."

After the Nestlé team left, the task force was faced that evening with a difficult decision about how to treat Nestlé. Smooth talk is easy when you're trying to win a concession, the members agreed.

"I sense a change of tune but not a real change," said Anita Anand. An official of the United Methodist Board of Church and Society, she not only led the successful effort to get that agency behind the boycott but also was one of the ones behind the failed attempt to get the 1980 General Conference to approve the boycott.

Paul Minus, though, said the task force was faced with an important theological question, "I think Nestlé is trying to recoup and pull out of its abysmal performance so far. Theologically, I believe that for us to err on the side of excessive caution would be a grave error. I'd like to see us test this new attitude and go for a new beginning."

Bishop Armstrong suggested that there appeared to be hard-liners and soft-liners in Nestlé's head office. What the task force was seeing, he said, might not represent the ultimate corporate authority but might be worth encouraging in the hope that the soft-liners might win out.

At the end of the evening, Wogaman astutely appointed Paul and Anita as a committee to write a statement of position for the task force to consider the next day.

First, though, Anita insisted that to work out some tension a swim in the hotel pool was in order. I joined her and Paul in the pool where we splashed cold water on unpalatable views.

I enjoyed watching the interaction between Anita, the young India native and boycott loser at General Conference, and Paul, the professor who sponsored the resolution that won and established the task force. One of the things that made this task force effective was the honest attempt at diversity in membership. Oh, ethnic, geographic, gender, and lay/clergy diversity was built into all church committees. For the most part, that was good, but often it disguised a lack of real diversity in experience and view.

President Kegerreis and Dean Wogaman were among the contrasts. Kegerreis was heavily invested personally in corporate America through membership on several boards of directors of large corporations. For him the task force was an opportunity to prod necessary reform, if it was needed, in a system he believed in.

Wogaman, on the other hand, had long expressed his feeling that various forms of capitalism were not as close to Christian ideals as some form of socialism. The dean of Wesley Seminary in Washington D.C. said he was "tempted" by democratic socialism, while quickly acknowledging there had been no models to test his belief in its moral superiority. He had deep concerns about the very nature of multinational corporations, but pragmatism ruled out any advantage from discussing whether or not they should exist, he said. Rather, the key question was "how to structure a fabric of law and institutionalization on a world scale to bring the industries into social accountability." Wogaman had never been accused of being a capitalist tool. Not yet.

The morning after our swim, the task force unanimously approved a statement that urged United Methodists in all nations to seek enactment of the WHO code by their own government. "Only those provisions that are clearly and demonstrably impracticable should be modified in national implementation," the members said. It was a bow to the flexibility the company officials had requested.

In another gesture that indicated they'd paid attention to the descriptions of overwhelming Third World infant health problems, members placed the code in perspective by acknowledging that misuse of infant formula caused far fewer deaths than bad water supplies. But the water was a far more costly and difficult problem to clear up.

Because of Nestlé's lobbying against the code at the WHO meeting, several of the members had come to the meeting expecting that at the end they would begin preliminary discussions of strategies for joining the boycott. Instead, all decided not to even discuss that until the September meeting. The perceived change in Nestlé deserved more observation, they said. They decided to look for additional signs of whether Nestlé could be trusted to continue to improve.

GCOM shows confidence, won't boycott Nestlé hotel
—Reporter, July 14, 1981

The Methodist General Council on Ministries decided Nestlé's more conciliatory attitude deserved affirmation and notified Stouffer's Hotel in Dayton that it wouldn't boycott it at the fall meeting.

Nestlé woes welcomed by boycott proponents
—Reporter, Aug. 14, 1981

INFACT and its boycott coalition members issued excited press releases in August about a 16 percent drop in Nestlé's profits. With Nestlé more vulnerable, now is the time to intensify boycott pressure, an INFACT official said.

My succession of articles was beginning to draw a moderate

stream of mail. I was getting helpful affirmation from people long involved with the infant formula issue and strong questioning from others about what this issue had to do with church, anyway. The latter comment was a prevalent one on the Sunday school tour, as well.

I routinely did guest teaching of adult church school classes around Dallas, and the Nestlé boycott had become my main topic. I typically taught on the major issues I was covering at a given time and got back more than I put in, because it helped me to understand and anticipate the questions, prejudices and wisdom of readers.

Many of the classes had bankers and business officials in them who were perturbed that something as radical as a boycott could even be considered by the church. Besides, some asked, what business did the church have sticking its nose into marketing practices?

But many of us mainline Protestants displayed a lot of our Christian discipleship through the way we didn't buy certain kinds of consumer products for ourselves or types of toys, like guns, for our kids. We regarded it as Christian stewardship of our money not to support corporations which had practices that demeaned humanity or desecrated the environment.

My son Jeremy's favorite cookie was butterscotch. But I had not been able to find butterscotch chips in any brand other than Nestlé. So Jeremy had to do without butterscotch cookies for several years.

I didn't try or want to persuade the people of the rightness of the boycott. Rather, I wanted them to understand that the issue was one demanding Christian attention, or at least deserving of it.

"If a person, a corporation, an organization, a neighborhood, a government treats a person as less than a full human being, or if they impede a person from living fully in God's grace, we as Christians have a strong obligation to do something," I said in every class.

I reminded the members of Isaiah's thundering proclamation that God called His people to cease to do evil, learn to do good, protest oppression, correct injustice, defend the poor and the powerless. I directed them to the 25th chapter of Matthew, where Jesus says we're destined for eternal punishment if we fail to stand up and help the hungry, sick and downtrodden.

But I was quick to point out that the power of those Scriptures came to bear on an issue only as the facts supported an action. Before Christians embraced a social action, they should be clear about the nature of a problem and the consequences and effectiveness of an advocated solution. Class discussion carried on from there.

Nestlé asked for proof of change
—Reporter, Oct. 2, 1981

When I arrived in Dayton for the fall meeting, task force members were inclined to start preparing the mobilization for a boycott. The bloom of Nestlé's spring change in attitude had faded during the last four months. Nothing new had happened. Members were concerned that they'd been subjected to a PR job intended to delay their actions.

Douglas Johnson, the brilliant and energetic young leader of INFACT, was there to encourage them to follow their instincts. If they weren't going to endorse the boycott, he beseeched them, at least stop diluting the efforts of other mainline denominations who had the courage to stand up to the international corporate villain.

Abruptly, Johnson, myself and the other observers found ourselves tossed into the hallway. A three-man Nestlé entourage whisked through the hall, into the room with the task force and shut the door.

This was unexpected to us. Nestlé was not on the agenda. Doug Johnson groused that Nestlé had its chance for the task force's ears in June.

Pagan had asked at the last minute for time on the agenda. Then he and his associates had flown from Washington with an "aide memoire" from Vevey, Switzerland. It proposed that the task force serve as a "hotline" to receive grievances against Nestlé from the public. Nestlé felt it would be a way to prove and ensure its sincerity in living up to its standards.

"We'll deal swiftly with any alleged marketing violations you pass on," Pagan said. People could be assured their complaints were not being ignored because the task force would have a record of complaints and the company's responses to them.

It was a tactical victory for Nestlé. Once again Doug Johnson left without a boycott endorsement, although he did get a meeting of sorts with Nestlé as he and Pagan talked about family while sharing lunch with the task force.

The task force declined to serve as the hotline, saying it should be more ecumenical in makeup. But the Methodists promised to help Nestlé formulate such a body.

After the Nestlé group returned to Washington, task force members decided they needed something more concrete to prove that Nestlé had changed its marketing policies, had communicated them to their worldwide outlets and had corrected problems when they occurred. They decided to ask Nestlé to open up its files and provide memos, letters and other documents to substantiate its claims. And to be sure Nestlé wasn't playing a delaying game, they put a December 1 deadline on their request.

Pagan had commended the task force "for your candor in expressing your concerns. . . .Nestlé, as a matter of company policy, is giving a high level of priority to working with you and other responsible church leaders."

"We'll see if they mean it," said the Rev. Ignacio Castuera, a hard-driving activist district superintendent from Los Angeles.

"If the company doesn't give us helpful information, let's forget them and vote on whether to boycott," said Eleanor Conrad, wife of a prominent Dallas black physician and an active hospital volunteer.

I pulled Anita Anand aside and asked her how she was feeling. Her opinion was changing. "I didn't believe they were sincere last June, but I feel there is potential for movement. Nestlé finally is in a position where it knows it has to change, I believe."

To move Nestlé in this way would aid far more infants than if the United Methodist Church joined the boycott as she earlier had advocated, she said. "To abandon negotiation could prolong the problem for infants around the world."

Members of the boycott coalition immediately went public with their distress about the nine-member task force's behavior. It came under heavy criticism for "hurting ecumenism" by its actions.

Friends stoke boycott fire;
UMC hoodwinked by Nestlé,
say numerous critics
—Reporter, Oct. 9, 1981

Boycotters noted that the boycott had the backing of the National Council of Churches, Presbyterian Church, Church of the Brethren, United Church of Christ, Christian (Disciples of Christ), American Baptists and 30 of United Methodism's 73 regional units.

A United Church of Christ official blasted the Methodist task force for working against all those groups. The close relationship with Nestlé was in danger of being "used to divide the religious community and to potentially undermine coordinated and ecumenical dialogue with Nestlé that might lead to a successful resolving of this issue."

Leaders of the Methodist mission and social action boards got together to discuss strategies to counteract the task force, which was the denomination's only official voice on the Nestlé issue. One might have thought they were plotting against Jerry Falwell and Ed McAteer. But they were trying to undermine a task force that included several certified church liberals, some a part of the national agency establishment.

The task force members noted that far more ecumenical friends of the United Methodists, such as Lutherans and Episcopalians, were out of the boycott than were in. They said the Methodist denomination had an obligation to pursue what it found to be the most effective and proper path.

Pagan used the tension to persuade top Nestlé officials to begin cooperating with the task force's request. On October 27, he sent the first installment from Vevey files.

"We realize the intense pressures you and your group are working under, and we share your desire to clarify the issues relating to the marketing of infant formula," Pagan wrote Wogaman. "As you know, it is not easy for any corporation working in an environment of competition and assumed privacy to open its internal documents. . . .The importance we attach to your review and our belief in your sincerity and trustworthiness has led to the enclosure."

When I talked to Pagan in November, he'd sent a second installment of files. But he expressed great frustration. Few religious activists were willing to give Nestlé credit for any changes, he lamented.

For three years, Nestlé had eliminated or changed one infant formula marketing practice after another. The broad "violations" had been eliminated. No more advertising on billboards and radio. No more labels on products with romanticized pictures of Western mothers bottle-feeding their babies. No more use of salespersons dressed like nurses to promote infant formula. No more indiscriminate handing out of free packets of infant formula to all mothers as they left hospitals.

Yet, Pagan said, the boycotters' literature vilified Nestlé even more now than before. "It would seem that nothing we do to bring our policies into conformance with the WHO code has any effect on what they say," he said. "The old charges continue without foundation."

INFACT, the coordinator of the boycott coalition, continued to put out letters that seemed to hold Nestlé responsible for 10 million cases of malnutrition and a million infant deaths a year. Actually, all figures were from estimates and included the results of the practices of dozens of other companies, which even the boycotters admitted were worse than Nestlé. The numerous specific cases cited in the literature were from before Nestlé made its changes, Pagan protested.

By the time Pagan sent documents on January 14, 1982, he was especially concerned that church women's groups were treating Nestlé with the worst possible epithets. He enclosed a newsletter from a Long Island women's group that reprinted a Nestlé boycott flier with a large headline, "How To Kill A Baby And Make A Fast Buck."

I was perturbed, too. There were a lot of factual and philosophical angles to all of this. But at base, there was a question of whether you were going to treat the "enemy" (Nestlé) as totally demonic or with a love that might nurture a redemptive relationship. There was an ugliness and "my-cause-at-any-cost" tone to some of the boycotter's pronouncements that did not speak to Third World babies being their overriding concern.

I saw that this issue—much like the Tchula, Mississippi, issue—was tossed lightly around by a lot of people who agreed with the philosophy behind the boycott but took no time at all to know what the facts were. I'd seen enough signs of change from Nestlé to personally want to give it a chance. I especially felt that way after the boycott leaders acknowledged that Nestlé wasn't anywhere nearly the worst offending company. Nestlé had been chosen as the boycott target because it was the biggest. Now it was the biggest and probably the best.

It was butterscotch cookies for Jeremy and Nestea for me at the Beck household again.

Nestlé data said fairly convincing; task force reviews documentation
—Reporter, Feb. 19, 1982

The February meeting of the task force was a turning point in many ways.

I wasn't immediately aware of the rarified air of the meeting because I was cooling my heels in the hallway outside a Dayton, Ohio, hotel room.

"What's taking them so long?" I complained to Leonard Perryman, the rotund veteran of *United Methodist News Service*. "They said they'd let us back in after about an hour. That was over a long time ago."

On the other side of the closed doors were 500 pages of top-secret business documents from Nestlé. The task force had to decide if Nestlé's documents proved the corporation was living up to its promises. But it also had to choose whether to risk being seen as a demonic Nestlé accomplice by the members' friends in the ecumenical social action movement. The Rev. Frances Manson had raised a model for the task force during a devotional about her experience with a badly burned son. Pain is necessary for the healing; you have to scrub the wounds to bring healing, reminded the Kansas pastor. The task force might have to scrub the wounds in this controversy and suffer the painful consequences.

"OK, I think they've had long enough," Leonard Perryman said to us observers as he walked toward the door. Leonard repeatedly had led the way in keeping these meetings as open as possible. As he opened the door to interrupt the proceedings, I saw a puzzled look on his face. He stuck his head in farther and looked all around. "There's nobody here."

I joined him at the door and looked in: No people. No Nestlé documents. No hint of where they'd gone.

"Maybe they finished early and left while we were in the coffee shop," Leonard said.

"But we were just there a half-hour," I said.

We headed for the hotel phones and called the rooms of all the members. No answers.

They weren't in the restaurant where we all were scheduled to eat together in another hour. The desk clerks couldn't help us. We sat in the lobby and waited.

Past dinner time, the entire task force came rustling in, heavily bundled in coats, gloves and hats against the February outdoors they'd just left. They turned red and grinned sheepishly when they saw us awaiting them. Wogaman apologized for the charade of the afternoon but said they had given us the slip as soon as we left the meeting room. They had ridden to the home of Ned Dewire, the task force staffer and head of the General Council on Ministries.

"We had some very important guests to meet, and they insisted on absolute privacy," Wogaman said.

"Who?"

The head of Nestlé's executive committee had flown from Vevey and joined with the chief of U.S. Nestlé operations and Pagan. The seeds of final resolution of the world's most popular corporate responsibility issue of the time were sown that afternoon in the living room of Dewire's striking Frank Lloyd Wright home.

For months, Nestlé's U.S.-based negotiators had been waltzing with the task force, each sizing the other up. As the U.S. Nestlé officials came to trust the Methodists, they increasingly pressured the "soft-liners" in Vevey to make concessions in infant formula policy.

Finally, on this quick trip to Dayton, the Swiss moguls felt they could trust this small group of Methodists by discussing a scheme to try to make everybody happy.

They shared a plan with the task force that eventually would develop into an auditing committee headed by former U.S. Secretary of State Edmund Muskie. That autonomous group, which included Wogaman and another member of the Methodist task force, monitored all complaints about Nestlé's marketing of infant formula to make certain it backed its promises to abide by new world health marketing standards. And the result was that Nestlé made final adjustments in its practices, bringing an eventual end to the long, bitter worldwide boycott.

At this winter meeting the task force asked to see some specific follow-up documents and asked for further changes in some practices.

UM task force OKs
Nestlé plan, rejects boycott
—Reporter, Sep. 13, 1982

By the end of the summer, the task force judged that Nestlé had made all the major changes and most of the minor ones in infant formula marketing that the boycotters had requested.

The task force deliberated in a hotel across the Potomac River from the Capital. It not only rejected the boycott for the United Methodist Church but called on all boycotting groups, agencies and individuals in the denomination to re-examine their position and consider dropping the boycott.

The task force members had begun two years earlier with widely varying positions, but they'd started on the ground floor with each other. They'd trusted in each other's basic Christian goodness. They'd experienced and talked through everything at every step. In the end, they could unanimously back the same course of action.

Wogaman announced that he was ready for the first time in years to eat a Nestlé's Crunch.

The task force credited boycotting organizations with "raising the consciousness of people of good will around the world to serious ethical problems in traditional infant formula marketing practices."

But they should turn their attention and moral energy to other companies and things that have even larger impact on suffering and death, the task force said. To do otherwise would give the impression that the Christian community neither recognizes nor rewards corporations which make substantial changes in response to ethical concerns. "That would make it increasingly difficult to convince other companies to raise their standards to Nestlé's."

Boycott pullout plan meets resistance
Some agency execs criticize task force call to soften stand on Nestlé
—Reporter, Oct. 1, 1982

The ecumenical social action community resisted the Nestlé conciliation just as much as it was resisting reconciliation at the same time with the white and black leadership of Holmes County, Mississippi.

I attended a meeting of the United Methodist Joint Panel on International Affairs in the Methodist Building across from the Supreme Court and Capitol. A year earlier I'd been on the spit. This time it was Phil Wogaman's turn.

As the members from national agencies argued, I sensed the same obstinacy against incorporating new information and revising opinions. There was a pride of ownership of an issue and the inability to let go.

More than anything, it seemed, people were saying, "This was our issue. How dare you jump in and negotiate a solution on your own." Symbolism and "solidarity" were everything.

They made it clear they would continue to push the boycott. They acknowledged that Nestlé probably was the best infant formula marketer in the world. But the boycott was necessary to push Nestlé to perfection so the boycotters could claim a victory and use the power of it to push other companies to the same high standard, they insisted.

A Presbyterian leader was there to say how much her denomination objected to the task force's work with Nestle' instead of falling in line with the boycott.

Afterwards, I walked several blocks with Wogaman back to his car. It was hard, he acknowledged, to be treated as such an enemy by those with whom he so often had been allied.

He told me he'd never intentionally put the task force on a solo course. He'd always tried to include and incorporate the boycotting leaders and groups. He told me of specific incidents in which the boycotting people had refused opportunities to negotiate a completion of the boycott with Nestlé because they wouldn't accept Wogaman and the task force as mediators. Nestlé had refused to go into the ring with the boycotters without such an intermediary.

Formula debate
takes new turn
—Reporter, Feb. 4, 1983

Nestlé was practically on its knees when the task force met again in New York.

Pagan provided data to show a drastic loss of infant formula sales in the Third World. In one way that could be good news because it might indicate a return to more breast feeding. (Nestlé, by the way, always maintained that there was a large need for the formula because of malnourished mothers.) But Pagan reported all its sales had been picked up by other companies.

Nestlé was at an extreme competitive disadvantage as it was the only company following the WHO standards, which only a few nations had adopted. Those companies, boycotters and Nestlé agreed, were far more unscrupulous in their marketing than Nestlé had been even in its bad old days.

Pagan asked the task force to please help turn the boycotting community's efforts to persuading other companies and nations to follow the WHO code. Why should Nestlé suffer for making the improvements, only so other companies could make the situation for Third World mothers worse?

Anita Anand had just returned from a fact-finding trip to Bangladesh and her native India, where she found Nestlé was not a problem. "The practices of India's semi-government infant formula company are terrible," she said. "This is often true around the world, where the local companies are worse than the multi-nationals."

But boycotting organizations attended the meeting and made their case for increased boycott pressure against Nestlé.

Anita told me she increasingly was being isolated in the social action communities in which she moved. Once she had been a darling of the people concerned about the infant formula issue because of her work for the boycott. Now she was made to feel like a traitor. "I thought I was still working for the same goal," she said.

(Wogaman's task force worked the following months with the U.S. infant formula companies, eventually getting similar agreements from them as with Nestlé. But the Japanese and Third World manufacturers remained out of reach.)

Nestlé boycott must go on, says global board
—Reporter, April 23, 1983

The United Methodist Board of Global Ministries reflected the fierce tenacity of the boycotting groups to keep the boycott going for "total victory." Re-affirmation of the Nestlé boycott at the board's April 1983 meeting took place alongside the re-endorsement of the national Eddie Carthan campaign even after the black leaders of Holmes County begged them not to do it.

The mission board was furious with Wogaman's task force because it had moved its focus from Nestlé to Methodist hospitals. The task force and a Global Ministries department had worked together to survey whether the WHO infant formula code was being followed in the 65 United Methodist hospitals in the United States mildly related to Global Ministries. Board officials were angry because the task force had publicized the fact that of the first 21 responses, 18 hospitals were violating the code.

Anticipating the board of directors' later vote to continue the Nestlé boycott because the Swiss company hadn't met absolutely all requests, Wogaman stood before them and asked, "Would anybody urge United Methodists to boycott those United Methodist hospitals until their compliance is strict, universal, scrupulous and permanent? Would we assume that the boards and administrations of these hospitals could only respond to the pressure of a boycott? We think not!"

The directors were so angry they voted to continue the Nestlé boycott and to stop sharing hospital information with Wogaman's task force. That and the Carthan vote helped make that week's agency directors' meeting one of the most petty, hypocritical, shortsighted and anti-rational displays I'd seen in a dozen years of reporting, most of them outside the church.

Nestlé boycott support wanes
—Reporter, July 1, 1983

Most of the United Methodist annual conferences pulled out or put on hold their boycotts during their spring sessions.

By now the boycott was over for nearly everybody except the vocal remnant that always has to have a boycott to prove it hasn't been sucked into the capitalist system.

Plan proposed to force agencies
to end boycott of Nestlé products
'You have twisted the tail
of a major Swiss company
and made it behave'
—Reporter, Nov. 18, 1983

Eventually the task force pulled a power play and won denominational approval for a plan that forced United Methodist agencies to drop from the boycott to preserve the good results the task force had achieved in the name of Christ and the United Methodist Church. Some time later, the international Nestlé boycott coalition was able to sit down with Nestlé and declare an end to the protest, freeing the hierarchies of the boycotting denominations that had stuck with the boycott to the end.

The boycott had accomplished a lot, especially in the early years, and was an essential reason for the improvement at Nestlé. But I was thankful that I'd experienced the full activity of the United Methodist Church's task force that didn't need a cause nearly as much as it needed to solve a problem for suffering people.

"Working with the task force was no path of roses," Pagan told me. "They were very tough. At times during the two years of discussions, we felt we should walk out. What kept us in was the faith we had in the personalities and the United Methodists' process."

He said Nestlé did not abdicate to the task force the corporation's right and responsibility to make its own decisions. But as the two parties developed faith in one another, the task force was able to help Nestlé officials view some of the issues in a different light and help them form new standards.

Back at the *Reporter* offices we discussed the underlying learnings from all of this. Although the application was not exact, I continued to be drawn to Paul's second letter to the church of Corinth, in which he described Christ's reconciliation. That spirit, it appeared to me, always seemed to produce the sweetest fruit.

Interesting to me was the fact that one of Nestlé's top negotiators ended up joining the church where Wogaman attended and became the head of its outreach commission.

As Paul wrote:

> From now on, therefore, we regard no one from a human point of view. . . .All this is from God, who through Christ reconciled us to himself and gave us the ministry of reconciliation; that is, God was in Christ reconciling the world to himself, not counting their trespasses against them, and entrusting to us the message of reconciliation (2 Cor. 5: 16-19, RSV).

8

'60 Minutes' and Counting

Millions of people turned on their TV sets January 23, 1983 and heard a rather sensational assertion on the theme of, "It's Sunday evening, do you know where your church offerings are?"

The issues of honesty and trust in the church with which I'd been wrestling went public, I mean really public, on CBS' "60 Minutes" that night.

Shirley and I barely returned from dropping Jeremy off at our church for choir practice in time to watch, while Andrew raced midget cars around us. We and some 40 million other Americans heard and saw the ticking-stop-watch opening of "60 Minutes" that had become as much the sound of U.S. Sunday evenings as church bells on Sunday mornings.

Morley Safer's voice immediately began giving the first introduction, "Americans give more to their churches than any other charity, and this congregation is as generous as any—money to do God's work at home and abroad." A congregation was shown putting money into offering plates.

"But what if some of that money is doing this man's work?" Fidel Castro ominously filled the screen.

"Or these people's?" Soldiers in Red Square marched by.

The image of Lutheran minister Richard Neuhaus was next. He said, "What worries me most—indeed, outrages me most—is when the church starts telling lies, when we start just sheer telling lies."

Harry Reasoner introduced another piece. He, Mike Wallace and then Safer identified themselves. And Ed Bradley concluded, "Those stories and more tonight on '60 Minutes'."

What followed was, by most analysts' accounts, one of the most savage reporting jobs ever done on the National Council of Churches and the World Council of Churches. And both were accustomed to decades of merciless criticism. Under attack were not only the councils but also the dozens of other mainline Protestant denominations and agencies housed in the high-rise office building at 475 Riverside Drive, New York City, as well as all 32 NCC member-denominations.

"I Think I Know That Guy"

Central to the rare 40-minute, double segment was the First United Methodist Church of Logansport, Indiana, and its pastor, the Rev. Michael LeSaux.

"I think I know that guy," I told Shirley.

LeSaux and the members of his church were angry that some of the money they sent to denominational agencies to be passed on to the councils might be supporting highly political causes with which they vehemently disagreed.

"I think most of our parishioners feel like their outcries of total frustration are falling on deaf ears," the last of three members who appeared said. "I think there's a bureaucracy there that—maybe it's so large that we can't get to it."

My hunch was that I might be a little bit behind the frustration of this congregation that now was bellowing to 40 million people.

A later check of my correspondence files confirmed that Michael LeSaux was one of the scores who wrote to me after my South Africa conference story in October 1981. The *United Methodist Reporter* had heavy circulation in Ohio and Illinois, but very light in Indiana. LeSaux asked me for permission to reprint my full story in his church's newsletter.

He waited until February 10, 1982 to reprint it and devoted his front-page message to the subject. He said the National Council's and the Methodist agencies' participation in the conference wasn't nearly as troubling as the lack of accountability. He told his church members that he was furious with the officials' casual brushing aside of criticism by saying 50 letters of protest were not enough to be distracted by "peripheral issues." His "Pastoral Jottings" continued:

Never once did they admit error in not investigating the

agenda of the conference. Never once did they admit misuse of Board of Global Ministries' funds. Never once did they apologize for the use of staff and office space to promote the conference. I joined the protest with letter number fifty-one.

He described a run-around in which he never got a direct response.

I noticed an irony in the back of the newsletter. A full page was devoted to encouraging generous contributions to the Human Relations Day offering, "As your pastor, I, too, encourage you to give and give and give, not til it hurts, but rather til it helps."

Soon after that newsletter, he and the congregation would learn from my coverage what that money was doing in Holmes County, Mississippi. The Human Relations Day offering was the chief supporter of Sheila Collins' network.

That pastor and his congregation had failed to get candid, gracious responses from the Protestant hierarchy in New York City and now were spewing their distrust in front of 40 million Americans on TV.

There was a lesson in that.

I'd never met him or talked to him and didn't know whether I agreed with him on much of anything. But I knew enough of what Michael LeSaux knew to understand the frustration.

South Africa Conference Revisited

Not too many minutes into "60 Minutes," Safer talked about the South Africa conference. My heart sped up. *With the way this program was bashing the nation's Protestant leadership, I don't need my name attached to this,* I thought.

Marti Galovic, the show's producer, had come to the *Reporter's* Dallas offices the year before to talk to us about my South Africa conference story. She interviewed Spurgeon and me in his grotto. Spurgeon took control of the session and was extremely cautious, giving uncharacteristically short answers. He said afterwards that he anticipated a hatchet job on the church and didn't want to assist in that. I gave Marti a copy of my story and some background papers.

Safer didn't mention us at all but attributed his statement about the conference to the FBI. It turned out that Marti had discovered that the FBI had investigated the conference and reported its findings in July 1982 to the House Permanent Select Committee on Intelligence.

I hadn't heard about that.

Members of Congress were told that the supposedly church-sponsored conference was an example of "a commonplace Soviet tactic of creating a conference to focus on an issue for which there exists broad support in a way that direct Soviet involvement is not apparent." Safer told his giant audience that the FBI discovered the conference "was run by the U.S. Communist Party and was entirely manipulated by the Soviet Union."

Strong words! And to think I remained "persona barely grata" in many church offices for my first-hand report, which merely had said the conference "appeared" to be manipulated by "pro-Soviet" forces!

At the end of the show I took the eight-minute drive over to the *Reporter* offices and started writing my story for that week's paper. Sharon Mielke had reserved a three-column, nine-inch hole.

"60 Minutes / Alleged leftist support by NCC, WCC probed," was the headline we decided on for my description of the show's main points.

I noted that Safer had provided no examples of NCC money given to a government or a revolutionary movement. He had, however, provided more details about several organizations receiving grants from the NCC which he said have demonstrated support for Marxist governments and Marxist revolutionary movements, particularly in their literature, but not in guns.

I called Warren Day, NCC communications officer, who was ready with a quote for the Monday morning newspapers. Bishop James Armstrong and Claire Randall, the NCC's president and chief executive, lamented the program's "irresponsible selectivity." Instead of the thousands of churches which support the councils of churches, "60 Minutes" focused only on the Logansport church, they said.

At the end of the story, I gave an address for people to write for a point-by-point NCC response to charges made on the TV show. The NCC was deluged by requests the next week.

Paper-Storm of Rebuttals

Many of the NCC member-denominations put out their own defenses. It was a paper-storm of rebuttals in private mailings and reprints in church publications.

At 10:30 a.m. the day after "60 Minutes," the *Reporter* staff began a meeting that overran lunch by a few hours. The key question Spurgeon had for us was, What is our responsibility both as a news organization and as a part of the church to deal with the questions and allegations raised on the program and by a *Reader's Digest* attack a few weeks earlier?

We didn't like the "60 Minutes" approach. I was especially disappointed that legitimate questions were not posed or were lost in the sensationalism of supposed revolution links. Those links were made with barely a shred of justification for using those images. I complained of that later to CBS people.

I told my colleagues that we ought to do our own investigation, the one "60 Minutes" had flubbed. I particularly thought we ought to concentrate on the charges of lying and definitely see if we could clear up or prove the image of gun-running. Others weren't so sure.

Spurgeon didn't really want to talk about an investigation right then. He was most interested in the *Reporter's* setting up a forum to which we would invite representatives from the NCC and critics, such as the Institute on Religion and Democracy which was featured prominently on "60 Minutes" and in an earlier scorching article in *Reader's Digest.*

"Such an event would be rife with potential for leaders of the NCC and its member-denominations to seize the offensive and begin converting many negative perceptions to positives," Spurgeon observed.

Our staff members spent the rest of the day making up a list of potential participants and talking logistics. We started contacting people and floating our balloon. We also decided to cover the news of responses as it happened.

"Support and questions: Survey finds mild response but many wanting answers," headlined my February 4 story, after I spent a week calling church offices around the country.

At the end of January I attended a Methodist Joint Panel on International Affairs meeting in New York. Members said the United States was entering a new McCarthyism era like the 1950s.

Bishop Jesse DeWitt of Chicago commented that he believed the church's critics had organized in the way mainline Protestant churches organized during the '50s when various church people created all kinds of coalitions to bring about desired changes in society, including less paranoia about communism. But those coalitions had broken down, while others who were strongly anti-communist had banded together in their own coalitions, he explained.

The panel, a supporter of that Soviet-manipulated conference on South Africa, determined it must fight back to turn away the new "Mc-Carthyism" sweep, I reported, in "New McCarthyism era possible / Criticisms demand response, UM leaders say."

I chuckled at the meeting as I thought of another possible head-line, "Panel fears anti-communists behind every bush."

On February 7, Bishop Armstrong severely disappointed Spurgeon by blessing him for his foresight but adding he doubted sponsorship by the *Reporter* of a reconciliation conference would be acceptable to the NCC leadership.

Concern in the churches mounted, however. We began to get reports of people pulling their membership out of some churches and of whole congregations withholding their denominational offerings because of concern about the charges of "60 Minutes." They didn't trust their New York church officials enough to believe the responses. United Methodist district superintendents of the entire Southeastern region urged creation of a special investigating committee to determine if any of the charges had any truth to them.

"All Of It?"
It was clear, though, from checking with church leadership that nobody was in the mood to do further investigation. *That is a big mistake,* I thought.

Trust is everything when a person puts money into an offering plate. It really wasn't reassuring to be told that only tiny parts of those offerings actually went to the NCC; a loss of trust in how even a small part of gifts are used can affect the attitude about the rest of them. People needed credible evidence that they could feel good about the tiny amounts of their money going to the NCC, and they wanted to know that all their offerings were being used well.

Our little Jeremy had reminded us of that the last autumn. After spending the night with a friend in East Dallas, he'd come home terribly excited to tell us he'd seen a man digging around inside a garbage can.

"Why would he do that?" he asked.

We explained that the man probably was hungry and that hundreds, if not thousands, of people in the city didn't have enough to eat. We said that was why Shirley and I, through our Sunday school class and the congregation, had helped with several emergency food and clothing efforts. Jeremy was horrified. The image of that man in the garbage can haunted him.

That Sunday between church-school classes and worship, Jeremy approached Shirley at a table set up in the traffic flow.

"What are you doing?" he asked.

"I'm selling Christmas cards. I'm on the Outreach Commission, and we'll use the money for projects that help hungry people."

Jeremy looked at the cards a moment. "Can I buy some?"

"Well, they cost $5."

During the next week's family race-and-test-of-love endurance trial—also known as getting ready for church—Jeremy remembered to check his bank, where he'd just deposited enough money to buy the Star Wars figures he'd been saving for.

At church, he approached the Christmas card table again. He thrust the wad of bills and change forward, then pulled it back.

"Are you sure this will help the hungry people like the man in the garbage can?"

"Yes," Shirley answered.

Jeremy still hesitated.

"All of it?" he asked.

Shirley pulled a card out, turned it over and showed him a line that said all the proceeds would fund projects for the hungry. Satisfied, he parted with his $5.

His gift was, relatively, far greater than our tithe, but we understood his caution. We regarded the tithes and offerings as money belonging to God, to be put to use only in ways that glorified God. We had great confidence that various church agencies which shared that money wrought more good than any other organization we might have chosen. All the more cause, we thought, why the church organizations should be open to the utmost scrutiny.

That's one reason I was bothered by the angry defensiveness to the "60 Minutes" assault. There were reasons to be angry, for sure, but all resources seemed to be devoted to rebutting "60 Minutes," with no acknowledgement that some of the criticisms deserved to be probed in a more thoughtful way. Based on previous experiences, I feared that some of the rebuttals might contain half-truths, thus justifying some of the charges made on "60 Minutes."

Even most daily newspapers and magazines wrote defenses of the NCC or at least criticisms of the attacks. That was a good public media

balance to "60 Minutes'" overwrought, negative reporting. The NCC
and WCC rarely got public media attention except to be scorched with
withering denunciation. They deserved better.

I addressed a letter to CBS in early February, commenting on my
small role in helping with the research. I suggested that the network
ought to consider looking for achievement stories in the NCC.

> For instance, it was an NCC delegation that was essen-
> tial to the bargaining for the release of the Amerasian
> children last fall. But I don't believe one word was said
> about that role in the national media.
>
> As your program said, the NCC primarily is involved
> in a lot of non-controversial, heart-warming activities. That
> work is not just syrup. There's some real guts to it. That's
> why major news media ought to have reporters regularly
> scouring the churches for stories that relate to that segment
> of our society. More than 50 percent of Americans make
> their church an important part of their lives. They spend
> more money there than on any other charity and most busi-
> nesses. Why does the church rarely appear in the national
> media except when there's some sort of scandal involved?

Nonetheless, I said in the letter that I felt some key issues about
church honesty remained unanswered.

More Wanted

I had a small stack of letters on my desk from readers who felt the
475 Riverside bunch was being let off the hook too easily and accusing me of whitewashing everything. A California man who criticized
my coverage wrote:

> It is my opinion that McCarthyism is not a fault con-
> fined to the right wing. The left can also be guilty of Mc-
> Carthyism, since the essence of McCarthyism is to repeat
> unsubstantiated allegations. To repeat charges of Mc-
> Carthyism without substantiating such allegations is in it-
> self McCarthyism, and this is what you did.

He said I had cavalierly dismissed charges against the NCC by referring people to the NCC's point-by-point denial papers; I should have investigated the charges myself.

He suggested I would find that the church leaders were trying to recover lost zeal in traditional Christian doctrines through a zeal to political causes evident in the theology of liberation. He continued:

> I am sympathetic to some aspects of this theology, such as helping the poor and oppressed and changing political and social conditions to alleviate their suffering. But it seems to me that it is too easy for Christians on the left to follow the example of right-wing Christians in making a religion out of their political views. They become less capable of feeling compassion for the suffering of people in "liberated" countries. . .like Vietnam.

I found myself being accused of rightist and leftist McCarthyism from the left and the middle and of white-washing Marxist misdeeds from the right.

A lot of old, untreated wounds were festering out there.

I thought of the strange experience Shirley had shortly after we moved to Dallas. A mother of a boy in nursery school with Jeremy told Shirley that she just had to tell her how difficult it was to not hate her. Shirley was astonished as the woman went on to say that she was connected with Wycliffe Bible translators and was a friend of a man killed by leftist guerrillas in South America.

"I know you are a Methodist and that the Methodists support organizations that support the guerrillas," she said. "I know you wouldn't have wanted to kill my friend, but you are partly responsible."

That was three years ago. Now, "60 Minutes" and *Reader's Digest* were pushing the same idea. If there was truth to this, it should be exposed and acknowledged inside the church. If false, the *Reporter* might have the credibility to shut down a lot of false rumors.

Many church officials were not helping their credibility by spending more time attacking the Christian intentions of the church people in the Institute on Religion and Democracy than dealing with the legitimate questions the critic group had posed. I shared the officials' keen dislike for the ultra-right foundations that were providing grants to the IRD. That might affect how one weighed the IRD's criticism, but it shouldn't have affected at all whether the IRD's questions deserved honest answers. It reminded me of the pro-business attempt to discredit Nestlé boycotters.

Heavy Baggage And An Empty Suitcase

When it was clear that nobody else was going to pursue those and other unanswered questions, the *Reporter's* editorial staff agreed that we would launch an investigation. We limited it to the NCC because it was closer to home and because the United Methodist Church dominated the funding.

Sharon Mielke gathered Garlinda Burton and me into her office where we worked out key questions to pursue. We plotted strategy to get them answered and went to work.

After a couple of weeks of research through the mail and over the phone, Garlinda and I flew to New York for a week at the fabled 475 Riverside Drive featured so forbiddingly in the "60 Minutes" episode.

Each morning at the entrance, we had to cross through a picket line of clerical employees chanting scripture and union slogans for better pay. The uninspiring, boxlike building looked more like a business than a church and reminded me of the Procter & Gamble Company's headquarters in Cincinnati, with similar security procedures. After all, 475 Riverside was the corporate and bureaucratic headquarters of much of American Protestantism.

On the West Side of Manhattan overlooking the Hudson River, across the street from the cathedral-like Riverside Church and a block away from Columbia University, the building was widely known as the "God Box." The majority of the money controlled here came from the pious Midwestern and conservative Southern churches, where many constituents harbored innate suspicions about anything located so solidly in the fleshpots of New York City.

Garlinda and I were armed with questions, and I with an empty, large, brown Samsonite suitcase, to find out if the radical epithets so long slung at this power center had any basis.

Perhaps it was the suitcase into which I began stacking documents. Maybe it was the *Reporter's* reputation for not coddling clerics or maybe it simply was the shell-shocked paranoia after the *Reader's Digest* and "60 Minutes" onslaught. At any rate, I was not welcomed into the NCC offices with total openness and delight. Secretaries gave me little help in getting to department heads. Department heads had little time for me.

In one office I visited early in the week, I realized I was carrying some heavy baggage, and I don't mean my suitcase. In that office I mainly was pursuing a story for the next week's *Reporter* about threats on the Council of Churches in South Africa. The man I was interviewing kept looking at my calling card and me and then, instead of answering my question, asked: "You're the one that wrote that story about our conference aren't you?"

"What conference?" I asked, feigning ignorance.

"On South Africa. We haven't forgotten."

NCC people involved in the campaign for Eddie Carthan and the United League of Holmes County were totally unhelpful. Those tied in with the Nestlé boycott chewed on my ear about why I should distrust the Methodist task force.

I'd been seen around this building before.

But I'd also written defenses of the NCC against Religious Right attacks and given detailed, sympathetic coverage of some of the NCC's efforts. I tried to remind people of that as I made my rounds.

Garlinda was doing fairly well on her rounds, as her primary assignment was to tour all NCC offices and report on the unsung great work of the NCC. Harriet Ziegler, Warren Day's assistant in the NCC communications office, was leading her around on that tour.

Warren and Harriet had been very encouraging to us when we arranged our visit by telephone. They said the NCC had nothing to hide. Although they stated that they knew we could bite, they felt we would come out with a mainly positive report if we were fair and that our saying it would mean more than the church rebuttals in convincing the folks in the pews. Their refreshing and enlightened, if a bit cautious, openness was shared by a lot of people in the building, I was pleased to discover by the end of the week.

But the first day was different. After several hours of resistance on my solo journey around the NCC offices I ran into Harriet and Garlinda in the hallway and told them of my difficulties. Harriet took my *Reporter's* note pad, opened it to a clean sheet and scrawled, "To whom it may concern, Roy Howard Beck is a legitimate reporter. Please give him your time and consideration in his inquiries. (Signed) Harriet Ziegler"

I paper-clipped the note to my shirt pocket where it could be seen when I pulled back my suit jacket. I felt like a plainclothes detective or maybe a school kid with proof of permission to be walking in the halls. It worked like a charm. If only legitimacy were always so easy to attain.

In Search Of A Cause For Tilted Image

Based on our readers' letters the key question people had was the one about leftist political ideology.

For years critics had complained that the ideology and not Christian principles guided the NCC. Defenders just as steadfastly contended there was absolutely nothing to the charge. But the charges and widespread impressions of an ideological tilt always continued. Why?

I depended a lot on a relatively new *Reporter* employee, Stephen Swecker, to help me tackle the question. Stephen was our East Coast intellectual who was taking over the duties of drafting editorials. He was trained in Christian social ethics under Phil Wogaman at Wesley Seminary in Washington, D.C. and had almost completed a doctorate at Boston Seminary. A sensitive, caring, pastoral-type of minister, Stephen was learning the journalistic ropes while adding keen insight to our discussions of how best to approach issues.

I knew that most ways of measuring a "tilt" could be shot down as using worldly and not Christian values. Stephen suggested I measure the NCC by the values *it* claimed were important.

NCC defenders kept saying the organization only operated within policy statements approved by its governing board, a collection of representatives from its 32 member-denominations.

I borrowed the bound volumes of policy statements and carried them to a vacant desk made available to me by the United Methodist News Service on another floor of 475. I found that since 1963 the NCC had operated under a human-rights policy that detailed some 50 freedoms and rights believed to be due to all persons everywhere in the world. Any government's denials of these rights and freedoms inherent to a person's worth before God, "are not simply a crime against humanity; they are a sin against God."

That would be my measure, I decided. It would not be based on a secular U.S. or Western idea of freedom but on rights believed by the NCC to be God-given and universal.

I began calling human rights organizations to find if their judgments could be used as a way to determine if the NCC was following its own human-rights policy in a balanced way or if there really was an ideological bias.

I found that Freedom House's Annual Comparative Survey of Freedoms judged nations on almost exactly the same criteria as found in the NCC policy. As an advocacy organization, Freedom House had a conservative reputation. But the part of its staff who worked full time on the survey of freedom had proven itself committed not to ideologies but to measuring each nation only by the freedom standards. By adding Amnesty International's rather narrow but important survey on political prisoners, I had the NCC values covered.

Garlinda and I spent hours poring over every press release issued the last five years by the NCC and every resolution passed by the governing board to find out what the NCC had been telling the public about itself. We listed on a yellow legal pad every action related to human rights. "Sixty Minutes" had us counting.

Soon after we had arrived in New York, Garlinda admitted to being wary of the whole project. As a black woman, she said, she had treasured the NCC's work for social and economic justice. In 1981, not long out of a college in Tennessee where she'd been a rabble-rousing columnist, Garlinda had come to us by way of a feisty stint at a daily newspaper in a "very white" Iowa town. Whether standing her ground or bellowing with husky laughter, the short, young reporter was rarely a receding presence.

Garlinda made it clear she wasn't going to be a part of a bald effort to "get" the NCC.

Yet, the documents, especially since they were the NCC's own words about itself, began to convince her, as well as me, that the NCC had a problem.

We kept on reading even after 4:30 p.m. when the offices emptied and workers hurried to catch their car pools and trains for long commutes into the suburbs. The more we read the clearer became the reason for the NCC's leftist reputation in the public mind.

The 36 nations with the worst human-rights records during the last five years were almost evenly split between right-wing and left-wing governments, according to Freedom House, with a similar split suggested by Amnesty International's reports.

Thus, if the NCC operated without regard to ideology and only on the basis of speaking for the oppressed, one might expect a somewhat evenly divided set of actions showing concern for victims of communist and other Marxist governments (such as Vietnam) and victims of military and semi-fascist governments (such as South Korea).

But the NCC had been telling the world something different.

Callous, Insensitive Neglect Of Oppressed Victims

Garlinda and I found that four-fifths of the NCC's human-rights' actions were related to abuses of people by right-wing governments. And even that purely mathematical statistic severely understated the tilt. That was because we counted a month-long flurry of actions on a single issue as one "action" in our tabulations. A rather bland resolution counted the same.

We found that NCC actions aimed at helping victims of left-wing governments almost always were superficial, single occurrences. Often, a resolution was the extent of it. Actions to help victims of right-wing governments, however, were extensive affairs with demonstrations, consultations, speeches before Congress and the United Nations.

"Look at this," I said to Garlinda. "Here's a case where the NCC expressed concern about the Siberian Seven, the Soviet Pentecostalist family that was in a sort of house arrest back in 1979. It doesn't mention anything about why or what they were trying to flee, nor whether religious persecution was a factor."

I held up another press release, "But here's a situation in 1980 where the right-wing government of Taiwan jailed a Presbyterian minister. The NCC not only expresses concern for him but also condemns religious repression in general in Taiwan. It held a public forum to fully air 'systemic problems' related to Taiwan's government."

When I saw condemnation of the right-wing government of Turkey for expropriating five churches, I remembered reading public news reports during the same period of the left-wing government in Bulgaria closing and demolishing a number of church buildings which had large worshipping congregations. I looked for some comment on that. There was none.

Did the tilt matter? we asked ourselves.

It wasn't so much the tilt as the neglect that mattered to victims of left-wing oppression. It was a callous, insensitive neglect. Ignoring those victims or dismissing their plight with a token resolution violated NCC policy which regarded citizens of communist and Marxist-led countries as no less children of God and no less deserving of God-given freedoms than citizens under right-wing rule.

Confronted with our findings, many NCC staff people acknowledged that indeed a tilt existed. The reason, they explained, was that the U.S. government had more clout with the right-wing governments, and the U.S. itself sometimes was supportive of the repression. Thus, the NCC focused its pressure where it could achieve the most results— on its own government and allies.

I tended to believe that was an accurate explanation for most 475 Riverside workers I knew and talked with that week. It wasn't a matter of their being Marxists or Marxist-sympathizers as their worst critics charged, but of their concentrating resources where they would be most effective.

But what about the millions of human-rights victims under left-wing oppression? If Christians in the U.S. and European democracies didn't speak up for those victims, who would? Was it right or realistic to leave it to Soviet Christians to speak prophetically for the victims of oppression in Lithuania, Angola and Czechoslovakia, to name a few?

It wasn't just the neglect that mattered. I believed that the tilt, although it was in favor of victims of right-wing abuse, actually worked against those victims, too, because the tilt made the churches' human-rights work appear at times to be more of a political movement than a fulfillment of Christian ministry. Conservative members of the churches were easily turned off by what appeared to be an imbalanced "picking on" the United States and its allies, while conveniently winking at similar human-rights problems on the left. Thus, the church was denied the prayers, financial and other kinds of support of large portions of its members to help victims of right-wing oppression.

Garlinda left the document search each night at about mid-evening. She was staying with an uncle who lived in New York. He was pretty squeamish about New York safety, insisting that she not ride the subways and sending a taxi for her. I gave her a rough time for leaving the white guy to roam the subways alone.

Sometime after each midnight I left the nearly darkened building and walked a few lonely blocks down into the infamous Broadway subway station from whence I had emerged two years earlier for the Soviet-manipulated church conference. Garlinda's uncle would not have approved of the characters who shared the platform with me. Of course, Garlinda said he wouldn't have approved of me, either.

Upon arrival near my mid-town hotel, I prowled the streets for something to eat and found myself resenting Frank Sinatra. "I want to wake up in a town that never sleeps, New York, New York," I kept singing under my breath as I approached one "closed" sign after another on Manhattan eateries. I had to go without food each evening because I couldn't get back into 475 Riverside if I left to get supper, and I was famished by this time. *The lyrics oughta say, "I have to go to sleep in a town that never eats, late night, New York,"* I thought as I plugged quarters into a hotel candy bar machine.

"Not If You Want To Stay Alive"

Maybe it was the lack of nutrition that clouded my mind one morning on the subway back up to 475. I got off at my regular 116th Street stop. But I started feeling disoriented even as I climbed the stairs. Loud urban-blues music blared down the tunnel. *Maybe there's a street carnival going on,* I thought.

But when I stepped into bright sunshine, it was like one of those "Twilight-Zone" movies where a person comes up from a bomb shelter and where a town used to be only rubble remains. Broadway had been flattened. I was surrounded by half-demolished buildings, rubble-filled vacant lots and a few run-down stores, one of which had giant speakers hanging over the door providing accompaniment to the scene.

"You lost?" an old black man said, approaching me and talking in a hushed, private way.

"I'm a little confused," I said. "This is 116th Street isn't it?"

"Yes."

"Where's Columbia University?"

"You're on the wrong line, son. That's 116th and Broadway. This is 116th and Lennox. You done got out in the middle of Harlem." I looked around at the crowded sidewalks. I guessed he must be right.

"You'd better get right back down there and catch the next train out of here," my acquired shepherd said.

"Why? Because I'm white? I don't mind. I can just walk 116th Street over that way a few blocks and that ought to get me there, hadn't it?" I pointed west.

"You can't get there from here."

This sounds like the Ozarks, I thought.

"There's a park in between," the old man said.

"I'll just walk through the park."

"Not if you want to stay alive. . . .Drugs," he whispered suggestively.

I thought, *Either this old guy is having a great time putting one over on a gullible outsider or he's being awfully considerate of my well-being.* I chose to chance erring on the side of trusting him and caught the next subway to where it parallelled the line I'd intended to be on in the first place.

Troubling Records In The Vietnam File

Trust was a big issue in my continuing research inside 475. Perhaps more important than the ideological tilt question was the one raised by Lutheran minister Neuhaus about lying, although it tied into the tilt subject.

Neuhaus specifically cited officials of the NCC and other mainline Protestant denominations for painting a "rosy picture" of Indochina after the U.S. withdrawal in spite of large numbers of people being imprisoned and tortured. In addition, he lashed out, those same church officials have "consorted with the persecutors of the church of Christ."

The official rebuttals had stated categorically that the NCC "does not fund or otherwise support Communist governments or movements or any other government anywhere in the world."

As I dug into financial and other documents, I found contradictions. In fact, hundreds of thousands of dollars of NCC aid to Vietnam had gone to a quasi-government organization there. The NCC designated where the aid was to be used, but the specified projects were governmental ones. That wasn't emergency food aid, but non-emergency development aid intended to improve the quality of life.

Confronted with my findings, NCC officials said their assurances of no aid to communist governments had been a "shorthand." They said they had little choice in a centrally-planned economy except to go through the government. They acknowledged that their aid probably strengthened the power of the government, but that it also strengthened Vietnamese churches in the eyes of government leaders because the NCC insisted on their participation in the planning for the use of the aid.

I checked on how the NCC-aided Vietnamese government was treating its citizens during that time. Amnesty International condemned it for mass detentions for political reasons and mistreatment of intellectuals and people of Chinese origin. Freedom House gave Vietnam its worst (number 7) rating on political rights and a number

6 rating on civil rights.

During that time of NCC aid through the Vietnam government, the NCC also was involved in a massive effort to help the tens of thousands of boat people who were risking their lives to flee that government. I looked through all the NCC press releases for actions that expressed concern for the conditions driving the Vietnamese people to sea. The pronouncements and actions to help the boat people rarely mentioned anything about why they were refugees. There was no record of NCC actions concerning Vietnam's aggressive abuses of human rights.

Late one night in my lighted corner of a dark office, I ran across a blood-curdling document. It showed an NCC delegation returning from Vietnam and talking to the public about how the Vietnam government placed a high value on "respect for human dignity." One member of the delegation claimed that most of the refugees fleeing Vietnam were people who had enjoyed "the good life" from the spoils of U.S. involvement there and now were fleeing for economic reasons.

So much for the church as a champion of the oppressed.

I was pleased a little later that night to find a later NCC statement placing some blame on the Vietnam government for the boat-people problem. But it also stated that the NCC would continue to send aid to the Vietnam government development project. NCC officials told me they had been relaying their human rights concerns to Vietnamese officials privately.

Richard Neuhaus' language on "60 Minutes" seemed a bit intemperate in describing a somewhat complex Christian aid program. The NCC's continuing presence in Vietnam, even when the U.S. government eschewed any role, may have helped prevent the bloodbath so many predicted.

Nonetheless, the NCC documents convinced me that the NCC had been involved in a lot of half-truths and convoluted priorities that suggested insensitivities to victims. Even well-intentioned people through history have been guilty of "consorting with persecutors."

Now-You-See-It-Now-You-Don't Links

I took a taxi over to Neuhaus's Manhattan townhouse. I was most interested as he told how he and many of the 475 Riverside people he was criticizing were allies during the 1960s in opposing the U.S. military involvement in Vietnam. Neuhaus was one of the founders of

Clergy and Laity Concerned which led the religious opposition. He said he and others split from the group about 1976 over the human-rights situation once the communist government took over. The fundamental difference, he observed, was that people like him opposed the Vietnam war as an aberration of U.S. principles. The others opposed the war as representative of an evil U.S. system. They don't care so much about victims in Vietnam as about punishing the United States, he said.

It was a dichotomy of reform or revolution that I'd run into often in my reporting of religious controversy. Why do you choose revolution over reform? Because you feel the chances of reform are hopeless or because you feel so much hate for the power to be toppled?

It seemed to me that the radical groups on the left and right were mobilized by hate. I remembered Bishop Armstrong referring to that just a year earlier, "I am alarmed by a new mood of permissive hate-fulness—that it's perfectly all right to think violent thoughts and enter into unethical practices if for the right reasons." He was referring to right wing religious activist groups. But his words seemed to apply to many of the organizations with which his NCC had links.

Trying to put your finger on the church definitely siding with those groups was a slippery business, though.

We constantly found the NCC and other Protestant agencies being linked with radical groups. But the church leaders usually denied any real responsibility for words and actions from those groups that drew criticism from church members.

Garlinda was trying to track down an example we had pulled from the "60 Minutes" presentation, The Interreligious Task Force on El Salvador and Central America. In 1981 it prepared a background statement that included explanations of how the Democratic Revolutionary Front, the political arm of the Marxist guerrillas in El Salvador, was the legitimate representative of the majority of people in that country. A unit of the NCC included the statement in information packets mailed to churches nationwide.

When some churches criticized the ideological bias of the task force statement, the NCC's Latin American office denied responsibility, saying it had no control over the independent group.

That same task force also had coordinated a speaking tour through five U.S. cities for officials of the Democratic Revolutionary Front. *The Guardian*, an independent U.S. Marxist newspaper, touted the tour as "sponsored" by the NCC. The NCC, when criticized by some church members, denied any connection or responsibility.

So was the NCC connected to the task force or not?

Garlinda and I combed the labyrinth of NCC offices and found the controversial "independent" task force on the sixth floor. It was surrounded by NCC cubicles and desks and was on the same floor as the NCC's Latin America office that denied any accountable link. The "non-linked" task force got the space rent-free from the NCC, Garlinda discovered. Also, all task force bookkeeping was done by the NCC financial office at no charge.

Some of the "confusion" that the NCC somehow was linked with task force activities might have been related to the fact that it sometimes advertised its activities, like the tour of the El Salvadoran revolutionary front, on letterhead stationary borrowed from adjoining NCC desks.

The task force had received some NCC grants. Harriet explained that the task force was started as a private project of some of the NCC staff. The task force had formal endorsement by the NCC's Latin American office.

Yet, the NCC claimed no responsibility for any of the task force's activities.

Garlinda was losing some of her good feelings from the "unsung-story" tour because of the run-around she was getting from the task force's two executives. The only answers they would give her were, "We work out of a Christian concern for the poor and the suffering. We shouldn't have to answer the questions of insecure critics."

Playgrounds For Hobby Horses

Meanwhile I was nosing around the building finding more examples supporting the growing theory—pressed by, for one, James Wall of the liberal *Christian Century*—that many NCC offices were being used as a political playground for staff members of denominational agencies and the NCC at 475 to ride personal hobby horses. It simply was dishonest to set up or support radical groups and let them use the NCC name when it gave credibility but to deny NCC responsibility when the groups were criticized.

I was finding another blatant untruth in the massive church-sent rebuttals of "60 Minutes." Nearly all included phrases like, "Representatives of the member denominations oversee and approve all the work of the NCC. The 260 members of the NCC's Governing Board are appointed by the member communions and are accountable to them."

Members of local congregations were encouraged to use "established channels" to voice criticisms. But I found those channels nearly impossible to find.

Accountability might have been possible if the Governing Board had more power. But I learned something insiders were well aware of: the Governing Board had no say in most actions and expenditure of money by some 50 NCC program offices. Each of those offices, like the one on Latin America, had its own oversight committee that had nothing to do with the Governing Board.

The oversight committee members sometimes were self-selected and in some ways, self-perpetuating. They consisted primarily of staff members of denominational agencies on other floors of 475. In their own agencies those staff people were required to get approval for their actions from their agency's directors elected from across the church, but on the NCC oversight committees, they *were* the directors.

In the NCC documents, I found many examples of where denominational staff people voted on the NCC oversight committees to use money supplied by their agency to the NCC to support a project. Then they'd use that NCC support to persuade their own agency's directors to kick in direct support of the project.

It dawned on me how the Eddie Carthan campaign snowballed.

A couple of denominational staff people enlisted some others with whom they rode in the 475 elevators and ate with in the 475 cafeteria. They organized the bogus investigation tour to Mississippi, used that to get NCC-Governing-Board support, then used that to persuade their own agencies to join in the "broad ecumenical movement."

A denominationally diverse 475 car pool could cook up a scheme and quickly make it appear that several of America's giant and diverse denominations had studied an issue and concluded a clear moral vision of the answer.

So how about a member of a denomination contacting the real powers?

I went from one NCC office to another for a list of the people on the some 50 oversight committees. Nobody seemed to know of such a list. I checked with some denominational ecumenical offices to see if they knew what members of their denominations served on the committees. They didn't know. So much for working through established channels.

Garlinda and I flew back to Dallas with a bulging suitcase and dizzy heads.

Terminal Highjinks Finish Off A Story

We had one more trip to make before trying to write. We wanted to confront NCC president Bishop Armstrong with everything we had found so he could set us straight where we were in error and so we could give the NCC a chance to have its explanation represented fully. The *Reporter* staff felt we needed to lay out our yellow legal pads in person.

The bishop was in the midst of a busy schedule and could give us only an hour-and-a-half.

Timing was of the essence. Air schedules were horrible. We couldn't get a direct flight to Indianapolis and had to have a layover on the way. We had to leave at 7 a.m. and would not get there until afternoon.

Garlinda was nervous. She didn't like the way I cut my schedules short. She'd never missed a plane and didn't intend to start. I told her not to worry, that I'd pick her up at her apartment at 6 a.m. That would get us to the airport 30 minutes early, which was a compromise between her favored longer time and my favored 10 minutes.

I awoke the next morning at 6:00 with the phone ringing. It was Garlinda. I'd slept through my alarm. She had a few choice words about my accountability, but I told her we could still make the flight.

Garlinda jumped from my car at the terminal door.

"You get in the doorway of that plane and refuse to move until I've parked this car and join you," I ordered. My plan was to park in the one-hour parking right there and call Dan Louis when we got to our next city and have him arrange for somebody to drive out and move my car to the proper parking lot.

Garlinda went running through the terminal. She did not look happy. She was not a jogger.

As I dashed around the corner and up to the concourse where our plane was leaving, I saw Garlinda walking toward me.

"It's left already?" I asked. "But it's only five after!" A whole new set of connections got us to Indianapolis just in time for Indiana communications director Jim Steele to pick us up and rush us into our meeting with Bishop Armstrong.

The bishop had us sit on a couch next to a window with a table in front of us. He sat on the other side of the table. We laid out everything. Garlinda and I had rehearsed on the plane so we could do it clearly and quickly.

"What do you think?" I asked at the end.

The activist bishop put his feet on the table, leaned back and spoke deliberately, as if dictating.

"You have done research that I'm not sure has been done before, but I'm not surprised at what appears to be an imbalance. Period. New graph." The bishop looked startled at what he had said and began to laugh with the two of us. He really *was* dictating—a bishop for the media age.

Armstrong gave reasons for stressing human-rights abuses in right-wing countries and for using "quiet diplomacy" with left wing governments. I read him a recent Amnesty International statement about the importance of not only balance and impartiality regarding governments of different ideologies but of the *appearance* of balance. It also emphatically stated the need for public expressions of concerns.

"I have to agree with that," the bishop said. "The NCC must devote far more attention to the mistreatment of people by their left-wing governments. We can find ways to speak out without endangering the persons we are trying to help. The imbalance you have found in our actions hurts our influence."

He also agreed that lines of responsibility were a mess at the NCC. The Nestlé boycott imbroglio had given him a personal taste of it. As a member of the United Methodist Infant Formula Task Force, he felt Nestlé was ready to negotiate a final settlement. But as president of the NCC he was powerless to budge the oversight committee of the NCC-related organization that absolutely refused to accept those negotiating conditions. He expressed great hope that an NCC presidential commission currently studying ways to reform the NCC would propose structural changes to improve the situation. We got an unscheduled extra half-hour from him before he whisked out of the building.

Jim Steele rushed us back to the airport. When he pulled up at the terminal, we had only a couple of minutes. I looked at Garlinda's shoes and remembered a failure that morning to emulate the success O.J. Simpson always found in catching his plane in TV commercials.

"I'll run ahead this time," I said. "You just try to keep an eye on me and come along as fast as you can. I'll hold the plane."

The Indianapolis airport was a maze. It was a right-turn here and a left-turn there, weaving and bobbing through the pedestrian traffic, tossing my brief case into the scanning machine. When I rounded what seemed to be the dozenth corner, my heart cheered as I saw there still was a line of people at the check-in desk. I strolled up to the line.

"Whew, I missed the plane in Dallas this morning. I thought I'd miss it back tonight," I said to nobody in particular.

One of the businessmen turned and said, "This line is for another flight. They've already closed out the plane to Dallas." He pointed to a stewardess who was closing a door.

"If you see a young, black woman running toward you, wave her that way," I called back to the line of businessmen as I dashed for the door. "Wait. I'm on that plane!"

The stewardess stopped, then picked up a phone, telling the pilots to stop. She looked at my ticket and told me to get on board.

"Uh, can we wait just a minute? I have a companion who'll be coming around the corner any second now."

"It's too late. Get on now or the plane's leaving."

"OK, but if you see a black woman running around the corner, motion her in."

"I don't care what color she is," the black stewardess snapped, "this plane is leaving if she doesn't arrive immediately."

"I just mentioned her color because. . ."

"The plane's leaving," she said sternly.

I turned slowly, but out of the corner of my eye I saw the whole line of businessmen waving wildly in unison in my direction. I turned back and saw Garlinda following their signal. We sprinted down the snorkel and around its final bend where we could see the plane already had pulled away slightly. We leapt the small gap and went crashing into the wall just inside the plane's door and behind the cockpit.

We slowly turned our heads to the right and found ourselves facing a hundred-and-fifty faces in various stages of perplexity. We straightened ourselves up and tried to walk to our seats with the dignity of reporters who had just gotten the final go-ahead to run with some hot stories.

Garlinda never traveled with me again.

The pressure was great to get the stories out. The entire editorial staff stayed at the office almost all one night to plan and haggle about what to report, when and where. We decided to fill two weeks' issues of the paper.

April 1 looked like the right first issue. But we didn't like coming out on April Fool's Day or hitting people with such potentially controversial material on what also was Good Friday. But *Time* magazine already had run a story that said our investigative report was coming out soon, and we felt we needed to run it while interest was high.

Everybody on the staff was involved. John Lovelace flew to Washington to do his own investigation of the Institute on Religion and Democracy. I was carrying the burden of the writing load, though and somewhat typically was missing Spurgeon's deadlines at every step. Everybody was a little frantic. For about 10 days, I rose at 4 a.m., fixed a cup of hot chocolate and and sat down at my home typewriter until 7:15 when I'd drive Jeremy to his bus. I took Andrew to nursery school at 9:00 and was back to writing in the office soon after. I stayed there until 10:00 or 11:00 each evening.

But when that first issue rolled off the press all of us felt the effort had been worth it.

Big Response

The National Christian Reporter and *United Methodist Reporter* ran nearly identical pages the first week in issues publicized through the nation's religion reporters.

"4-1 imbalance found in NCC human rights actions / Documents suggest indifference to leftist abuses," proclaimed the banner headline over my top story and a big graphic.

"Council leaders: Tilt blamed on priorities set by member-denominations," was the head over my story just below it.

"Silence seen benefitting leftist tyranny; NCC must speak louder, president says," introduced Garlinda's and my story from the Armstrong interview.

Garlinda's "Writer finds major unsung story / 'I felt good about the NCC' " started on the bottom of the main news page and jumped to fill most of another. It was a warmly crafted first-person account of how nearly every office at the NCC related to something she used or had used in local churches. It was especially fine in showing how a number of conservative churches such as the Southern Baptist Convention which weren't NCC members, almost secretly were active members of NCC divisions because the NCC work was so essential.

Spurgeon introduced everything with "A letter FROM the editor /
Special report reflects our best effort to determine truth or falsity of
charges against NCC and its supporters." The entire staff helped polish
that and my stories and contributed to a big box of "Findings lay some
myths to rest." Under that was my "NCC in Vietnam: 'Delicate
diplomacy' or 'big lie' argument raised in case study."

Response was immediate.

Despite "60 Minutes'" incredible investigative organization, the
Reporter was seen as having done far more to expose the flaws of the
475 Riverside Drive complex. And most NCC supporters and en-
thusiasts were grateful to the *Reporter* for having put to rest with a
great deal of credibility the inflammatory gun-running-type charges.
That was done mainly by revealing that we couldn't come up with a
single specific allegation of such a thing, let alone proof that such a
thing had occurred.

Warren Day called me from the NCC. "This is just exactly the kind
of critique we need," he said. "The care and caution was so obvious. I
doubt very few people in the NCC have ever done as careful research
as you all have."

He went on into a philosophical discussion on why so many
church agency people tend to identify more with the left when they
veer into political ideology. "The left has better rhetoric. The communists talk about feeding, clothing and housing the poor and giving
them all jobs. It sounds like Jesus' parable of the Last Judgment. You
don't hear right-wing dictators talking like that."

"But we must get beyond rhetoric to see reality," I said.

"I know. I think what you've done reminded us that we aren't
aware of the statistics, of how the leftist governments are as abusive
as the rightist ones."

Naturally, not all million potential readers were pleased.

A few right-wing die-hards still felt we had white-washed the evil
NCC. They wanted a revolution that did away with the NCC, not
reform. They seemed guided by their hate for the institution and by
their entanglement in nationalism that sought baptism of any nation
considered a strategic ally of the United States.

Hatred of U.S. allies and conservative U.S. politicians similarly
seemed to guide several readers on the left.

A Chicago pastor fumed:

Your articles expressed a tragic lack of perspective and
an outright attack on what it is to be engaged in the liberating Gospel of Christ in the 20th century. . . .There is a need
to remember that the Christian perspective is that of being
prophetic and being rejected as we try to bring about a more
just world. Do the opponents not want us to carry out the
call to "love your enemies"? Do those who oppose really
want to create systems that share the earth's resources with
all the people or do their salaries and lifestyles show them
buying into and wishing to maintain their affluence while
the great masses of the world remain oppressed?

I felt we were talking past each other. That letter, like other similar
ones, got a point-by-point response from me.

The primary thrust of our articles was that the NCC has
not been engaged in the liberating Gospel of Christ in half
the repressed world. There was no challenging of the
NCC's liberating work on behalf of victims of right wing
repression.

The man had justified the NCC's tilt/neglect behavior by saying
the NCC has special responsibility for the Western Hemisphere. That
was a wild statement. Part of the NCC's neglect was its failure to speak
up for human-rights' victims in Cuba, Nicaragua and Grenada, all
Marxist-ruled Western nations, while extolling them. The point is not
to do less about abuses by the rightist governments of El Salvador,
Guatemala and others, I wrote, but to do more for the victims of leftists.

Are we to love only our left wing enemies, or do we include our right wing enemies in that? And does loving an
enemy mean extolling that government while it commits
atrocities against its citizens?

Exposing Tangled Power Lines

As news media around the country began to relay some of our
findings we hit the mail with our second issue. "NCC's tangled power
lines: 'Like no other organization anybody likely has ever seen'," was

the banner headline. I'd worked with Mike Hill from our composition department to do an illustration of a tangled marionette that quickly showed the NCC's structural problems.

My story began:

> Trying to sort out the lines of accountability within the National Council of Churches is a lot like trying to operate the strings of a tangled marionette.
> When you pull strings that look like they're connected to arms, the arms don't always move.
> Strings that would appear to control the main body of the NCC are only partly attached.

Garlinda's explosive story on the Interreligious Task Force on El Salvador and Central America ran below. Because Bishop Armstrong had pledged to tackle the problem, she led with him and framed the story as a flaw that was being corrected. "NCC president identifies 'linkage problem' / Latin American task force subject of case study," was the head.

John Lovelace's lengthy probe of the Institute on Religion and Democracy ran under "NCC critic group: 'Conservative adversary' or 'reluctant prosecutor'."

Spurgeon did a two-thirds-page analysis, "Reformed NCC needed: more balance, accountability, strength." Once again he had staked out the militant middle ground he so loved. A stronger NCC was needed, he said, but to be stronger it needed to be more accountable to its member-denominations and unentangled from ideological motives, or the appearance of them. Spurgeon concluded:

> We need to recall Paul's words to the church at Corinth, 'We have this treasure in earthen vessels, to show that the transcendent power belongs to God and not to us. . . .' We urge concerned Christians. . .to recall these words, and to pray that out of this difficult period of division and debate, the Body of Christ may grow stronger and more unified in its witness to the treasure of God's love.

Just to be sure our coverage wasn't forgotten, Spurgeon suggested that readers express their views to their bishops.

We knew that the bishops were resisting efforts to get them to do a full-scale review of the United Methodist Church's relationship with the NCC and WCC. Bishop Finis Crutchfield of Houston, the current president of the Council of Bishops, was pushing the idea but not getting anywhere.

A consistent liberal critic of the *Reporter* in Texas wrote to all bishops, apparently hoping to persuade them not to buy into the reform movement. As he'd often done before, this critic attributed our exposure of flaws in the church to the evangelical Good News caucus. "Must the *Reporter* burp most every time Good News has strong dissident indigestion?" he asked.

A few weeks later, the council met in Little Rock, Arkansas and set up a full-scale review. Bishop Crutchfield told me after the overwhelming vote that it never would have happened without our coverage.

The year-long review committee would find that Methodist agency staff people were among the sources of the NCC's problems. The second installment of our reports brought private response from NCC officials who said that for years their problem had been that the member-denominations did not control their own agency staff people, instead allowing them to move NCC units into actions that squandered the credibility of the NCC as a whole. These officials said they hoped our reports would shake up some denominational officials to take responsibility.

We offered a six-page reprint of the entire package for what seemed to me to be an expensive price. The orders flooded in and continued for years. We sold 40 to 50 thousand. Many religious publications of various denominations chose to advertise our reprints out of a feeling that they would calm the emotions in their own churches and foster creative discussion.

A Kentucky pastor was one of many pledging prayer support to my own personal work.

> For that and the many other contributions that you are making to the life of our church, I just want you to know I appreciate it and am grateful for your sensitivity and your sense of fairness amidst the task.

A high official in a Methodist agency wrote:

In the midst of charges and counter-charges, you have cut through the verbiage to provide information and analysis on the key issues. You have helped us to replace heat with light and emotion with information and reason. You have opened the door for us to build stronger and more faithful ecumenical relationships and ministries. May God help us do that!

Prof. Wagner's comment to me on the need in the church for more information was definitely being affirmed once again.

Our middle-ground style of coverage in the broad American journalism tradition was being noticed in the New York offices of the Religious News Service. For 50 years the National Conference of Christians and Jews had subsidized the service, which was a daily religious news wire to most religious publications and a number of daily newspapers, including some of the nation's largest. Tight financial times had pushed the national conference to put the news service on notice that it had to find a new angel or close down.

RNS leaders said they looked around for an organization that had financial stability and which exemplified the same journalistic commitment to balance as the RNS had pursued. By the end of the year, the *Reporter* was operating RNS and eventually would turn it into a self-supporting subsidiary.

Signs Of Change

In mid-May I flew to San Francisco to observe the NCC Governing Board. We had mailed our special reprint to each member. The presidential panel gave an interim report of its work, and the chairman said the way the NCC operated almost certainly would change within the next two years.

The nation's religion writer corps noted numerous signs that the Governing Board was taking into account the months of stinging criticism. Human-rights actions showed a remarkable richness in their concerns for abuses from all kinds of governments. A major policy statement on Latin America was sent back for more work because of concerns that it presented an unbalanced view. And much talk centered around the inevitability of bringing the NCC's dozens of offices under the control of the Governing Board.

It was an affirmation of hope in the ability of unvarnished information to make a difference. And it indicated promise that the level of trust among grassroots church members for their institutions might be raised. As in all such matters, time would tell.

Unfortunately, I was plunged into other discussions in San Francisco that pointed to more trust problems—far stickier ones.

9

Fidelity

The timing was terrible from a public relations standpoint.

The location wasn't much better.

Considering the public relations nightmare of the past several months, the last thing the National Council of Churches' governing board would appear to have needed was to immediately consider the membership of a "homosexual denomination"—while meeting in San Francisco, no less.

For months the national media spotlight had been on charges against the NCC of leftist ideological excess and lack of fidelity to its own policies and its 32 member-denominations. But the NCC's steps toward responsibly dealing with concerns at its spring meeting didn't get much media attention.

Those steps were mostly lost in the reporting of a more sensational item of business. The long-pending application of the Universal Fellowship of Metropolitan Community Churches just happened to come up for mandatory consideration at the San Francisco meeting.

The 27,000-member, 200-congregation denomination was founded primarily as a church for gay men and lesbian women. Despite its unconventional nature, it met all the NCC requirements for membership: It was Trinitarian in doctrine (belief in God as Father, Son and Holy Spirit), national in scope and had at least 20,000 members in 50 local churches.

The delegations of Presbyterians, United Church of Christ, Disciples of Christ and United Methodists appeared fairly willing to accept the new church on the basis of justice to all groups of people. But the black Baptist, black Methodist, Orthodox, American Baptist and Lutheran denominations expressed unequivocal opposition to accepting that a church could be based on the type of sexual practice of its ministers and members, especially a sexual practice considered invalid in their traditions.

About a fourth of the governing board went to a Universal Fellowship worship service the first night and sat in the balcony to observe. I sat with a group of reporters in a corner.

The Communion service at the altar appeared faithfully to follow "high church" Christian liturgy. But as couples of the same gender embraced and occasionally kissed after receiving the bread and grape juice from their avowed homosexual ministers, it was obvious that this was not just any Christian church.

"It's good to be exposed to this," one liberal Methodist said afterwards, "but I'm afraid my tolerance has been worn out."

As I was to learn on different occasions, the decision for church organizations was much easier than might first appear. They were being asked by the homosexual advocates to do much more than depart from church tradition and accept that two people of the same sex could unite in a lifelong, faithful commitment to each other under the same blessing God gives to a man and a woman in marriage.

Rev. Nancy Wilson, a Universal Fellowship minister, explained to me that her church did not consider lifelong monogamy and sexual fidelity as necessary standards for a Christian lifestyle. Although the denomination performed "Rites of Holy Union" for homosexual couples, it did not necessarily advocate that they live in lifelong monogamous relationships, Rev. Wilson said.

The church leaders made a lot about the fact that a sizeable minority of their members were heterosexuals. Most of them, Rev. Wilson told me, were people with non-traditional lifestyles. The church also conducted rites for heterosexual couples so they could demonstrate their covenant with each other but not commit themselves to a legal or life-long relationship, she added.

The NCC voted overwhelmingly not to accept the denomination.

Rev. Troy D. Perry, founder of the Universal Fellowship, told me the denominations had their heads in the sand, and what many didn't seem to realize was that a substantial percentage of mainline Protestant agency leaders were homosexual. He claimed at least a fourth of those working at 475 Riverside Drive in all the denominational, NCC, WCC and related organizations were homosexuals. They blended easily into New York's influential and large homosexual community, he said.

That was a rather easy claim to make and obviously was designed to bolster his position, I concluded and asked Perry, "Will you name them?" He declined, of course, saying individuals had to make decisions on their own about "coming out of the closet." He insisted, though, that he knew from experience about the preponderance at 475, and that he had talked with many of the homosexual staff people and knew of the others from those talks. I heard him repeat those claims to others in the press corps.

Lifestyle Tales

Walking San Francisco's hilly streets and dining with others in the press corps, the subject of the lifestyles of church leaders came up. Several people said they knew a number of lesbians and gays in high offices at 475 Riverside. Some influential names were tossed around, as well as that of a bishop whose story created a sensation a few years later after his death from AIDS.

I filed the rumors in my memory but essentially forgot about them for awhile, choosing to assume they were only rumors. But as the months passed, more and more stories about agency workers and leaders came my way from a number of sources.

Some people told me of sitting in bars with some of the individuals and getting an earful as the night and the drinks passed. Others had been in gatherings where the travails of homosexual church leaders were discussed openly.

I encountered a meeting like that once at the beginning of my stint at the *Reporter*. My arrival was a surprise to the participants. When I sat down I noticed several people looking awkwardly at me and whispering among themselves. A couple of people eventually asked me to step into the hall.

Several minutes later, a man came out and explained that a number of people were nervous about the presence of the press. The group would allow me to attend the meeting, he said, if I agreed not to quote anybody by name unless given permission.

I realized rather quickly that some of them were homosexuals. Public knowledge of that could ruin their careers. The United Methodist Church recognized practicing homosexuals as "persons of sacred worth" who were welcome as church members but who generally were deemed ineligible for ordination because the sexual practice was considered "incompatible with Christian teaching."

Part of the agenda of the meeting was to talk about increasing and supporting the number of gay men and lesbian women in church leadership. (As the years progressed, several of the national boards and agencies—with many of their members having a very personal stake—joined the effort.)

Bit by bit, there seemed to be some validating of claims made by Troy Perry. Some kind of informal network of lesbians and gays did appear to be present in high Protestant offices.

All of us on the *Reporter* staff were accumulating these rumors and claims. We weren't really probing for them at first. The stories probably were flushed out by the increasing politicization leading up to the United Methodist Church's every-four-year General Conference. More than half the 73 annual conferences were pushing for more explicit prohibitions against homosexuals serving as ordained clergy. Already the United Methodists had one of the most conservative standards among the mainline denominations. But the conferences were stirred by the refusal of Denver-area clergy to dismiss a pastor who had left his wife and children to pursue a public, homosexual lifestyle.

At the *Reporter*, we weren't sure how to handle all the tales. But we talked about them a lot, trying to ascertain their significance. They came from liberals, conservatives, "straights," homosexuals, pastors, lay people, agency staff people and bishops.

One high official at 475 confided to one of us that the reason he couldn't bring about a solution to an entirely unrelated situation was because of the cohesive power of what he euphemistically called "the single women" on staff.

Another 475 staffer said outward gestures among some homosexuals had become common enough in one of the restrooms that higher officials had to ask the employees to "cool it."

We weren't sure how to assess the reports. But even if they were only partly true, they held potential to greatly undermine the support for the denominational and ecumenical agencies at 475 from large numbers of the people in the pews.

My perception was that most local mainline Protestant congregations were not on the lookout to uncover discreet private actions by their members. But homosexual activity was not something most church members wanted their church leaders to model as exemplary behavior.

I began to inquire carefully among some of the severest critics of the church agencies to find out if they'd heard any of the stories.

As it turned out, the critics already were aware of most of the ones we had heard and many more through their networks of ministers, district superintendents and even bishops. We were a bit surprised that they had not unleashed those stories as part of their open criticism of the agencies. But they were as frightened of publicly raising the subject as we were.

Hidden Explanations Of Sexual Politics

Increasingly it was appearing that one couldn't fully understand the complete measure of critics' dissatisfaction with national church leadership without knowing a lot about the sexual conduct of the people in whom they had lost trust. Even some promotions, staff changes and decisions in some agencies couldn't be understood without knowing the sexual politics.

Most everybody, including those of us at the *Reporter*, shrank from confronting the issue, although many thought that painful, open dealing might be preferable to the whispers blowing against the foundations of the churches.

One person who spoke of the advantages of openness was Morris Floyd, gay leader of a United Methodist activist group for gay and lesbian concerns. In a lengthy interview with me, he said many of the church's most creative and committed leaders were achieving only a fraction of what they could because of energy spent concealing their true identity. He only recently had left an executive job at 475 Riverside.

"Most of the gay and lesbian people that I know in the church agencies are clergy or they are laywomen associated with the women's organization," he said. "The closeting of them is a professional loss to the church. This leads to high-stress levels for them, and that reduces their effectiveness. In those church agencies you relate to other people in significant kinds of ways. If you are holding back about yourself, you can't do as well."

Morris hoped some day the church would bless the homosexual staff members' lifestyles, but he admitted that probably wouldn't solve their relational problems with the grassroots church members.

I asked Morris if his group wanted a recognition of homosexual marriages which then would be guided by the same principles as marriages of Christian men and women.

"That's a difficult question," he answered. "I have trouble with gay men and lesbian women unthinkingly emulating heterosexual models. Lots of gays would subscribe to and live lives that reflect lifetime monogamous relationships, but I don't know that that is necessary. I'm not opposed to sexual responsibility, but the church should have no concern in the specificity beyond that sexual activity be done in the context of loving relationships."

"Well," I asked, "if we had church guidelines that blessed non-monogamous lifestyles for homosexuals but not for heterosexuals, might some heterosexuals think that unfair?"

"Oh, I don't think that openness for sex outside of marriage is much different from what we have at present among heterosexuals," he said. "Infidelity among heterosexual clergy is consistently winked at, or at worst they are banished to hinterland appointments."

My story on that interview was one of only three or four during my tenure at the *Reporter* that were prohibited from running. I was disappointed. I thought the interview might serve to open up the festering issue for church consideration. The editor saw it mainly as inflammatory.

Straight Talk

I felt Morris and other homosexual advocates likely were exaggerating "straight" sexual infidelity for their own purposes. But reports also were pouring into the *Reporter* that lent some credence to Morris' point.

Affairs between unmarried female secretaries and married male executives were reported. Affairs between colleagues that led to divorce and new marriages were spoken of. Affairs between staffers and officials were sometimes claimed to explain promotions, demotions and lack of administrative control. Although the homosexual stories tended to come from New York, these heterosexual tales were centered more heavily in other cities, such as Nashville.

I felt the stories were getting out partly because the agencies still had people who were more like classical liberal Christians from earlier decades. They were people who crusaded in the name of God from a base of spotless, conservative personal lives and deep spirituality against social immorality that victimized workers, the poor, women and minorities. Some of them were deeply disturbed by the sexual activities around them.

One prominent agency executive arranged a clandestine meeting with a *Reporter* colleague to unload his personal burden about illicit sexual liaisons among staff that he felt were undermining the operation of the agency.

Did we know something other church leaders didn't know? we wondered.

Little by little, we realized many of the bishops were struggling with the same stories. Indications of that would pop up in subtle ways—a comment in the hallway here, the choice of Scripture in a devotion there. One southwestern bishop took just two sentences in a talk to an agency to comment on the lack of local congregation responsiveness to agency leadership. It's hard for people in the pews to follow folks they think are immoral, he said, before quickly moving to another subject.

Only a couple of times did we decide to try to track down a specific rumor with the thought of reporting it. That kind of research and reporting was so fraught with problems we quit in frustration and squeamishness each time. It was one area in which the *Reporter* would not be a leader. Yet the oral evidence coming from so many different believable sources left no doubt of the magnitude of the problem.

Spurgeon and I were invited to speak to the special bishops' commission that was investigating the NCC and WCC. They were giving a lot of attention to the Methodist agencies which seemed to be influential in the ecumenical councils' problems. This session, like all of them, was closed. In a basement room of a hotel near O'Hare Airport, I wondered if this was what it was like to be called before the early church elders in Jerusalem. And one of the earliest concerns of those first-century leaders came up deep into our interview.

"Do you think the lifestyles of our agency people are ones the people in our churches would be proud of?" one bishop unexpectedly asked us, taking what seemed like a sharp turn from the subject at hand. "Lifestyle" was a euphemistic term widely used in the churches to deal with sexual relationships outside those encouraged under Christian tradition.

Spurgeon paused a second and then shifted the emphasis to the entire church. No, much of the church would not be pleased with the lifestyles of many agency people, he said. But then, neither would they be pleased with the lifestyles of many more pastors and perhaps some bishops. Nervous episcopal grunts were barely audible around the table.

Spurgeon noted the explosion of clergy divorce around the nation and the high percentage of cases in which "third parties" were involved. One bishop said he hoped they could "bell the cat" and bring a more personally disciplined standard to the staffs of the agencies.

In a few instances over the next few years, that seemed to happen. Complaints of philandering sometimes got results. Staff people sometimes quietly left their posts after a particularly convincing charge was made from people with high influence—such as overseas church leaders. Unfortunately, there were signs of a certain kind of blackmail, too, something possible because of the conspiracy of silence. Publicity was avoided in most cases.

But not much was done because of church legal systems that had been set up out of the admirable concern for the protection of clergy from precipitous and unjust dismissal. It was very difficult to correct a situation in which a clergyperson denied accusations and absolute proof of wrongdoing was unavailable. Without the power to subpoena witnesses, church courts often protected a minister even in the face of overwhelming evidence of immorality in the public domain because the court didn't hear from key witnesses.

It wasn't a matter of expecting perfection in the clergy. Failure and sin were certain to occur among the clergy. But unrepentant behavior in a clergyperson became a kind of advocacy for that behavior. True, the New Testament was full of examples of Jesus consorting with and embracing sinners rejected by society. But his forgiveness included the admonition to go and sin no more.

Most American religious institutions—liberal, conservative, liturgical and charismatic—had lost the ability to do any more than embrace the fallen among their clergy. The admonition was missing.

A Legislative Response

That clearly was dominating thoughts of the most broadly American of denominations in May of 1984. The every-four-year General Conference of the United Methodist Church which has a worshipping, missional presence in more U.S. counties than any other denomination took up the awkward topic in Baltimore, where the denomination had begun exactly 200 years earlier. Methodism had ridden with its circuit rider preachers to every new corner of the expanding American frontier. The morality of Methodism had become the morality of America. And the immorality of Methodism, such as its North-South split in the face of failure to deal with the slavery issue, often became the immorality of America. After the first 100 years of the American Methodist Church, one out of every three Americans was reported to be a Methodist of some kind. In 1984 the largest of the Methodist denominations no longer dominated the religious scene and was in a period of steep membership decline. But the importance of its actions remained significant.

The thousand-member, top legislative body of the United Methodist Church devoted almost half of its two-week deliberations to what appeared to be homosexual issues. But the homosexual issue was merely the lightning rod for the larger morality issues because homosexual advocacy groups publicly pushed their cause. There were no organizations formed around promoting the acceptance of heterosexual adultery or lasciviousness as an acceptable lifestyle for ordained clergy, although delegates knew that lifestyle was a reality among the clergy.

The rounds of votes indicated that overall sexual morality was the key concern. The delegates voted 525-442 to add to church law language that specifically prohibited "self-avowed practicing homosexuals" from the ordained ministry. But it voted by more than a 4-1 margin for more-encompassing language that held clergy to a sexual standard of "fidelity in marriage and celibacy in singleness." Most people previously had thought that was assumed. But the stories and rumors rampaging below the surface of public discussion had spurred the action.

Unfortunately, that didn't calm things much. Predictably, the problem couldn't be legislated away. The stories continued to come in. The legislation had some effect on leaders who felt shame and, in effect, policed themselves. The shameless leaders were virtually untouched.

A pastor called me once to say an African missionary had been in his home and complained of an affair between two mission executives. Pastors told me they had gone to bishops about specific situations and been told there was little they could do.

A wife of an agency official told of fruitlessly seeking help from district superintendents and bishops for years as her husband had one affair after another.

Such stories were multiplied about local pastors. Some bishops told me General Conference had taken so much power away from them over the last two decades that there was little they could do if an accused minister denied wrongdoing and if others weren't willing to appear before a full-fledged church trial.

I began to receive phone calls from secular reporters of daily newspapers around the country alerting me to rumors of outlandish behavior by ministers in their cities.

Paul's word to the Christians in Corinth came to mind. He chastised groups of Christians whose personal conduct violated even the pagan world's idea of morality (1 Corinthians 5:1). It would be only a matter of time, I thought, before some of what we in the church feared to challenge would burst forth into the public and severely compromise our ability to work toward the kingdom of God—beyond the compromise already occurring.

In fact, a few years later, bizarre immoral actions involving sex, violence and finances of a rather large number of Christian leaders became a mainstay on the pages of supermarket scandal tabloids and tittering TV comic monologues. Some instances of efforts to manage the original breaking of scandals, as also in decisions to suppress the news, just seemed to extend and heighten the public sensationalism.

Caught in the act were TV evangelists, tall-steeple mainline preachers, bishops, well-known charismatic leaders, highly-visible lay leaders, revered small church pastors, priests, Pentecostals, liberals, conservatives—you name it. What a commentary on the church's role in uplifting society!

At the same time that glossy-magazine trend writers and flip newspaper style page journalists were telling of the U.S. society's return to marriage and more traditional lifestyles, the Christian institutions were being shown as riddled with the old "new morality" of the '60s. The loss of leadership, influence and authority were phenomenal in one religious sector after another.

In my own denomination, a poignant example was in a *Time* magazine article in the aftermath of the "60 Minutes"/NCC controversy.

Pictured were Bishop Finis Crutchfield, United Methodism's most conservative bishop, and Bishop James Armstrong, the best-known liberal Methodist bishop whom *Time* called the nation's most powerful Protestant leader. Both were important leaders of reform movements in their own way. They were pictured in *Time* because of their importance to the NCC discussion. But both later took highly publicized plunges into infamy. After Bishop Crutchfield died of AIDS, the news media reported many sources detailing a long double life divided between being a family man and a promiscuous homosexual. Bishop Armstrong was forced to resign his episcopal office, his NCC presidency and his leadership in Christian public policy issues, eventually surrendering even his ordination credentials, because his own secret life of heterosexual violation of his marital vows.

Fundamental Importance Of Fidelity

As I examined my own feelings, I thought I detected a major part of the problem. For those of us who had concentrated on Christ's message of challenging unjust systems, driving out the money-changers, feeding the hungry and loving the unloved, the issue of personal sexual morality just hadn't seemed a high priority. American churches always had devoted disproportionate time, as far as I was concerned, to such individual morality matters while letting members off easy in the way they ran their businesses or voted selfish interests above the public good at the polls.

I was changing my mind.

And although liberals might seem more likely to fall into rationalizing the neglect of sexual morality, events showed conservatives were just as skilled.

In nearly all cases, it seemed, a common ingredient was pride, the sin Jesus condemned more than any other, I think. People thought their work for a particular part of the kingdom of God was so important, and they were so fatigued from the work, that they deserved some special physical and emotional rewards, even at the expense of other people to whom they were committed.

At a time when key ingredients of the growing poverty in the United States are divorce and illegitimate births, the church should be modeling a personal ethic of responsibility, not experimenting with a never-before successful openness in sexual lifestyles, I thought.

Some clergy looked on the issue as a kind of civil rights question. Why should they be held to a higher standard than the laity? they asked. Actually, the same standard was held up for all. But while it seemed important to keep the church broad enough even for people who landed well wide of the standard, such failure could not be tolerated on a continuing basis for leaders.

At the *Reporter* we watched notable leaders come crashing down in the morass of their lifestyles of unfaithfulness to marital, friendship, professional and ecclesiastical relationships. They weren't private matters. We saw the ripples which became like waves that crashed down on the sometimes multitudes of lives around them.

I saw some of those surrounding lives ruined—really ruined— from the disorientation caused by the fall of leaders who apparently thought their personal lives were of no concern to anybody but themselves. Several times my own family experienced the victimization by religious leaders in various locales who tried to live and justify a life of infidelity.

Fidelity in marriage was a principle that I never had doubted for my own life but had been hesitant to advocate forcefully for others. It seemed like such a private matter. I came to see that forceful advocacy indeed was needed as a loving way to try to warn others from creating their own tragedies. Still, we at the *Reporter* were unsure how to do that without getting into supermarket-style journalism.

So we, like most of the bishops, presbytery heads, agency directors and congregational pastor-parish relations committees of most American denominations, kept out of the sticky mess.

Ironically, the job of discussing matters such as standards and advantages of morality was left to the secular news media. We at the *Reporter* did, however, sound a general cry of concern. Spurgeon was in Kenya for a half-year sabbatical as Dan Louis guided our staff in wrestling with the fidelity question. We decided to float an editorial in our ecumenical and denominational papers to see if there was at least general consensus around the churches about the importance of the issue. We got no protests.

It was a fairly typical *Reporter* editorial effort. Members of the staff talked informally about the issue for weeks, finally hashing out the possible points of an editorial in a concentrated session. Stephen Swecker took the notes from all of that, mixed it with his own special insight and wrote an editorial that was refined by further evaluation as it was passed around the office.

I remembered Minnesota Bishop Emerson Colaw's preaching about the concept of biblical commands as not being intended to spoil the fun. Rather, he said, they are gifts from God to protect us from the painful consequences of certain behaviors. If you follow them, you are in a sense released to enjoy richer fruits of life.

Stephen's final editorial rationally and almost lyrically explained the pivotal importance to an entire society of the biblical commands concerning personal morality.

> ... We are particularly disturbed by the implication that one's ability to be a leader in a moral struggle, such as the effort against apartheid, is unrelated to one's sexual morality. ... Similarly outrageous is the implication that one's moral leadership in the public sphere excuses one's personal moral failings. ...
>
> From a theological perspective, we as Christians believe that faithfulness in marriage is an integral part of human life. The quality of faithfulness that makes possible the marriage covenant between a husband and wife is similar to that required for a less formal, but no less real, covenant between leaders and their followers.
>
> If one cannot remain faithful to the vows of marriage, there is justifiable reason to think that person may not be faithful in other moral covenants and responsibilities.
>
> Thus the Sixth Commandment against adultery is not simply a call for personal sexual morality. The commandment is a recognition that the entire fabric of human relationships and human survival rests on our ability to make and keep our covenants with each other just as God does with us.
>
> Even if we are not a recognized leader of any cause or movement, our personal example in such matters—if only as a leader of our own family—is urgently needed in a world where marital faithfulness has been sadly trivialized.
>
> As Christians, we should hold each other to an uncompromising biblical standard of faithfulness in marriage. We also should make it clear to our actual and would-be leaders that their moral leadership in public cannot properly be separated from the conduct of their personal lives.
>
> We should be prepared to offer the healing love of God to all who fall short of that high standard. We should not delude ourselves, however, that the standard does not exist. Even if marital infidelity does not "create problems" for

some, it does for God and the whole human family.

As I read Stephen's finished editorial, I noted the positive, active thrust of it. Maybe we in the modern church had not been drawn to emphasize personal morality so much because we've seen it as a matter of a negative, a "thou shalt not," merely an abstention from certain actions. It's difficult to feel terribly constructive by emphasizing the absence of something.

I thought the Methodist General Conference had done well to put emphasis on the word *fidelity*. Nothing passive about that. Fidelity is not the absence of illicit sexual activity. A person easily could have such an absence and not be anywhere close to having fidelity in a relationship. Rather, a life of fidelity in one's sexuality is one of bold, enriching action. Fidelity, as the dictionary notes, means devotion, allegiance, faithfulness, loyalty, honesty and integrity.

The lack of sexual fidelity among some in the church certainly was not the only or main reason for the church's lack of moral power in American society. But it was one. Without fundamental ingredients of discipleship like fidelity in thought, deed and relationship, how could Christians hope to challenge the frailties of the world's principalities?

10

Judgment Day for Sacred Cows

By spring of 1986 the ice had gotten thin indeed.

At a national gathering of black ministers and church leaders in Dallas, my writing was being denigrated in the same breath with South African apartheid. Angry at several of my recent stories, the keynote speaker raised the possibility of boycotting the *Reporter* and encouraging local congregations and church regions to discontinue publishing with the *Reporter*. I'd really raised temperatures this time.

And the ice was melting all around my colleagues, too. They good-naturedly complained that I'd gotten mainline church leaders so stirred up that they felt like they were walking into an ambush every time they went out on assignment.

Roberta Sappington came back shaken from an Oklahoma City meeting of the United Methodist Church's national watchdog commission on racism. She was as committed to Hispanics and their culture as she was to Mexico missions in which she had worked several summers, but she encountered hostility from the multi-ethnic commission and was barred from some parts of the meeting. She brought back word that the commission members voted to try to counter my recent work.

Douglas Cannon went to a denominational special committee on stopping the long membership decline and heard worries that my reporting "only makes United Methodists more discouraged."

Another national agency meeting was like a mine field for Susan Aguren, who kept stepping into pockets of anger about what I'd been doing.

What had I been doing?

Some pretty sensational stuff, I had to admit.

But this time journalistic excitement wasn't nearly enough to compensate for the personal disappointment. Critics were striking me where it hurt, suggesting I was insensitive to ethnic minorities or that I was trying to undermine ministries to and by ethnic minorities or that I might be motivated by racism itself or that I had set myself on a course to destroy faith in the church as an institution.

A Sacred Myth Shattered

I had shattered a sacred myth of mainline Protestants with a series of stories about who truly was showing concern for ethnic minorities in this country.

One story began:

> While so-called liberal mainline Protestants have talked a lot about ethnic inclusiveness during the past decade, Baptists and the Assemblies of God have brought the most ethnic-minority members into their denominations.
>
> In a survey of Protestant denominations, each with more than one million members, the *Reporter* found stagnant or small ethnic membership growth among most mainline Protestant churches during that period. But the Assemblies of God, Southern Baptists and American Baptists have burgeoned.

An age of innocence. . .no, blissful ignorance, was ended. As far as I know, I was the first person to gather that information—certainly the first to go public with it. Previously, the common assumption was that the conservative Baptists and Pentecostals had been growing numerically by emphasizing white homogeneity.

Mainline Protestants had taken some comfort that although their denominations had been losing members for two decades, at least they weren't racist and had been faithful in reaching out to all God's children. Nobody took more pride in that than we United Methodists.

For a decade we had celebrated ourselves as a rainbow. The most ethnically inclusive denomination in America, we said about ourselves. The claim was in our literature, speeches, sermons, brochures and periodicals. I'd been as proud of it as anybody.

For 10 years, the "missional priority" of the denomination had been to develop and strengthen black, Native American, Asian-American and Hispanic congregations. Every congregation, white and ethnic, was assigned an apportioned part of the cost.

Five percent of our members were ethnic minority, but we made certain that closer to 30 percent of agency staff, agency directors and bishops were ethnic minority. We looked really good—at the top.

I had been warmed by that fact at my first national church agency meeting outside Louisville back in 1981. As I looked up and down the rows of directors, I saw that the people themselves created a multi-fabric tapestry. This was the way the church ought to look in the American society, I thought at the time. I'd long been troubled by the cultural separation in our churches. For years I had craved being able to find a multi-ethnic congregation in each new city to which I moved. Failing, I pushed for racially inclusive efforts in each of the 99-percent-white congregations I ended up in.

But my excitement from the multi-ethnic leadership meetings was tempered by initial disappointment when I found that the liberal white and minority leaders in the denomination had given up on racially-inclusive congregations as a short-term goal. Rather, nearly all the creative energy and racially-targeted finances were being expended on strengthening the congregations in each culture. It wasn't that segregation still existed, they said, but that the cultures of most people in each ethnic group caused them to prefer to worship in their own kinds of services. Lots of evidence supported that premise.

During my first years at the *Reporter* I began to worry about our much-touted "missional priority." A sign here, a half-finished spoken comment there seemed to suggest that reality might not be matching the proud public claims. But I put off doing a good, clear journalistic evaluation of the nationwide program.

This was one of the most serious errors in my time with the *Reporter*. That long-delayed search for truth could have brought forward information years earlier to help the church wrestle more honestly with the tough questions of its ethnic ministries.

My deep desire for the work among ethnic minority people to succeed caused me to let down in my responsibility as a journalist and, as it turned out, my responsibility as a Christian steward. I probed just enough to know that nobody in the vast church bureaucracy was evaluating the net effectiveness of the millions of dollars that were being spent.

Some events in 1985 caused me to agonize further.

A few black pastors with inspiringly effective ministries had been telling me that the denomination's ethnic minority program not only was of little help but probably was also counter-productive in many of the ways it was carried out.

Hearing much the same thing in Atlanta at a special meeting of black pastors of growing black congregations was my colleague Sheron Covington Patterson, who in mid-1986 chose to become a pastor of a black congregation herself.

Many of them saw the ethnic priority program as more of a welfare or reparations program than a missional program; it failed to place resources in the hands of congregations showing the most likelihood to reach out into their communities with the transforming power of Jesus Christ. Leaky church roofs and decaying parsonages, regardless of whether vital ministry or its potential existed, were more likely recipients, some black pastors said.

Revelation Beneath A Baptist Revolution

In 1985 I also I encountered an important revelation at, of all places, the Southern Baptist Convention. It was my second year to cover the spectacular annual meeting of the nation's largest Protestant denomination.

The main personal effect from being at the conventions was to feel happy I was a United Methodist. All decisions were made by 30,000 to 40,000 angry "messengers" with minimal time for study or debate. There was virtually no limit to how many people could come and vote. Orderly, rational decision-making was not possible.

The political scent of an infamous soap salesman was strong at nearly every session. The Religious Roundtable's Ed McAteer clearly had helped engineer his dream for the Southern Baptist process. A highly-organized Religious Right opposition had begun busing in thousands of people to wrest control from the moderates. And they got the power. Old Baptist fundamentals like the separation of church and state and the priesthood of all believers to interpret the Bible for themselves were turned on end.

And how different it was in complexion from mainline Protestant gatherings. Of the scores of people who stood at the convention podium at one time or another, I don't think more than a half-dozen were other than white men. So imagine my surprise when I walked down the ramps, far below the ground and the convention hall to find displays proclaiming burgeoning work in ethnic minority neighborhoods across the country!

Rev. Oscar I. Romo in effect told me I didn't have any idea what was happening in American ethnic minority ministries. He was head of the Southern Baptists' language ministries. He told how the black ministries department had started 400 new black congregations in the last decade, boosting black membership to nearly 340,000. And his department now could point to 4,600 congregations with nearly 250,000 members divided among 87 languages in the United States.

I was flabbergasted. Romo hadn't said it, but I suspected we United Methodists were living a lie concerning our treasured claim to unequaled concern for ethnic minorities.

At *Reporter* editorial planning meetings, we had decided to take a full overview of United Methodist ethnic priority work. I led the push for that and had taken responsibility to get it going. But I continued to drag my feet until the end of 1985. Then I went back to the records of the original debates 10 years earlier that led to the denomination's ethnic minority priority. I found the key purposes were to stop the ethnic United Methodist churches from vanishing altogether and to begin a bold new evangelistic thrust to the ethnic minority communities of America.

But that was not to be.

I spent weeks gathering statistics that had not been previously put in one place. I uncovered that we United Methodists lost our claim to being the most ethnically inclusive church almost as soon as we began our ethnic priority.

I was able to report success at halting a rapid decline of ethnic members even while our white membership losses continued. So, there was success.

But during a decade of explosive ethnic minority population growth in the United States. . . .

During a decade when larger and larger numbers of ethnic minorities were outside the nurturing community of a worshipping congregation and while family breakdowns, poverty and illegitimate births soared. . . .

During a decade when United Methodists were spending at least

20 million dollars to provide all that a church can offer to suffering communities. . . .

During all of that, the United Methodist Church had been unable to reach out to any significant increase of ethnic minority people other than in the unique situation of Korean-Americans.

I called the leaders of each of the four ethnic minority caucuses in the church. They unloaded their frustrations at the denomination's lip service instead of roll-up-the-sleeves service.

I pounded away at my findings with stories five weeks in a row, including dramatic charts by Roberta Sappington:

"Ethnic membership barely grows in priority decade."

"Ethnic minority churches succeed by avoiding vanishing predictions" and "Data void points to commitment problem."

"Baptists, Assemblies pass UMs in ethnic inclusiveness."

"Others excel at ethnic church 'planting'." "'Mothering' replaces money in most 'planting'." "Mission vision lies with ethnics."

"Black pastors assess 'priority' weakness / Ethnic church grants, fanfare given little credit for fast-growing congregations" and "Four impediments cited by pastors as barriers to UMC ethnic growth." Sheron aided me on the final week's installments.

Defending The Myth

My prayer had been that the stories would be like a stinging aftershave lotion to the face—(slap) "Thanks, I needed that"—and we, as a denomination, would be stirred to get honest, get bold and get going in ministry to the pain-filled ethnic minority communities of this country.

Mainly the response seemed to be to get Beck and get the *Reporter*. The almost universal public response from ethnic group leaders, agency leaders and regional conference leaders was that we had set out to "do in" ministries to ethnic minorities. Nobody proposed re-evaluating the ethnic minority programs and spending. Defending what had gone before was the priority.

The moderate Baptists loved the stories and ran them in their publications—whose own independence at seeking truth was severely under challenge by their denomination's new power figures.

Our denomination didn't even come close in any category to being the most ethnically inclusive in America, yet some leaders insisted on continuing to use the claim.

Mainline Protestants would have been better off not being told that the conservative Southern Baptists and Assemblies of God were acting out the mainline Protestants' pluralistic dream, several leaders complained. "Hasn't Roy Beck ever heard of a ministry of silence?" fumed a Northeastern leader.

Letters and phone calls began to come in indicating that we had butchered a sacred cow this time. Massive subscription cuts due to displeasure among regional leaders loomed in the midst of thinly veiled threats.

Spurgeon had to devote major blocks of time to salving oozing wounds. I flew to Minot, North Dakota, where a prairie fire of dissatisfaction was blazing toward us.

An Illinois leader complained to Spurgeon about the "predictable anti-United Methodism of Roy Beck." A Western bishop blasted us in a national mission magazine and suggested "ulterior" motives on our part.

Hints and actual charges of racism emerged. And I had found that once the word "racism" got attached to any endeavor, person, organization or line of thinking, rational discussion usually was ended. Just as people sometimes can shut off discussion by accusing a person of being a Marxist, the same effect was ensured by labeling people as racist, sexist, homophobic, McCarthyite and a number of other epithets.

I remained convinced that the chief reason for the abject fiasco in Holmes County, Mississippi, had been the intimidation of the racist charge. Almost everybody involved was afraid to search for the truth because searching—and any doubting—were labeled early on as racist.

How the criticism toward me was intended, I don't know. Always, the tendency is to allow criticism to feel more personal than it may have been intended. But I took this criticism to heart. I was hurt, bewildered and angry at the responses to my reporting on ethnic minority ministry.

I certainly wasn't without my own racism struggles. But coming out of an all-white Ozarks background, I long had attempted to understand and deal with race issues. When Shirley and I began moving from city to city, we fought with realtors who didn't want to show us houses in integrated middle-class neighborhoods. We practically insisted on buying in such neighborhoods. By so choosing, we'd lost money by missing out on the phenomenal 70's inflation escalator in all-white neighborhoods. We'd always chosen to live near downtown. We made certain our children had ethnic minority playmates in every city. We sent the boys to urban public schools, including one at the crime-ridden public housing project near the *Reporter*. In Dallas we lived in a neighborhood where whites were the minority in nearly every store where we shopped. Often we found ourselves the only whites in a sea of blacks and Hispanics and usually found little awkwardness.

We voted with ethnic minority interests in mind and were politically represented by ethnic minority people. We'd broken politeness and challenged racial slurs and slights among friends and family for years. We had led our Sunday school class in a years-long project of hundreds of hours of work in an emergency children's clothing project in a black Methodist church in a poor Hispanic neighborhood. We had given considerable time to a weekly children's drama workshop that included field trips and camping and became the primary entrance for ethnic minority people in our local congregations.

But our efforts at racially inclusive living felt like failures much of the time. We often became discouraged. We sometimes let bad individual experiences creep into our generalized thinking. We were inept and fearful in bridging deep economic class divisions in social relations.

But none of my accusers had asked me about my real motivations for reporting those ethnic minority ministry stories. If they had, mine would have been a common sanctimonious journalist's response: I was seeking truth. In this case I cared deeply for the ethnic minority goal and felt one of the worst things for it was to allow people to live in a state of fantasy about efforts toward achieving it.

With human frailties, I'd tried to live out Paul's admonition to the church in Ephesus.

> Therefore, laying aside falsehood, speak truth, each one of you, with his neighbor, for we are members of one another. . . .And do not participate in the unfruitful deeds of darkness, but instead even expose them. . . .all things become visible when they are exposed by the light. . . .take up the full armor of God, that you may be able to resist in the evil day, and having done everything, to stand firm . . .

having girded your loins with truth (Ephesians 4:25;
5:11,13; 6:13-14, NASB).

The intensity and longevity of the criticism this time were greater
than I'd ever seen. For the first time at the *Reporter*, I did not feel encouraged to aggressively pursue the next questionable action that came
along—and certainly not to seek one out. Criticism of our highly-con-
troversial profile was not just coming from institutional die-hards now.
Longtime friends of the *Reporter* who stood in the mainstream of
church life were suggesting that mainline Protestantism, a weakened
part of the Church universal, needed a gentler voice.

For all its circulation, the *Reporter* was a physically small paper.
We couldn't begin to print all the newsworthy truth from the world of
religion each week. Why not shift some to report more of the truth
about parts of the church that were alive, thriving and which could
serve as inspiring models for the parts of the church that weren't alive
and thriving?

Spurgeon listened thoughtfully to those comments. Since his sabbatical in Africa two years earlier when he was widely acclaimed for
his constructive mission reporting, he had seemed to me to be in a new
phase, less of a maverick, even more concerned than before about the
overall effect on the church of all that we did.

The *Reporter* always was shifting emphases from one month to
the next. But we appeared in general to be shifting to putting somewhat more energy into aggressive reporting of the fruits of the church
and somewhat less energy into aggressive reporting of the thorns.

If so, I had to acknowledge that the shift fell within the realm of
a legitimate journalistic decision, since it did not at all desert the hard
side of news. But I felt uneasy.

None of our friends was suggesting that we falsify or cover up disconcerting news in the church. It was more a question of how much
energy to apportion in pursuing it.

As the key staff member in that pursuit, I felt quite ambivalent
about the appropriateness of my continued presence on the staff. A
report of my feelings reached Spurgeon in a roundabout way, and he
confronted me and said he was not harboring such feelings about me.
But my sense of ambiguity remained.

Almost six years earlier, I had left daily newspapering to spend "a
couple of years" in service to the church, not to be destructive. *Per-*

haps, I thought, *I've overstayed.* That thought became even more for-
tified by late summer when I wrote about El Salvadoran refugees.

No Sanctuary From The Storm

I'd been following that refugee problem since 1981 when I
"broke" the story in the United States of the daring underground railroad for the refugees. I spent three weeks along the Mexican border
in Texas and California and reported on the fledgling sanctuary movement and the deep concerns about our nation's policies toward Central
America and the refugees fleeing the suffering there.

But, through the years I'd become increasingly concerned by the
apparent willingness of "sanctuary" supporters to make claims that
could not be proved and often were easily disproved.

The movement objected to the Reagan administration's insistence
on sending the El Salvadorans back to their war-torn country. The
movement did all it could to keep the refugees here. But the government was deporting thousands. For years I'd heard people stand up at
church meetings and say that up to 40 percent of the deported refugees
met death or persecution. I'd never been able to find a source for that.

I'd also never been able to prove that any of the groups involved
with the sanctuary movement were trying to protect the deportees once
they arrived back in El Salvador. I'd been privately suggesting to
people for years that somebody should set up a reception program that
documented deportees as they arrived in El Salvador and attempted to
keep track of them to let the death squads of left and right know their
actions would be noticed.

Late in the summer of 1986, I discovered that a 35-year-old,
Geneva-based refugee organization was trying to do just that. Run as
an intergovernmental operation representing 32 European, Latin
American and North American nations, it conducted this deportee
reception work on grants from the United States and El Salvador.

After a year and a half, an internal report of the effort slipped out
that showed the difficulty in keeping up with the 4,800 deportees from
the United States during 1985. Nonetheless, it was significant that the
organization did not come upon a single case of a politically-motivated
torture, killing or jailing of a deportee during that period.

Checking names against those on lists made by human rights organizations failed to find any of the deportees among the many victims of the government. None of the swarms of journalists and activist

groups in El Salvador had come forward with such a case.

I called several advocacy groups in this nation, including various "sanctuary" leaders and people in the churches who had been talking of 40 percent becoming victims of the El Salvadoran government. None of them was able to point me to a single incident—let alone the suspected thousands—during the last two years. And only a couple of incidents could be cited during the previous years of the civil war.

I pointed out in my story that all of that did not speak to the continuing violence, death and destruction of the civil war, or to the economic devastation and resulting poverty or to the many incidents of persecution and cruelty toward other citizens by governmental soldiers, right-wing extremists and left-wing guerrillas. But it did suggest that the U.S. immigration and court systems and the international reception program might be doing a pretty good job of screening out potential persecution victims before deporting refugees.

It was a story so at odds with so much that we in the church press, as well as much of the public press, had reported, that we at the *Reporter* thought we needed to get the word out in a highly-visible way to our readers.

They were a thought and action soon scorned.

Blood On My Hands?

Various leaders of the sanctuary movement and of church agencies went public and private with strong charges that I might have the blood of deported refugees on my hands by supposedly giving encouragement to the Reagan administration's immoral immigration actions.

One of my colleagues was at a meeting of church leaders where one stood and said, "I think the time has come for us to ask just who *is* this Roy Beck." Resurfacing were earlier conspiracy notions that I might be some form of undercover agent for the ultra-right political strikeforce of the Reagan administration.

Personal attacks on my ability and even my character were so numerous that the conversation over one of our *Reporter* barbeque luncheons was whether I had become so controversial I could no longer effectively cover the church. I was the first to raise the concern.

At one point in this year of deep dissent, a Southern bishop told me that he conceded that the *Reporter* and I had done what we had to under good journalistic practices but that he wished we were guided less as journalists and more by a sense of loyalty as part of the church. *Was a journalistic search for truth outside the church's vision of truthfulness,* I pondered?

Some of the deep criticism came from people for whom I had great respect. Many were honestly attempting dialogue. "My disappointment in this article does not diminish my regard and respect for your talent and commitment to high standards of journalism. It is in the spirit of these standards that I write you my personal concerns," a Pennsylvania leader wrote. Many were lucid discourses that often misunderstood what I had done but nevertheless contained thoughts that challenged me.

Private Prayers And Support

Thankfully, not all response to my hot 1986 reporting was negative. Little positive reaction came publicly, but we eventually received considerable appreciation privately from lay people, pastors, regional and national leaders and bishops who found the subjects too hot to tackle themselves. Throughout the year we received a large amount of private support for our effort to face the facts in ethnic minority ministries, for example.

One Midwestern leader wrote in a letter labeled "not for publication":

> Your series took a lot of courage. Ultimately, I think the denomination will be the better for it. And clearly the *Reporter* is the only outfit which could have even considered such an undertaking.
>
> This is not to suggest I'm against the ethnic minority priority; however, even its most ardent supporters acknowledge (in private) that it has been only marginally successful, at best. Yet, so often we in the church maintain a public facade bordering on hypocrisy as we pretend not to hear the little boy telling us, "The Emperor has no clothes!"

As had happened throughout my six years at the *Reporter*, expressions of personal concern and prayer support came unexpectedly from people known and unknown to me. That was especially true in the middle of all the 1986 controversy as, coincidentally, Shirley's multiple sclerosis, which had been progressively attacking for years, took a sudden, but as it turned out only temporary, incapacitating dive.

In the midst of that, a story I was researching necessitated a call to a Methodist seminary professor near Chicago whom I had talked with only once, six years earlier.

Part way into the interview he dropped his professional role for a moment. He reminded me that I had told him during our previous meeting about Shirley's personal health challenge as she continued to conduct a very special private practice as a physical therapist. He not only had remembered but also said he had prayed for us weekly for six years. Upon learning of the present developments, he pledged to multiply his supplications. A warm sense of God's grace enveloped me from the revelation that a virtual stranger in a far-away city would intercede for us with such regularity.

Later the same afternoon I was interviewing a research official in the Assemblies of God denomination when I was interrupted by a call from home. When I got back on the line with the researcher and told her that I had to make a run to the hospital emergency room, she expressed her concern and asked, "What's her name? I'll pray for her until you call me back tomorrow."

"I'll pray for you" can be as glib as "have a nice day" from the tongues of Christians. But some of the most meaningful surprises while covering the church came as the offer of prayer broke through the business of journalism and revealed true Christian concern from people whose main or only contact with me had been professional.

Sixteen years of newspapering had built up a thick skin and the expectation that when people didn't like what I wrote they were more likely to blame bad motives than bad information. At the *Reporter*, a writer's loyalty and state of sanctification quickly became an issue with some irate readers, especially those considering themselves protectors of orthodox belief. "I'll pray for you" sometimes was attached to the end of a letter not as a comfort but an acerbic reminder of how much the help was needed. Nonetheless, my former years with metropolitan daily papers didn't prepare me for the humbled but uplifted feeling I got from so often opening mail from complete strangers who expressed concern for me in my role with the newspaper and added, "You are in my prayers."

The impact is longlasting, as our younger son Andrew reminded us. If ever a kid needed prayer and a guardian angel it was Andrew. During my years at the *Reporter* he developed a rare, life-threatening blood syndrome just after his first birthday. He later took a 25-foot free-fall from the top of our magnolia tree. He dangled half-outside the back of our careening stationwagon in an accident in heavy interstate traffic. And an ugly lump on his shoulder was diagnosed by three doctors as most probably being cancerous.

In every case he was enveloped with prayer from those near and far through a wonderful network of friends and relatives who involved far more people—strangers to us—so that Andrew was lifted up in all kinds of spiritual communities. We told him about every group and locality we knew of where that was happening. And for years Andrew ran into people who told him they had prayed for him during one or another of his dramatic episodes.

It was difficult for Andrew to think of himself as an isolated, insignificant person after so much attention and divine invocation. "Momma," he asked unexpectedly one day when the dramatic events were in the past, "are all those people still praying for me?"

Shirley hesitated a second to register what he was talking about. "Maybe not all at once like when you were sick. But there are many people who still remember you in their prayers. And *I* thank God for you and Jeremy every day."

I wrote about these many prayer experiences in a column and noted that I really didn't understand prayer. But the one who prayed and the one for whom a prayer was offered seemed nearly always changed by it. During the important and heartfelt disagreements that were so commonplace in the church, I often observed what a difference it made when opponents dealt with each other in an attitude of prayer.

Among the people who showed loving concern for Shirley and me in our situation were some of the church agency people for whom my investigative and controversy-covering reporting caused the most difficulties. The church can and ought to be different from other institutions, not because disagreements are rare but because of the spirit in which disagreements are fought and settled.

When I was considering taking the job at the *Reporter* in 1980, the departing Bud Herron had asked me if I had a background of exceptionally warm and vital local congregation experiences. Without that, he said, religion reporting could become a bitter personal experience.

I had great congregational experiences in the past and had more while in Dallas. I didn't lose my faith reporting on the church despite my keen disappointment in its willingness so often to perpetuate dishonesties. By November of 1986, however, I realized that I may have spent more time in the trenches dealing with the church's deepest tensions than was personally helpful to me. So I was receptive when I received a job offer that came as much out of the blue as the late-night call in 1980. In early 1987, I turned my reporting attention on Washington D.C. for a daily newspaper chain. But I didn't leave the *Reporter* with the idea that the often unpleasant search for truth should stop in the church. I was certain it would continue, that I would be a part of it as just another layman, and that the *Reporter* would be part of it.

My experiences during the previous 12 months had added even more passion to my belief that the things and issues most dear to us are the ones that we most need to hold up to vigorous examination.

I felt as though I had tried to live that philosophy. I'd done the toughest reporting on my own denomination, its wider mainline Protestant community and on social stances that were similar to my own. That was much more painful than pointing out the foibles of others. I was certain that I could have found just as many sensational stories of integrity breakdown if I'd concentrated on other Christian communities. But each community primarily must be responsible for holding its own members accountable in the faith. We must not fall into the dangerous "judge not" ethic that erroneously interprets Jesus' comments in the sixth chapter of Matthew as a reason not to hold one another—and especially sacred cows—accountable.

Insight From Ghana

Just before I left Dallas the head of the Ghana Methodist Church visited the *Reporter*. He shared some of the joy of the numerically growing Christian community in Africa. But he offered a sobering and troubling insight.

Corruption and issues of honesty were a major impediment to development in Ghana as in many African nations, he acknowledged. Unfortunately, the increase in the number of Christians was not necessarily improving the situation.

"There are certain things you'd expect of Christians that are dashed to pieces on some of these values like honesty. For instance, after a recent stealing binge in one part of our country we found that maybe 80 percent of the people involved were Christians," the Rev. Jacob S. A. Stephens said. "The question is, how far do they extend their Christianity into their business, the community and their family? We are trying to make this more a part of our evangelism."

What a tragic story!

What a warning for the United States where fundamental character traits so often are treated carelessly! If the church and individual Christians don't model character, whom can society count on for character formation? If individual Christians are not transformed in the way they live and think and act, what is the hope for the transformation of institutions and societies? Where will the unswerving personal integrity come from to do battle against the dishonesty and injustice of worldly powers?

In looking back over my six years of religion reporting, the overarching theme seemed to be the absolute need for intellectual integrity in Christian living. Without it, dishonesty creeps in under many guises and leads to myriad failures and misery.

In what is commonly called the "Great Commission," Jesus did not command His followers to go into all nations and persuade people to express their faith in Him. Rather, Matthew tells us that Jesus said to "make disciples of all the nations. . .teaching them to observe all that I have commanded you." All that He commanded.

Being a disciple begins with faith, but it demands so much more. It is not just what we believe, but what we do and how we do it.